REFUGEES, SELF-RELIANCE, DEVELOPMENT

A Critical History

Evan Easton-Calabria

BRISTOL UNIVERSITY PRESS

First published in Great Britain in 2022 by

Bristol University Press
University of Bristol
1–9 Old Park Hill
Bristol
BS2 8BB
UK
t: +44 (0)117 374 6645
e: bup-info@bristol.ac.uk

Details of international sales and distribution partners are available at bristoluniversitypress.co.uk

British Library Cataloguing in Publication Data
A catalogue record for this book is available from the British Library

ISBN 978-1-5292-1908-1 hardcover
ISBN 978-1-5292-1909-8 paperback
ISBN 978-1-5292-1910-4 ePub
ISBN 978-1-5292-1911-1 ePdf

Cover design: Nicky Borowiec
Front cover image: The author
Bristol University Press use environmentally responsible print partners.
Printed in Great Britain by CMP, Poole

This book is dedicated to the bookends of my life: To my Abuelo, Edison Easton, whose conversations about entrepreneurship and global economics inspired my interest in this topic, and to my Abuela, Joyce Lindberg Easton, who helped me find the poetry in my words.

And to my daughters, Lilah Joyce and Edie Marie, who joined me for the final stage of this project and are the newest chapter of my history.

I would like to write the history of this prison, with all the political investments of the body that it gathers together in its closed architecture. Why? Simply because I am interested in the past? No, if one means by that writing a history of the past in terms of the present. Yes, if one means writing the history of the present.

Michel Foucault, *Discipline and Punish*, 1977

While too we talk in terms of statistics and demarcation of responsibility and finance, we have to remember what all this means in terms of human distress and pauperisation, and loss of initiative and hope if the right course is not taken. Reference to … Tanzania with the people in a semi-starved condition eating their crops before they are ready for harvest and selling their clothes to keep themselves alive, cannot leave us unmoved, the more especially when we realise that for a good or a bad plan, for one which brings hope and positive achievement and for one which perpetuates human misery, the cost is the same.

T.F. Betts, Field Director, Oxfam,
'Refugees in Eastern Africa: A Comparative Study',
6 May 1966

Contents

List of Figures and Tables		vi
Abbreviations and Acronyms		vii
Notes on the Author		ix
Acknowledgements		x
1	Introduction: Why Refugee Self-Reliance?	1
2	Self-Sufficiency out of Necessity: Refugee Self-Reliance Assistance in Interwar Greece	25
3	Socialism and Self-Reliance: Refugee Self-Reliance Assistance in Post-Colonial East Africa	59
4	Warriors of Self-Reliance: Refugee Self-Reliance Assistance in Cold War Pakistan	94
5	Dignity in Informality? Urban Refugee Self-Reliance Assistance in Kampala, Uganda	127
6	Livelihoods 2.0? Refugee Self-Reliance and the Digital Gig Economy	162
7	Conclusion	193
Annex: A Note on Methods and Sources		206
References		208
Index		231

List of Figures and Tables

Figures

2.1	Letter by Ignatios Tsakalopoulos	41
2.2	'Sister Sarra's busy day'	46
2.3	AWH Bulletin, 1923–1924	47
6.1	Overview of actors involved in digital livelihoods creation at different levels of the international system	177

Tables

1.1	Historical overview of refugee self-reliance assistance	12
5.1	Livelihoods training for refugees in Kampala	141

Abbreviations and Acronyms

ACTV	African Centre for Treatment and Rehabilitation of Torture Victims
APRRN	Asia Pacific Refugee Rights Network
AWH	American Women's Hospitals
CRRF	Comprehensive Refugee Response Framework
CTA	Community Technology Access
FRC	Finnish Refugee Council
GBP	Great British Pound
GoP	Government of Pakistan
GoT	Government of Tanzania
GoU	Government of Uganda
GRN	Global Refugee-Led Network
GRSC	Greek Refugee Settlement Commission
GTZ	German Technical Cooperation Agency
HOCW	Hope of Children and Women Victims of Violence
ICARA I and II	International Conferences on Assistance to Refugees in Africa
ICVA	International Council of Voluntary Agencies
ILO	International Labour Organization
IMF	International Monetary Fund
IRC	International Rescue Committee
JRS	Jesuit Refugee Service
KCCA	Kampala City Council Authority
LWF	Lutheran World Federation
MDB	Multilateral Development Bank
NWFP	Northwest Frontier Province
RAD	Refugee Aid and Development
RBTU	Rädda Barnen Training Unit
RLP	Refugee Law Project
RTV	Refugee Tentage Village
SAFRON	States and Frontier Regions Ministry
SAP	Structural Adjustment Programme
SRS	Self-Reliance Strategy

TANU	Tanganyika African National Union
TCRS	Tanganyika Christian Refugee Service
TDA	Targeted Development Assistance
UK	United Kingdom
UN	United Nations
UNDP	United Nations Development Programme
UNHCR	United Nations High Commissioner for Refugees
UNRISD	United Nations Research Institute for Social Development
UNRRA	United Nations Relief and Rehabilitation Administration
US	United States of America
USD	United States dollar
WFP	World Food Programme
YARID	Young African Refugees for Integral Development

Notes on the Author

Dr Evan Easton-Calabria is Senior Researcher at the Feinstein International Center, Tufts University, and Research Associate at the Refugee Studies Centre, University of Oxford, focusing on refugee self-reliance, self-governance, and the contemporary humanitarian system. She previously worked at Oxford's Refugee Studies Centre, specializing in contemporary urban assistance to refugees, including by refugee-led organizations in East Africa. She is the author of over 70 publications for academics, practitioners, policymakers, and the public on refugees, and co-author of *The Global Governed? Refugees as Providers of Protection and Assistance* (Cambridge University Press, 2020). She holds a Master's and Doctorate from the University of Oxford.

Acknowledgements

Thank you to my friend and mentor Professor Alexander Betts for our conversations about refugee self-reliance for over a decade. Our shared interests mean much to me. Thank you to Mitch Yasur Artman for your endless edits, bottomless morning coffee, and being my loving mirror. My best friend and husband, always, all ways. Thank you to Maurice Herson, friend and editor, and William Allen, friend and colleague. And thank you to my mother, Leslie Easton, whose hours with my infants allowed me to finish this initial PhD project on time.

This project would not have been possible without generous support from: The National Geographic Society; Vice-Chancellors' Fund, University of Oxford; Santander Academic Study Award, University of Oxford; Frances Stewart Bursary, Oxford Department of International Development; Europaeum Oxford-Geneva Study Bursary, The Europaeum; Economic History Society, School of Social and Political Sciences, University of Glasgow; and the Gilbert Murray UN Study Award, London School of Economics.

1

Introduction: Why Refugee Self-Reliance?

Their labour is often all that refugees have to sell.[1]

I often start discussions on refugee self-reliance with an example of success. Have you heard, I ask, about the successful settlement of 15,000 refugees, mostly farmers, in 15 villages? They were given tools, seeds, and livestock for their first year; schools and hospitals were built in the area which locals could also use. Different cottage industries were started for those uninterested in farming. They were provided emergency rations until the harvest. After their first year, most of the refugees were entirely self-reliant.

Where, you might ask, did this take place? It hadn't come across your inbox recently, although it does sound similar to a lot of development programming for refugees today.

Oh, I explain, this was done in the 1920s in Greece. And it was not the United Nations that undertook this work, it was the League of Nations.

Indeed, despite the near century-long gap in between programming, there are striking likenesses in work conducted by the League of Nations and other organizations to foster refugee self-reliance (what I term here *refugee self-reliance assistance*) and that being undertaken today. A 2018 evaluation of the United Nations High Commissioner for Refugees' (UNHCR) livelihoods strategies and approaches from 2014–2018 found, for example, that the most common interventions were vocational training, agricultural interventions, and artisan livelihoods opportunities – shockingly similar to the farming and cottage industries of embroidery work and carpet weaving documented in League of Nations reports on refugee assistance from the 1920s and 1930s. Yet the long history of refugee self-reliance assistance is often obscured by an emphasis on current challenges or by the promises of new solutions to protracted displacement.

---

[1] Chambers, R. (1979) 'Rural refugees: what the eye does not see'. Paper for the African Studies Association Symposium on Refugees. London, 13–14 September 1979.

That said, a heightened focus on refugee self-reliance is clearly present. Since the beginning of the 21st century, UNHCR and other humanitarian and development actors have increasingly promoted self-reliance as a desirable goal for both individual refugees and their communities. In 2018, UNHCR had livelihoods programming for 75 countries with a budget of over $70 million USD.[2] As a Women's Refugee Commission report reads, 'Everyone, from local community-based organizations to international non-governmental organizations to policy makers and donors, wants to support, fund and implement more effective programs to support the self-reliance of the displaced'.[3] Its importance in contemporary policy efforts to support refugees is evident: 'enhance refugee self-reliance' is one of the four core objectives of the 2018 Global Compact on Refugees, a widely heralded international commitment to promote refugee responsibility-sharing, which UNHCR's 2019–2023 Global Strategy Concept Note on Refugee Livelihoods and Economic Inclusion builds on.[4] However, as these chapters will go on to show, this centrality in the international refugee regime is much more of a resurgence than an innovation.

This introduction lays the groundwork for the following chapters through an overview of the contemporary discourse on refugee self-reliance and a sampling of the literature on the topic. It then turns to the primary focus of this book, an exploration of self-reliance and refugees as economic subjects in the 20th and 21st century. Over many years now, the persistent financial focus in current rhetoric on refugee self-reliance has engendered both my criticism about how it is viewed today, and my curiosity about which practices were undertaken to foster it in the past. Today's economic focus on the topic equates refugee self-reliance with jobs and livelihoods, on one hand, and assistance to foster it with a reduction of aid tied to funding shortfalls, on the other. Thus, the topic of refugee self-reliance retains a focus on money when it could instead be associated with so many other aspects of life, such as political freedom, community self-determination, or sustainable and sovereign food production. Why is this so? And has this always been the case? Such questions led me to the writing of this book, a reading of history focused on linkages between refugee self-reliance assistance and material interests and influences. Ultimately, my focus on the economic side of refugee self-reliance is not to promote but rather to problematize it, with the hope that doing so can elevate its many other existing and potential components.

2 UNHCR (2018) 'Evaluation of UNHCR's Livelihoods Strategies and Approaches (2014–2018) – Global Report'. December 2018. Geneva: UNHCR.

3 WRC (Women's Refugee Commission) (2009) *Building Livelihoods: A field manual for practitioners in humanitarian settings*. New York: WRC.

4 UNHCR (n.d.) Refugee Livelihoods and Economic Inclusion: 2019–2023 Global Strategy Concept Note. Geneva: UNHCR.

Discussions of refugee self-reliance today

The importance of self-reliance has arguably only increased with the COVID-19 pandemic. Countries have redirected humanitarian and development funding and closed their borders, restricting two of the three so-called durable solutions of resettlement and repatriation. Only the third, local integration into host countries – which by many accounts requires refugee self-reliance – remains within reach, albeit still elusive. With shrinking donor budgets for humanitarian and development work, refugees living without humanitarian aid become ever more appealing for agencies and donors alike. Indeed, some might go so far as to posit that the objective of refugee self-reliance has de facto replaced that of the durable solution of local integration. This of course raises a slew of protection (and ethical) concerns. But, really, in a world where one out of every 95 people is displaced, how can helping people live independently from limited humanitarian assistance be anything but good?

Yet current policy and practitioner rhetoric around refugee self-reliance is vague. The most common definition of refugee self-reliance comes from UNHCR:

> Self-reliance is the social and economic ability of an individual, a household or a community to meet essential needs (including protection, food, water, shelter, personal safety, health and education) in a sustainable manner and with dignity. Self-reliance, as a programme approach, refers to developing and strengthening livelihoods of persons of concern, and reducing their vulnerability and long-term reliance on humanitarian/external assistance.[5]

Despite the multiple components of this definition, much of the recent discourse and programming has an individual, economic focus.

And despite its prominence in the Global Compact on Refugees, the definition generally goes unchallenged, with self-reliance presented as a positive widespread goal and even a panacea to the seemingly perennial 'refugee problem'. In a 2015 policy brief, for example, former UN Deputy High Commissioner for Refugees Alexander Aleinikoff advocates moving 'from dependence to self-reliance' and thus 'changing the paradigm in protracted refugee situations'.[6] The World Bank also explains why fostering self-reliance is important: 'Refugees are vulnerable, having lost their assets and livelihoods, and without the ability to plan their lives. They need help

[5] UNHCR (2005) Handbook for Self-Reliance. Geneva: UNHCR.

[6] Aleinikoff, A. (2015) *From Dependence to Self-Reliance: Changing the paradigm in protracted refugee situations*. Policy Brief, Transatlantic Council on Migration. Washington, DC: Migration Policy Institute.

regaining their voice, becoming self-reliant and rebuilding their lives.'[7] Nowhere in texts such as these is there an explanation of what self-reliance actually is. Livelihoods creation is presented in current discourse as a main way for refugees to attain self-reliance; thus refugee self-reliance and livelihoods are often presented in tandem, with livelihoods as a vehicle to 'reach' self-reliance.

Alongside the humanitarian and development focus on refugee self-reliance has come the engagement of the private sector. The IKEA Foundation has donated over 198 million dollars to UNHCR in a variety of key areas, including livelihoods.[8] In 2016, the billionaire George Soros stated his intention to invest 500 million dollars in start-ups, social enterprises, and businesses founded by migrants and refugees.[9] The founder of Chobani yoghurt began hiring refugees, and started a non-profit grant-making organization known as the Tent Foundation to bring together the private sector to fund innovative solutions to displacement. Richard Branson, the CEO of Virgin, has supported refugees and advocated for the role of the private sector in refugee assistance, stating: '[B]usiness has enormous opportunities to put refugees on a pathway to economic self-sufficiency, not simply through employment, but also through the integration of refugee-led businesses into supply chains.'[10] The involvement of such actors in refugee assistance demonstrates today's market-based fixation on how best to foster refugee self-reliance and achieve other 'solutions', although the success of such endeavours by the private sector remains to be seen.

Accompanying this emphasis on self-reliance for refugees has been an outpouring of publications and policy papers on the topic. Some recommend self-reliance for refugees as an alternative to the failing 'care and maintenance' model used in protracted refugee settings.[11] Others view the concept as valuable, but consider it as a false panacea for refugees living in camps or constrained environments.[12] For others, the promotion of self-reliance is inherently flawed as an ultimately 'self-serving' strategy for donors 'focused on the reduction of

---

7 Bousquet, F. (2018) 'Doing things differently to help refugees and their host communities'. *Voices: Perspectives on Development*. Washington, DC: World Bank Group.

8 UNHCR (2018) IKEA Foundation. Webpage. Available at: www.unhcr.org/uk/ikea-foundation.html (accessed 18 August 2018).

9 Soros, G. (2016) 'Why I'm investing $500 million in migrants'. *Wall Street Journal*, 20 September. Available at: www.wsj.com/articles/why-im-investing-500-million-in-migrants-1474344001 (accessed 1 August 2018).

10 Branson, R. (2018) How Business Can Make a Difference for Refugees. Webpage (18 July). Available at: www.virgin.com/richard-branson/how-business-can-make-difference-refugees (accessed 18 August 2018).

11 Crisp, J. (2010) 'Forced displacement in Africa: dimensions, difficulties, and policy directions'. *Refugee Survey Quarterly* 29(3): 1–27. Available at: https://doi.org/10.1083/rsq/hdq031 (accessed 25 June 2018).

12 Omata, N. (2017) *The Myth of Self-Reliance: Economic lives inside a Liberian refugee camp*. Oxford: Berghahn; Easton-Calabria, E. and Omata, N. (2018) Panacea for the refugee crisis? Rethinking the promotion of 'self-reliance' for refugees. *Third World Quarterly* 39(8): 1458–1474.

material assistance' due to budgetary concerns.[13] Proponents of this view point out that a focus on self-reliance has increased as assistance programmes for long-term refugee situations became increasingly deprived of adequate funding, and a recognition by UNHCR that it is unable to ensure meeting essential needs for all prolonged refugee populations.[14] The rhetoric and practice of refugee self-reliance is thus perceived by different actors as fulfilling dichotomous functions, including either actualizing or neglecting protection and assistance.

Yet despite the widespread interest in achieving refugee self-reliance, the history of assistance to foster it remains largely unexplored, meaning that little is known of how and with which results these practices have changed over time. It is therefore difficult to speak convincingly of new or innovative practices toward refugees regarding self-reliance while there remains a significant gap in historical knowledge and institutional memory, particularly prior to the 1980s. This also means that important lessons may go unheard and unheeded.

Given all this, a critical question remains: what is refugee self-reliance – and is it actually anything new?

'Solving' refugees' lack of self-reliance

In the early 1980s, political scientist Robert Cox famously discussed the useful distinction between problem-solving and critical theory.[15] Problem-solving theory views the world in its current structure, focusing on solving the issues present within it without questioning the social and power relationships and systems they exist within.[16] Critical theory, on the other hand, 'is directed towards an appraisal of the very framework for action, or problematic, which problem-solving theory accepts as its parameters'.[17]

Until recently the majority of literature on refugee self-reliance has been technocratic and policy-oriented.[18] Existing critical engagement often focuses on

---

13 Hunter, M. (2009) 'The failure of self-reliance in refugee settlements'. *Polis Journal* 2: 1–46, p 1.

14 Jamal, A. (2000) *Minimum Standards and Essential Needs in a Protracted Refugee Situation: A review of the UNHCR programme in Kakuma, Kenya*. Geneva: Evaluation and Policy Analysis Unit, UNHCR.

15 Cox, R. (1981) 'Social forces, states and world orders: beyond international relations theory'. *Millennium: Journal of International Studies* 10: 126–155.

16 Cox, 'Social forces, states and world orders'.

17 Cox, 'Social forces, states and world orders', p 129.

18 IFAD (1987) 'International consultation on strengthening national agricultural research systems: wheat and rice research and training'. 26–28 January. Rome: International Fund for Agricultural Development; Gorman, R. (1993) *Refugee Aid and Development: Theory and practice*. Westport, CT: Greenwood; Jacobsen, K. (2005) *The Economic Life of Refugees*. Bloomfield, CT: Kumarian Press, Inc; Betts, A., Bloom, L., Kaplan, J. D., and Omata, N. (2014) *Refugee Economies: Rethinking popular assumptions*. University of Oxford, Refugee Studies Centre (pp 1–44).

refugee self-reliance programmes in practice[19] and tends to be implicitly liberal, presenting refugee self-reliance and livelihoods creation as development 'solutions' upholding refugees' human dignity and respecting their right to work.[20] While a small body of literature on refugee self-reliance has cited a 'disconnect' between benefactors and beneficiaries, and stated and intended aims and outcomes,[21] many of these studies nonetheless fall within a problem-solving paradigm. Similarly scarce in discussions on refugee self-reliance are critical examinations of its politico-economic history and its relationship to larger structures such as economic systems. This obscures, however, linkages between Western domestic social and economic norms and international development policy, reflected in turn by changing refugee assistance policies, programming, and terminology.

This book fits within a growing body of literature in the English-speaking world offering a critical rather than problem-solving lens on refugee self-reliance (loosely defined here as the ability to live independently from humanitarian assistance but questioned throughout). While much of the work on refugee self-reliance is contemporary, the focus here is on historical case studies documenting 'model' practices to foster refugee self-reliance at different points in time. Through both archival and contemporary research, it is my intention for this work to challenge current thinking on assistance to foster refugee self-reliance, and in turn to contribute to a more critical examination of rhetoric, policy, and practice today.

In so doing, this work fits alongside other critical voices on the implementation and outcomes of refugee self-reliance assistance. In the mid-2000s, for example, Kaiser and Meyer explored refugee livelihoods in Uganda within the ambit of the country's self-reliance strategy (SRS), finding notable disconnects between the stated aims of the strategy and its outcomes.[22] Strongly echoed in Meyer's findings as well, Kaiser writes,

> [T]he handover of services from UNHCR and its implementing partners to the district authorities represents *a mechanism for the reduction of services*

[19] Daley, P. (1989) 'Refugees and Underdevelopment in Africa: The case of Barundi refugees in Tanzania'. DPhil Thesis. Oxford: University of Oxford (p 133); Meyer, S. (2006) 'The "refugee aid and development" approach in Uganda: Empowerment and self-reliance of refugees in practice'. UNHCR Working Paper Series No. 131. Geneva: UNHCR.

[20] See for example: UNHCR (2005) *Handbook for Implementing and Planning: Development Assistance for Refugees (DAR) Programmes*. Geneva: UNHCR. Available at: www.unhcr.org/44c484902.pdf.

[21] Kaiser, T. (2006) 'Between a camp and a hard place: rights, livelihood and experiences of the local settlement system for long-term refugees in Uganda'. *Journal of Modern African Studies* 44(4): 597–621; Meyer, 'The "refugee aid and development" approach'. As overviewed in the introduction, Omata's (2017) work is an important critical exception to this trend.

[22] Kaiser, 'Between a camp and a hard place'; Meyer, 'The "refugee aid and development" approach in Uganda'.

> *for refugees and a cost-saving strategy. The SRS is commonly perceived as designed to support the development of Uganda's refugee hosting areas, rather than the refugees themselves.*[23] [emphasis added]

More recent academic work interrogates the aims and methods of fostering refugee self-reliance today, finding a similar trend of its employment as a cost-effective exit strategy.[24] Omata's monograph on 'self-reliant' Liberian refugees in Ghana's Buduburam refugee camp questions whether the camp's high level of economic commerce resulted in high levels of economic well-being, and examines the role of UNHCR's withdrawal of self-reliance assistance.[25] He reveals that the central economic driver of the camp was access to overseas remittances, which was unrelated to UNHCR initiatives to increase self-reliance through aid withdrawal. While refugees who received remittances were able to satisfy their basic day-to-day needs, those who had no connections to the diaspora remained deeply impoverished. Similar to other refugee-hosting countries in developing regions, Ghana virtually excluded refugees from formal labour markets and limited their engagement in commercial activities outside the camp. With little access to meaningful economic opportunities, refugees survived by relying on mutual support networks with other refugees. This example alarmingly demonstrates how the concept – or 'myth' as Omata terms it – of self-reliance can enable aid agencies to fail to protect vulnerable refugee groups living in desperate conditions.

Other literature questions common suppositions about self-reliance, such as it being a fixed state once attained and largely enacted at an individual level. Barbelet and Wake reveal, for example, that refugees often fare better in the direct aftermath of displacement due to the prevalence of assets and prior social networks, and struggle more in later months and years – at a time when they are paradoxically assumed to be self-reliant.[26] The authors explain:

> [T]here is a strong case for early support to livelihoods, especially geared towards the protection of assets and the prevention of indebtedness. In Cameroon, for example, by the time aid agencies started thinking about livelihoods many refugees had exhausted the assets they had brought with them, and the small-scale livelihoods support they received – which was not designed with their input – failed to create sustainable livelihoods opportunities.[27]

23 Kaiser, 'Between a camp and a hard place', p 613.

24 Easton-Calabria and Omata, 'Panacea for the refugee crisis?'

25 Omata, *The Myth of Self-reliance.*

26 Barbelet, V. and Wake, C. (2017) *Livelihoods in Displacement: From refugee perspectives to aid agency response.* Humanitarian Policy Group Report, September. London: ODI.

27 Barbelet and Wake, *Livelihoods in Displacement*, pp 23–24.

Similarly refuting current rhetoric, Field et al's work on refugee self-reliance in Delhi finds that rather than existing at the individual level, refugee self-reliance is achieved at the household and communal level, though this often remains unacknowledged by humanitarian actors.[28] A range of other work problematizes the notion of self-reliance as individually and economically based and in so doing begins to reconceive understandings of appropriate support to foster it.[29]

While these accounts provide detailed technical and critical analyses of refugees' economic lives both within and beyond camps, the historical evolution of approaches to foster refugee self-reliance is rarely broached in Anglophone scholarship. The emergency nature of many refugee crises has encouraged forward-thinking and contemporary research instead of in-depth archival analysis.[30] This has, in turn, obscured the reality of refugees' historical involvement in development as well as recognition of longer trends and changes in refugee assistance. In this way, the lack of history on refugee self-reliance assistance also reflects a larger lacuna in historical literature within Refugee Studies.[31] Yet as Barnett (2011) reflects on humanitarianism, its history can only be understood when placed in global context. Why should the history of humanitarian and development efforts to foster refugee self-reliance be any different?

Refugees as economic subjects

Since the Second World War, refugees have most commonly been considered as humanitarian subjects, with the dominant perception being that of hungry people awaiting hand-outs in camps instead of productive employees or entrepreneurs. The history in this book presents a different story. In fact, the unemployment of refugees has been tackled throughout the history of the international refugee regime. This assistance has generally occurred in one or more of the following ways: rural agricultural settlement (farming), micro-finance loans (to start or stimulate businesses), employment-matching (placing refugees into employment), public works projects (to 'develop' land or infrastructure), and vocational training (training to become employable or

[28] Field, J., Tiwari, A., and Mookherjee, Y. (2017) 'Urban refugees in Delhi: identity, entitlements and well-being'. IIED Working Paper, October, p 54.

[29] Easton-Calabria, E. and Skran, C. (eds) (2020) 'Special issue: Rethinking refugee self-reliance'. *Journal of Refugee Studies*; Easton-Calabria, E. (ed) (2017) 'Rethinking refugee self-reliance: moving beyond the marketplace'. RSC Research in Brief, No. 7. Oxford: RSC.

[30] Crisp, J. (2003) 'No solution in sight: the problem of protracted refugee situations in Africa'. Center for Comparative Immigration Studies (CCIS) Working Paper No. 68. CCIS: San Diego, p 223.

[31] Crisp, 'No solution in sight'.

to foster entrepreneurship).[32] Notably, each of these practices targets refugees not just as beneficiaries but as people capable of regaining or developing livelihoods. In other words, refugee self-reliance assistance itself treats refugees as *workers*. Indeed, I argue that refugees have been considered economic subjects since the inception of the first international refugee regime which began with the League of Nations in 1919.

This focus on refugees' economic capabilities and rights is also present within the guiding document of the current international refugee regime, the 1951 Convention Relating to the Rights of Refugees (the '1951 Convention'). Article 17 stipulates that refugees should be provided the same treatment as nationals in relation to the 'right to engage in wage-earning employment'.[33] The article goes on to state that 'restrictive measures imposed on aliens or the employment of aliens for the protection of the national labour market' should not apply to refugees. Article 18 of the Convention concerns refugees' self-employment, and proposes that refugees be provided 'the right to engage on his [*sic*] own account in agriculture, industry, handicrafts and commerce and to establish commercial and industrial companies'.[34] Together, these articles and Article 19 on liberal professions demonstrate the labour rights of refugees, and a desire for them to be given the means to engage in labour markets in host countries. Although written in 1951, these articles draw on interwar year recommendations and arrangements, including one concerning wage-earning employment for Russian and Armenian refugees and refugees' exemption from national labour market restrictions in the 1933 and 1938 Conventions.[35] These articles are significant in that they demonstrate the historical recognition of refugees as holding the right to work.

Main arguments and themes

As the Refugee Studies scholar and activist Barbara Harrell-Bond once wrote, '[A]s relief is a gift, it is not expected that any (most especially the recipients) should examine the quality, or quantity, of what is given.'[36] Examining the quality and quantity and, furthermore, the intent and result of the 'gift' of refugee self-reliance assistance enables an understanding of refugees' implicit

32 Easton-Calabria, E. (2015) 'From bottom-up to top-down: the "pre-history" of refugee livelihoods assistance from 1919 to 1979'. *Journal of Refugee Studies* 28(3): 412–436.

33 UNHCR (1951) 'Convention and Protocol Relating to the Status of Refugees', Article 17. Geneva: UNHCR. Available at: www.unhcr.org/uk/3b66c2aa10 (accessed 1 August 2017).

34 UNHCR (1951) 'Convention and Protocol Relating to the Status of Refugees', Article 18.

35 Labman, S. (2010) 'Looking back, moving forward: the history and future of refugee protection'. *Chicago-Kent Journal of International and Comparative Law* 10(1): 2.

36 Harrell-Bond, B. E. (1986) *Imposing Aid: Emergency assistance to refugees*. Oxford, Oxford University Press.

and explicit links to the modern capitalist economic system, where both economic thought and events such as recessions play a role in shaping refugee assistance. In this sense, I follow Pierson's proclamation that 'the conditions that are placed on state [welfare] benefits ... are often orientated not to the meeting of recipient's needs but rather to the requirement not to undermine the dynamics of the labour market'.[37]

Questions driving this research include: How has the practice of refugee self-reliance assistance changed over time? How are practices of refugee self-reliance assistance situated within wider historical eras? Whose interests shape the practices of self-reliance assistance? And, crucially, what are the outcomes of these practices for refugees?

In five empirical chapters spanning three regions of the world in the 20th and 21st centuries, this book explores how long-term refugee assistance has sought to foster the self-reliance of refugees. Case studies ranging from refugees in Greece in the 1920s, post-colonial Tanzania in the 1960s, Pakistan in the 1980s, Uganda in 2015, and, more recently, in Egypt and beyond (2020) demonstrate that this has largely occurred through development projects that have treated refugees as workers in need of employment – or in cases as vulnerable subjects coerced into filling employment needs. This has largely occurred in the cases I cover through development projects targeting refugees and sometimes also locals and even entire regions. This self-reliance assistance has been a main feature of refugee assistance yet has rarely been explored in scholarship.

This book uses archival and contemporary evidence to examine continuities and changes in institutional assistance to foster refugee self-reliance. It draws upon programme and evaluation reports of the League of Nations, UNHCR, and other main refugee assistance actors, as well as contemporary qualitative research with refugees and international humanitarian and development agencies, to document the shifting aims and conceptualizations of refugee self-reliance over time.

In each of the case studies, I explain how refugee self-reliance has become an instrument that alternately serves and exemplifies changes in social, political, and economic structures. Indeed, the rhetoric surrounding refugee self-reliance reveals main interests at different times, which can be elucidated by examinations of both practice and rhetoric, such as whether refugee self-reliance is espoused as an economic imperative, a protection instrument, or a human right. The identification of these linkages has implications for understanding the conditions under which refugee self-reliance is 'fostered', for analysing the means through which it is intended to be attained, and its explicit and implicit outcomes. Based on the case studies examined here, refugee self-reliance is revealed as an end in itself, as well as a malleable instrument to achieve other ends.

---

[37] Pierson, C. (1991) *Beyond the Welfare State? The new political economy of welfare*. Cambridge: Polity, p 53.

The three overarching arguments of this book are as follows. First, fostering refugee self-reliance has been an ongoing aim of the international refugee regime. Second, efforts toward refugee self-reliance have mainly been sought through the involvement of refugees in host country development projects, thereby demonstrating that refugees have always been development as well as humanitarian subjects; however, the development aims of many countries in the Global South are also driven by international (Western) development interests and economic trends, which refugee self-reliance assistance also becomes embedded within. Third, refugee self-reliance has not always been attempted solely for its own sake – instead, in many cases outside interests have converged to influence the types and amount of self-reliance assistance offered to refugees (including whether it is offered at all).

This convergence of interests around a particular aim (here, fostering refugee self-reliance) is often referred to as issue linkages,[38] which I expand on here through the analytical concept of instrumentalization. Drawing on critical development theory, I use the term 'instrumentalization' to discuss benefits that particular actors receive through the concept and outcomes of refugee self-reliance. I identify types of instrumentalization in the archives through following the core functions of the modern capitalist state – processes of accumulation, reproduction, and legitimation/repression[39] – that different assistance projects upheld. I then examine how these aspects of projects provided benefits to different actors. This also leads me to analyse different programmes and projects through dissecting the function of assistance in relationship to capitalism by 'following the money' and asking 'who benefits?' from refugee self-reliance.

I argue that self-reliance assistance plays a crucial role in mediating refugees' engagement with and integration into local and national economies and the international and global economy. Crucially, the types of self-reliance assistance provided are not neutral or dictated solely by the needs of refugees, but instead influenced by economic, social, and political trends at different times. As the needs and the shape of the capitalist system change, so does the labour necessitated – in response, self-reliance assistance has changed to meet those demands. In this way, refugee self-reliance becomes instrumentalized.

As overviewed in Table 1.1, when examining the history of refugee self-reliance assistance, three main observations cut across the case studies presented here. First, refugee self-reliance assistance has shifted emphasis from rural agricultural production to urban vocational training and entrepreneurship. This

[38] Haas, E. B. (1980) 'Why collaborate? Issue-linkage and international regimes'. *World Politics* 32(3): 357–405.

[39] Gough, I. (1980) 'Thatcherism and the welfare state: Britain is experiencing the most far-reaching experiment in "new right" politics in the western world'. *Marxism Today*, pp 7–12 (p 9). Note: Gough draws on James O'Connor's analysis of welfare and capitalism: O'Connor, J. (1973) *The Fiscal Crisis of the State*. London: St James Press.

Table 1.1: Historical overview of refugee self-reliance assistance

	Main type of self-reliance assistance	**Labour practices**	**Economy supported by labour practices**	**Ideological aims of refugee self-reliance**	**Economy supported by ideological aims promoted**	**Historical trends**
1919–1945 (Case Study 1)	• Rural settlement • Employment-matching • Public works	• Agricultural labour • Participation in national development (for example, public works)	• National and international economy	• Upholding nation-state system • Promoting peace • Preventing social unrest/rise of Communism	• International economy	• *Political*: Nation-state dominance • *Social*: Nascent welfare state • *Economic*: Great Depression, attempts to return to international economy
1945–1979 (Case Study 2)	• Rural settlement	• Agricultural labour • Participation in national development (for example, cash crops, building infrastructure)	• National and international economy	• Contributing to the 'development project' • Preventing social unrest/spread of Communism • Tanzania national self-reliance agenda	• National and Western international economy	• *Political:* Nation-state dominance • *Social:* Rise of welfare state, modernization (development) • *Economic:* Keynesian economics, international economic expansion
1979–1995 (Case Study 3)	• Livelihoods training • Public works	• Small-scale entrepreneurs • Involvement in Structural Adjustment Programmes (for example, World Bank)	• Informal national economy/ global economy	• Political pawns of capitalism (fighting Communism) • Development aid to host countries • Structural adjustment	• Global economy	• *Political*: Cold War • *Social*: 'Decline' of the welfare state, shift from collective to individual welfare • *Economic*: Rise of neoliberalism

(Continued)

Table 1.1: Historical overview of refugee self-reliance assistance (continued)

	Main type of self-reliance assistance	Labour practices	Economy supported by labour practices	Ideological aims of refugee self-reliance	Economy supported by ideological aims promoted	Historical trends
1999–2015 (Case Study 4)	• Livelihoods training • Micro-finance loans	• Small-scale entrepreneurs (informal sector)	• Informal national economy/ global economy	• Promoting peace • Building democracy • Exclusion from economy	• Global economy	• *Political*: Private sector dominance • *Social*: Individual welfare • *Economic*: 'Triumph' of capitalism, informalization, neoliberalism, globalization
2015–2020 (Case study 5)	• Livelihoods training • Digital remote work training, including ICT and freelancer skills • Micro-finance loans/Graduation Approach	• Small-scale entrepreneurs (informal sector) • Digital entrepreneurs (online work platforms) • Gig workers	• Informal national economy/ global economy	• Dignity through work • Market-based protection • Exclusion from economy • Global outsourcing	• Global economy	• *Political*: Private sector, isolationism/ restrictionism • *Social*: Individual welfare • *Economic*: Neoliberalism, growing informalization, globalization, 'gig economy'

coincides with host countries' changing approaches to development as well as the rise of urbanization and globalization. Second, in the last century refugee self-reliance appears to have changed from constituting largely agricultural subsistence (and in some cases surplus) in rural areas to a wage-based market dependency in urban areas; since the 1980s refugees have increasingly been incorporated into the informal working urban poor. And now, with the advent of digital remote work for refugees, this role has extended into the digital gig economy. This has important implications for refugee protection.

Last, and more broadly, this history suggests that, as development has shifted from being considered an outcome created through state action to an outcome of market forces, refugee-serving agencies have shifted from working with the state to foster refugee self-reliance to supporting populations in a host state's absence. They have thereby increased the emphasis on integrating refugees into economies rather than state systems as a means of assistance and in this way continue to be important but problematic arbiters in the relationship between refugees and work. This is evident through the emerging transition to promoting remote, digital livelihoods as a means to support refugees who may lack the right to work and to social protection in restrictive host countries with high levels of unemployment.

Why historicize refugee self-reliance?

One question I asked myself throughout this project was a simple one: Why historicize? More specifically, why was it important for me to historicize refugee self-reliance assistance? By historicize I mean here to recontextualize with historical information and, as Fraser writes, to reread texts 'in light of categories and problems not available to their authors'.[40] I sought to bring a materialist historical reading to the topic of refugee self-reliance with the objective of seeking to better understand different actors' interests, namely assistance agencies and governments, as they undertook self-reliance programmes. I also undertook this particular reading of history in order to better identify the relationship between capital and refugee self-reliance assistance; I attempted to do this through identifying and analysing material interactions, interests, and influences such as wider economic phenomena. At the same time I accounted for the role of political and social interactions and events, which I analysed as part of the broader historical contexts I presented in each case study.

However, history is of course written and read from the perspective of a variety of intellectual disciplines, with their different methodologies and definitions of evidence. Comparative history, intellectual history, cultural history, and social history are only a few of the many different

[40] Fraser, N. (2003) 'From discipline to flexibilization? Rereading Foucault in the shadow of globalization'. *Constellations* 10(2): 160–171.

schools of historiography.[41] I chose a materialist reading of history as it enabled an opportunity to bring a new perspective to current discussions on refugee self-reliance and corresponding assistance, particularly as much of the contemporary rhetoric and academic research on this subject is economically focused.

In so doing, I provide three main contributions to knowledge. The first is a history of development assistance for refugees, as current literature on this topic rarely precedes the 1980s, meaning that refugees' historical involvement in development has not been visible. Through this history I seek to provide empirical evidence to challenge the longstanding perception that refugees' primary needs lie in humanitarian rather than also development support. Second, I seek to write a history of refugees as *workers*, and examine how refugees' economic participation is enabled through self-reliance assistance – itself shaped by and fulfilling functions necessitated by markets. This contributes toward a small body of literature that treats refugees not as humanitarian but as economic subjects.[42] Last, I explore the ways in which refugee self-reliance assistance has been intimately bound up with larger economic, social, and political trends and events, demonstrating how refugee self-reliance is a dynamic concept that reveals power relations and predominant modes of thoughts at different points in time. In so doing I contribute a critical perspective on refugee self-reliance to a field that has largely treated the concept as technical and ahistorical.[43]

This book also sheds light on a troubling facet of refugee assistance: the conflation of livelihoods and protection through humanitarian and development actors' focus on fostering refugee self-reliance. As the following chapters demonstrate, the concept of refugee self-reliance has shifted definitions over decades yet assistance to foster it has largely maintained the same practices for almost a century, thus revealing both change and marked continuity within the refugee regime. This evidence-based argument, which a historical approach enables, has enormous potential to contribute to conversations on how best to support refugee self-reliance today.

Situating the story: academic disciplines and theoretical approaches

This book is situated within the fields of Refugees Studies, Development Studies, and History. It draws on critical development theory and historical methods to contribute new theory and history to Refugee Studies. The

---

41 Cannadine, D. (ed) (2002) *Introduction: What is history now?* Basingstoke: Palgrave, p 37.

42 Rolfe, C. and Harper, M. (1987) *Refugee Enterprise: It can be done*. London: Intermediate Technology Publications; Jacobsen, *The Economic Lives of Refugees*; Betts et al, *Refugee Economies*.

43 IFAD, 'International consultation on strengthening national agricultural research systems'; UNHCR, *Handbook for Implementing and Planning*; WRC, *Building Livelihoods*.

chapters here offer an alternative to a liberal approach in reading self-reliance, placing an emphasis not on *how* refugee self-reliance can be achieved within social and economic structures but on interrogating the larger structures it is promoted within, *why* it continues to be promoted at all, and for whom and for which ultimate ends. In so doing, it examines the integration of refugees into the international global economy and self-reliance as part of a wider set of ideals and practices linked to the capitalist system. As mentioned previously, refugees are considered not solely as humanitarian subjects but also as economic actors whose economic participation is enabled through self-reliance assistance.

Examining refugees and work also raises the topic of development, and indeed, much of the literature on refugee self-reliance and livelihoods involves explicit or implicit discussions of it. However, while Refugee Studies scholars have engaged with many of the underlying concepts in Development Studies, the discipline has largely ignored Development Studies tools of critical analysis. This is evident in the modern boom in literature on refugees and development, which lacks critical theoretical engagement with refugees' relation to systemic causes of 'underdevelopment', dominant actors' aims in involving refugees in development, and even critical discussion of development terms, including 'self-reliance' and 'development' itself. Within Development Studies, however, these issues are well-theorized and have been examined both historically[44] and in contemporary settings.[45]

The relevance of themes of power, inequality, and economic interests for refugees in a development context suggests many unexplored parallels between Refugee Studies and Development Studies. Indeed, examining the relationship between refugees and development necessitates extending analyses of power beyond just refugees and assistance agents, and instead encompassing national development goals in host countries, Western influences in setting development agendas and terms, and the ultimate aims of development. All of these issues are connected to capital on national and global levels, which refugees become inherently entwined with as soon as assistance aims include 'putting refugees on the development agenda'.[46]

---

[44] Frank, A. G. (1966) *The Development of Underdevelopment*. Boston, MA: New England Free Press; Wallerstein, I. (1974) 'Dependence in an interdependent world: the limited possibilities of transformation within the capitalist world economy'. *African Studies Review* 17(1): 1–26; Arrighi 1971, 1978.

[45] Escobar, A. (1995) *Encountering Development: The making and unmaking of the Third World* (Princeton studies in culture/power/history). Princeton, NJ: Princeton University Press; Cowen, M. and Shenton, R. (1996) *Doctrines of Development*. London; New York: Routledge; Sachs, W. (ed) (1997) *The Development Dictionary: A guide to knowledge as power*. Hyderabad: Orient Blackswan.

[46] UNHCR (2005) 'Putting refugees on the development agenda: how refugees and returnees can contribute to achieving the Millennium Development Goals'. High Commissioner's Forum. FORUM/2005/4. 18 May.

In addition to providing a means to analyse linkages between macro and micro phenomena, critical development theory also offers Refugee Studies the opportunity to consider central development topics from a historical perspective, refugee self-reliance among them. Regarding critical theory in Development Studies, Schuurman states that, among other characteristics, it 'attempts *to uncover historic processes* which link the various elements of a particular social reality without falling into the trap of reductionism' [emphasis in text].[47] He goes on to characterize critical development research as:

> 1) an object of research which concerns the lack of emancipation of large groups of people, the structural causes thereof and attempts to do something about it; 2) an explanatory framework using the inner (but globalising) logic of the capitalist system in terms of production, market and consumption; and 3) challenging accepted ideas, ideologies and policies (... the 'subversive' side of critical theory).[48]

Critical development theory provides one way to examine refugee issues not only from the framework of the nation-state, as is commonly the case, but from that of the capitalist system. Indeed, this book takes as its starting point that since the creation of refugees as well as responses to them do not occur within the boundary of a single state, understandings of refugee issues must therefore come from an understanding of larger global systems, including the expansion and shifting forms of capitalism across the world.[49] Such a perspective offers new angles for analysis that can transcend borders and nationalities and instead delve into systemic issues related to capital at a variety of scales, including but in no way limited to local and global class systems and the transnational money flows of the so-called industrial humanitarian complex.

This work sits alongside that of a small handful of scholars in Refugee Studies who have broached discussions of the role of capital in refugee affairs. B. S. Chimni and Stephen Castles are two notable and widely valued contributors to the topic, whose structural examinations of capitalism and causes of migration flows, including refugees, demonstrate important connections between Refugee, Migration, and Development Studies.[50]

---

47 Schuurman, F. J. (2009) 'Critical Development Theory: moving out of the twilight zone'. *Third World Quarterly* 30(5): 831–848 (p 836).

48 Schuurman, 'Critical Development Theory'.

49 Daley, 'Refugees and Underdevelopment in Africa', p 133, p 2.

50 Chimni, B. S. (2004) 'From resettlement to involuntary repatriation: towards a critical history of durable solutions to refugee problems'. *Refugee Survey Quarterly* 23(3): 55–73; Castles, S. (1998) 'Globalization and migration: some pressing contradictions'. *International Social Science Journal* 50(156): 179–186; Castles, S. (2000) *Ethnicity and Globalization*. London: Sage.

Castles, for instance, has analysed the systemic role of capitalism in broader international migration,[51] and its effect on citizenry,[52] arguing that we cannot understand modern movement without taking economic factors into account. However, Castles' political economy work on migration generally discusses refugees as one type of migrant, mentioning them in relation to other migrants yet failing to acknowledge and theorize the particularities of refugeedom as related to political economy.

Chimni compellingly addresses the relationship between Refugee Studies and humanitarian practice to broader economic and social trends, including colonialism, geopolitics, transnational capital, and the needs and interest of hegemonic (Western) states.[53] However, his work generally utilizes a political economy framework that analyses these important linkages without breaking down the specific mechanisms through which grand concepts such as 'humanitarianism' and 'imperialism' operate in tandem.

Although focusing more broadly on aid and development, Mark Duffield contributes a similarly valuable critical perspective to the theme of capital, including its role in policies that promote the containment of populations in the Global South which might otherwise migrate to Northern countries to seek both jobs and welfare benefits.[54] He also directly addresses the topic of self-reliance, such as through his conceptualization of sustainable development as a bio-political technology for containing 'non-insured populations' which are required to improve their resilience and strengthen self-reliance within their given conditions.[55] However, Duffield's work is often not grounded in case studies or empirics, making it difficult to unearth the specific mechanisms and contextualized outcomes of the societal shifts he critiques.

Together, these and other scholars offer an important critical foundation for analysing refugee self-reliance assistance yet also provide considerable

---

51 See among other work: Castles, S. (2012) 'Cosmopolitanism and freedom? Lessons of the global economic crisis'. *Ethnic and Racial Studies* 35(11): 1843–1852; Castles, S. (2013) 'The forces driving global migration'. *Journal of Intercultural Studies* 34(2): 122–140.

52 Castles, S. (2005) 'Nation and empire: hierarchies of citizenship in the new global order'. *International Politics* 42(2): 203–224.

53 Chimni, B. S. (1998) 'The geopolitics of refugee studies: a view from the South'. *Journal of Refugee Studies* 11(4): 350–374; Chimni, B. S. (2000) 'Globalization, humanitarianism and the erosion of refugee protection'. *Journal of Refugee Studies* 13(3): 243–263; Chimni, B. S. (2009) 'The birth of a "discipline": from refugee to forced migration studies'. *Journal of Refugee Studies* 22(1): 11–29.

54 Duffield, M. (2008) 'Global civil war: the non-insured, international containment and post-interventionary society'. *Journal of Refugee Studies* 21(2): 145–165; Duffield, M. (2002) 'Social reconstruction and the radicalization of development: aid as a relation of global liberal governance'. *Development and Change* 33(5): 1049–1071.

55 Duffield, M. (2006) 'Racism, migration and development: the foundations of planetary order'. *Progress in Development Studies* 6(1): 68–79.

scope for more detailed critical analyses of refugees' specific relationship to capital as well as linkages between refugee assistance, development, and capitalism. Indeed, with these authors as important exceptions, the role of capital remains under-theorized in Refugee Studies, including in discussions regarding the formation of the international refugee regime, 'root causes' of refugees, and contemporary drivers of refugee self-reliance and livelihoods.

The geography of refugee self-reliance

The geographic focus of this book shifts from interwar and post-war Europe to early post-colonial East Africa, the Middle East, and contemporary East Africa. The history I present does not trace one country or case across time but instead captures cases of refugee self-reliance assistance in different countries based both on content availability and the geographic movement of the international refugee regime. By focusing on model assistance programmes and by examining the wider trends and dominant thought on refugee self-reliance in different eras, I seek to capture the broad arc of changes and continuities in refugee self-reliance assistance throughout the history of the international refugee regime. Given this, this book cannot by any means be considered a complete global history of refugee self-reliance. For example, I do not explore the work of the United Nations Relief and Works Agency (UNRWA) in fostering refugee self-reliance, despite its long history and successful endeavours in livelihoods assistance such as micro-finance.[56]

The idea that important information could be gleaned through examining continuity and change in self-reliance assistance in different parts of the world influenced the selection of cases. I also sought to find case studies through which I could discuss important contemporaneous social, economic, and political events and trends. I decided for example that, given their effect on wider refugee assistance, including cases which discussed decolonization and the Cold War in relation to refugee self-reliance assistance was important. It is also noteworthy that each case deals with different refugee populations (including some such as ethnic Greek refugees in Greece, who might be considered forced migrants today), meaning that the cases are not necessarily comparable. The thread that links them are the practices of assistance actors and the international refugee regime itself. While the time periods selected are not always comparable in length of time, they focus as comprehensively as possible on the self-reliance programming examined, which in each case varied in length.

56 Hanafi, S., Hilal, L., and Takkenberg, L. (eds) (2014) *From Relief and Works to Human Development: UNRWA and Palestinian refugees after 60 years*. London: Routledge.

Where does the story come from? Sources and methods

I employ archival and ethnographic methods in this book.[57] I view these as parallel methods of different time periods, in that each seeks to illuminate both specific behaviours and the broader context in which they take place. I supplemented archival research with several key informant interviews of former humanitarian aid workers working in, respectively, East Africa in the 1970s and 1980s and Afghanistan and Pakistan in the 1980s and 1990s; however, this often served as background information for myself rather than explicit material for chapter. The combination of methods I employed is highly valuable in offering researchers the ability to examine objects of enquiry from both present and past perspectives and is increasingly used in fields such as anthropology.[58] My decision to undertake both historical and contemporary fieldwork arose out of my aim to write 'the history of the present'[59] in regard to efforts to foster refugee self-reliance I observed while living in Kampala, Uganda, in 2011, and in subsequent trips. While primarily historical (case studies 1–3), this book extends to 2020 through contemporary qualitative fieldwork (case studies 4 and 5). This choice of case study also necessitated contemporary rather than historical methods, as many archives such as UNHCR's have a 20-year time limit on material, meaning that no documents produced prior to 1995 were available when I first began this work.

A note on terminology

As we all well know, the words we choose in conversations matter. Yet what does a discussion on self-reliance mean when the word doesn't exist in some refugees' own languages? And when the very concept changes from culture to culture? And when most written work on the subject is not written by refugees themselves? At the end of the day, self-reliance is just – significantly – an English word. But refugees span the world.

These reflections were important for me during my research and are also important to mention here due to the decisions and caveats they reveal. First, my archival research was limited to English-language texts. While this was rarely a problem due to my predominant focus on international

[57] For a longer discussion of my methods, see Annex 1.

[58] Merry, S. (2002) 'Ethnography in the Archives', in J. Starr and M. Goodale (eds) *Practicing Ethnography in Law: New dialogues, enduring methods*. New York: Palgrave Macmillan; Scheppele, K. L. (2004) 'Constitutional ethnography: an introduction'. *Law & Society Review* 38(3): 389–406.

[59] Foucault, M. (1977) *Discipline and Punish: The birth of the prison*. New York: Pantheon, p 31.

institutions and agencies, and English-speaking assistance actors, it of course influences the type of story I am able to tell. I sought to examine refugee self-reliance assistance from global to individual levels through my selection of archives and informants, but each of my case studies would surely have been enriched by local and national archives, and other data-collection methods.

Second, I chose as far as possible to retain the language of the eras that I found in archival documents and during contemporary research. Thus 'self-sufficiency' and 'population transfer' (rather than 'forced migration') emerge in Chapter 2 on refugee self-reliance in Greece, while 'self-reliance' and 'empowerment' are present in Chapter 4 on Afghan refugees in Pakistan, with an additional focus on 'livelihoods' in Chapter 5 on Congolese and other refugees in Uganda in the mid-2000s. This decision around terminology was an attempt to be faithful to the archives and my informants and provide the reader with a stronger sense of historical context; this flexing terminology ultimately also acted as a powerful unit of discursive analysis, which I compared and contrasted with the actual practices described in different places and time periods.

As I will go on to discuss, my research identifies many of the 'core' practices to foster refugee self-reliance by international institutions and agencies over the last century, which have (alarmingly) changed little. These practices as well as others seeking to achieve the same goal of refugees' 'independence' from institutional assistance, are what I have chosen to refer to as the – admittedly bulky – phrase 'refugee self-reliance assistance', sometimes replaced in this book with the equally unwieldy 'institutionally fostered refugee self-reliance'. While many of the other words surrounding refugee self-reliance in forthcoming chapters are directly from documents and interviews, these phrases are my own. Rarely used by other academics, practitioners, and policymakers, some of their focus, however, is encompassed by contemporary terminology such as 'self-reliance programming', 'livelihoods support', 'economic inclusion', and even 'development assistance'. It is my best attempt to clearly separate the efforts of refugees themselves to foster their own self-reliance from that of external actors, who often imposed their own understandings, objectives, and interests into self-reliance assistance to refugees of whom they often knew little. It is this latter story – fascinating and deeply problematic – that this book seeks to tell.

Chapter overview

Chapter 2: Self-sufficiency out of necessity: refugee self-reliance assistance in interwar Greece

This chapter presents the first international response to refugees led by the League of Nations through a case study of ethnic Greek refugees in Greece in the 1920s. It highlights the dominant self-reliance assistance practices undertaken at the time by the Greek Refugee Settlement Commission, created to assist the 1.5 million ethnic Greek refugees from Asia Minor forced to relocate to Greece between 1922 and 1924. The population exchange exemplifies the upholding of the post-First World War new 'world order', the creation of nation-states after the collapse and break-up of multi-ethnic European empires, and a corresponding attempt to return to the successful international economy of the pre-First World War world. This case study highlights the primacy of states at this point in time and examines the ways refugee development assistance explicitly targeted state needs (in this case, Greece's) through the dominant mode of production – agriculture. The population exchanges of the interwar years, of which the Greek-Turkish exchange was only one, and the focus on returning displaced people to their countries in order to 'reconstruct' economies and 'restore' peace demonstrates an economic motive of instrumentalizing refugees for both peace and labour through development.

Empirical material: League of Nations Archive (UN, Geneva); International Labour Organization Archive (Geneva); Ruth A. Palmeree Private Papers (Hoover Institution Archives, Stanford University); Brainerd P. Salmon Private Papers (Hoover Institution Archives, Stanford University).

Chapter 3: Socialism and self-reliance: refugee assistance in post-colonial East Africa

This chapter examines the nature of refugee self-reliance assistance within the post-war 'development project' in Tanzania following the wars of decolonization in the 1960s. I link the promotion of many East African refugee self-reliance settlements through mono-crop cultivation for national export to wider development policies at the time; these focused on domestic production and international economic participation as a means to achieve mass well-being. Refugees' economic value therefore came in the form of growing cash crops for both subsistence and export, supported by international actors such as the International Labour Organization (ILO) and the World Bank. Thus, refugees contributed to the so-called 'development project' through participating in programmes premised on modernization. In this way I demonstrate the ulterior aims of this assistance as related to the international economy and refugees' role as labourers according to exogenously determined dictates.

Empirical material: UNHCR Archives (Geneva); T. F. Betts Collection (RSC, University of Oxford); Neldner Collection (RSC, University of Oxford); Brainerd P. Salmon Private Papers (Hoover Institution Archives, Stanford University).

Chapter 4: Warriors of self-reliance: refugee self-reliance in Cold War Pakistan

UNHCR's biggest operation at the time, assisting Afghan refugees in Pakistan between 1979 and 1995, was largely focused on self-reliance and livelihoods. Contributing (at least in theory) to host country development, refugees served as 'development pawns' for Pakistan and donor countries alike, illustrating a broader trend of host countries seeking development and aid funding due to hosting refugees, and donor countries utilizing funding for refugees as a means to fight Communism and incentivize the restructuring of Southern economies. I present four phases of self-reliance assistance for Afghan refugees, which correspond to shifts in broader economic trends from Keynesian economics to neoliberalism. The practice of self-reliance assistance promoted large-scale employment, individual income generation, and ultimately acted as a protective mechanism for vulnerable populations unable to succeed in the market-based economy. These stages of self-reliance assistance encompass periods of humanitarian focus on so-called 'refugee dependency syndrome' and self-reliance as psychosocial support. This chapter demonstrates the dynamism of self-reliance as both a concept and a practice.

Empirical material: UNHCR Archives (Geneva); T. F. Betts Collection (RSC, University of Oxford); RSC Grey Literature Collection (RSC, University of Oxford); P. and M. Centlivres Afghanistan Collection (Geneva Institute); Digital archive of the Afghanistan Center at Kabul University.

Chapter 5: Dignity in informality? Urban refugee self-reliance assistance in Kampala, Uganda

This chapter presents a case study of urban refugee livelihoods trainings in Kampala, Uganda, in 2015. Here I explore how the contemporary global discourse of refugee self-reliance is transposed on to a local context. I examine livelihoods trainings offered by national and international organizations, including by interviewing and 'following' refugee informants through their post-training livelihoods creation. In so doing I present the impact of trainings on refugee self-reliance as well as the local constraints refugees face in achieving self-reliance in Kampala, including lack of access to capital and markets. This chapter also focuses on the impact of neoliberal tenets embedded within contemporary refugee assistance and the related impacts of urbanization and informalization.

Empirical material: UNHCR Policy Documents (contemporary, digitally accessed); primary qualitative research with refugees and livelihoods trainers, members of UNHCR and other national and international organizations.

Chapter 6: Livelihoods 2.0? Refugee self-reliance and the digital gig economy

The final chapter brings the history of refugee self-reliance assistance up to the pre-COVID-19 present through a focus on the emerging topic of digital livelihoods and refugees, set against the backdrop of the so-called European refugee crisis and the Global Compact on Refugees. Although the main research for this chapter was conducted pre-COVID-19, it also touches on some lessons for self-reliance and livelihoods programming that have emerged during the COVID-19 pandemic. Current scholarship, policy, and practice on refugee self-reliance rarely focus on the global emerging phenomenon of the changing nature of work, which include gig economies and innovations in technology, AI, and robotics. This chapter offers an original perspective on how refugees are involved in the so-called 'future of work' through a review of over 100 initiatives to help refugees and other migrants access digital work, and a case study of a Syrian refugee named Alaa in Cairo, Egypt, who created a website that helped him survive. In this way, the chapter highlights refugees who successfully engage with the emerging digital economy as well as those who are unable to do so. In particular, the chapter discusses the protection issues raised by humanitarian agencies acting as intermediaries between refugees and largely unregulated work in the global gig economy, with a broader examination of NGOs seeking to use technological means to foster refugee self-reliance.

Empirical material: Qualitative research with refugees and digital livelihoods trainers, as well as members of UNHCR; key informant interviews with experts in digital work and members of the private sector hiring remote workers; UNHCR publications; NGO and INGO publications.

Conclusion

As Nigerian author Emman Ikoku once wrote, '[S]elf-reliance is the oldest idea. It is the story of normal human existence.'[60] Examining this story more closely, and in particular the intent and result of the 'idea' of refugee self-reliance assistance enables an understanding of refugees' implicit and explicit links to the modern economic system, where both economic thought and events such as recessions play a role in shaping refugee assistance. A main aim of this project is to increase understanding of refugee self-reliance and the history of assistance that has both promoted and stifled it. The ability to become self-reliant in even the most disadvantaged of circumstances is worthy of respect and illumination. Understanding which forms of assistance support or hinder these endeavours – and how and why these practices arose – is worthy of the same.

[60] Ikoku, E. (1980) *Self-Reliance: Africa's survival.* Enugu: Fourth Dimension Publishers.

2

Self-Sufficiency out of Necessity: Refugee Self-Reliance Assistance in Interwar Greece

Introduction

On one mild day in October 1922, an American doctor named Ruth Parmelee arrived in Salonika, Greece. Although not her intended destination – she was meant to begin work in Smyrna after summer holidays in America – the activities she would undertake would become her life's main calling. 'I now began, this time in Greece, a period of service which lasted thirty years', she writes in the final sentence of her memoir.[1] She was not the only new arrival who would stay so long. On 9 September 1922, the Turkish army entered the city of Smyrna, spurring on the start of a population transfer between Greece and Turkey that would eventually uproot over 1.5 million people. In the course of that month, hundreds of thousands of Ottoman Greeks and Armenians left Smyrna for Greece. That October, Dr Parmelee estimated that there were 100,000 refugees in Salonika alone, and these flows were just the beginning. 'Many are flooding in from Thrace', she wrote in a letter to friends in November. '[O]ne day we walked [to] the market to buy a loaf of bread, and were told that the bakeries were empty, because seven shiploads of refugees had just arrived.'[2]

---

1 Parmelee, R. A. (1967/2002) *A Pioneer in the Euphrates Valley*. Ann Arbor, MI: Gomidas Institute Books.

2 Parmelee, R. (1922) 'Letter to family and friends'. Ruth A. Parmelee Papers, Box 1, Folder 1.2, Notebook 1. Hoover Institution Archives.

Over the following decades, through her prolific reports to the American Women's Hospitals' headquarters and letter-writing to friends and families, Dr Parmelee became a documenter of the Greek-Turkish population exchange and its aftermath – notably of the emergency and development assistance provided to refugees. In the same letter to friends that November, she wrote:

> This morning I saw evidence of the efforts on the part of the government to place families in the country where they may till the fields and make their living ... Aside from attempts on the part of the government to find some sort of shelter for these bodies, they are giving daily food rations, and furnishing some facilities for medical care. The Greek government is working and doing all they can, although they are a bankrupt institution. But they cannot begin to do it all and need the cooperation of all the relief agencies available.[3]

Beyond her role as a witness, Dr Parmelee became an active part of refugee relief and development work itself. As a doctor she directly assisted in emergency medicine, and in later years fought to open training schools for refugee nurses. In this way she simultaneously provided emergency and development refugee assistance. As we shall see, her work both documents and exemplifies the multi-pronged refugee assistance provided in the interwar years by relief agencies and institutions.

In the 1920s, the nascent international humanitarian system experienced its largest task to date with the compulsory population exchange. Similar to many humanitarians, Dr Parmelee was battling entropy, striving to make order from disorder, to bring new lives – in the form of obstetrics as well as vocational training – to those refugees from Asia Minor who had been forced into Greece. It is therefore fitting to include her work with the American Women's Hospitals (AWHs) alongside other humanitarian agencies and the broader work of the League of Nations and Greek Refugee Settlement Commission at the time. Short of trained staff, money, and even space for hospital beds, Dr Parmelee struggled to expand and institutionalize the ad hoc response to the Greek refugees. She sought to shift the humanitarian gaze from refugees' short-term emergency needs to the potential of longer-term skills they and their surrounding host communities could utilize throughout their lives. However, self-reliance was no easy task, for either refugees themselves or the outside entities seeking to foster it. Nor is it simple to dissect efforts to create self-reliance from the coinciding nationalistic aims or economic priorities of states and institutions. Refugee self-reliance assistance

[3] Parmelee, 'Letter to family and friends'.

was, and continues to be, embedded within larger social, political, and economic structures. It is often guided by invisible hands, and the archival texts designated to document it rarely hold explanations for its origins.

This chapter presents the main forms of assistance to refugees beyond the emergency phase – agriculture settlements, micro-finance, employment in public works, employment-matching, and vocational training – and demonstrates that they have existed since the 1920s. Although ranging in scope, these practices all target self-reliance, defined here as living without institutional assistance. This suggests a base belief by humanitarian and development actors at the time in the productive capability of refugees, evident in the discourse and corresponding construction of refugees as workers at different points in the history of the international refugee regime. This also suggests an instrumentalization of both refugee self-reliance assistance and the refugee labour that arose from it, wherein the types of development assistance utilize the productive capabilities of refugees in different ways – ostensibly to promote self-reliance yet with the larger aim of serving host governments' and others' interests.

The primary focus here is on ways that refugees' efforts toward self-reliance were guided by assistance projects that contributed to the national and international project of statebuilding. This project, in turn, was pivotal to creating the modern capitalist economy, which in the interwar years was incubated by states and fed by the international economy. Using the response to the Greek refugee crisis by the League of Nations and supporting organizations, the relationship between refugee self-reliance assistance and states' economic and non-economic aims both nationally and internationally is examined, with a focus on the pervasive nationalist ideology present in the interwar era. In this period, refugee settlement premised on employability was readily utilized as a solution when labour was needed in countries of resettlement – and refused when it was not. Examining the larger landscape at the time also demonstrates how refugee assistance by the League of Nations, Greek government, and international charities such as the AWHs were in many cases pivotal to successful refugee settlement and in this way became integral arbiters in instrumentalization.

The League of Nations and refugee self-reliance

The establishment of the formal commission on the League of Nations on 25 January 1919, provided an unprecedented basis for international cooperation and oversight as well as the first attempts by an international body to respond to mass displacement. The League was formed with the primary goal of maintaining peace, for the countries comprising it had in many cases been devastated by the First World War. With the League's creation, states envisaged a security system to prevent war by increasing international dialogue and accountability, and upholding newly drawn state lines, even condoning forced displacement through population exchanges to adhere to these borders.

In 1921, the League of Nations created the High Commission for Refugees (hereafter, the High Commission), in part to diminish the perceived threat of European destabilization posed by displaced people. Approximately nine to ten million refugees were in Europe during the interwar period;[4] those supported by the League included Russians, Greeks, Armenians, Bulgarians, Turks, Saarlaenders, and Jewish, mainly German, citizens.[5] The end of the First World War and the interwar years constituted a continuous era of humanitarian efforts based on states' developing but still nascent propensity to take responsibility for populations in need and respond through international coordination and organizations.[6] Yet throughout this era, welfare provision by states was largely unfamiliar, and they maintained an overall ethos of self-reliance for citizens as well as refugees.

This focus on self-reliance was evident through the aim of the few welfare measures created during this time. One of the League's main areas of focus was unemployment, which after the First World War was an area multiple countries needed to address. As Pironti writes, 'The regeneration of national economies at the end of war was closely linked to the need to find a solution to labour problems where the greatest social tensions were nested. All countries faced similar problems concerning labour reconversion and the risk of mass unemployment.'[7] Widespread unemployment and the social needs that accompanied it thus formed a premise for an international debate on social issues and solutions, and led to the creation of important social security models, such as the ILO's international model of social insurance.[8] A main means to combat unemployment proposed by the ILO and later more widely considered by the League was public works,[9] which were expanded as a main foundation of welfare assistance in the United

---

4 Marrus, M. (1985) *The Unwanted: European refugees in the twentieth century*. Oxford: Oxford University Press, p 51.

5 Fanshawe, M. and Macartney, C. A. (1933) 'What the League has done: 1920–1932'. League of Nations Union, O.LNU/1933, p 9.

6 Barnett, M. N. (2011) *Empire of Humanity: A history of humanitarianism*. Ithaca, NY: Cornell, p 87.

7 Pironti, P. (2017) Post-war Welfare Policies. Encyclopedia Online, 1914–1918. Webpage. Available at: http://encyclopedia.1914-1918-online.net/article/post-war_welfare_policies (accessed 18 June 2017).

8 Sauthier, I. L. (2013) 'Modern Unemployment: From the creation of the concept to the International Labour Office's first standards', in S. Kott and J. Droux (eds) *Globalizing Social Rights: The International Labour Organization and beyond* (International Labour Organization century series). Basingstoke: Palgrave Macmillan, p 80.

9 Sauthier, 'Modern Unemployment', p 79.

States of America (US) through the New Deal between 1933 and 1938. The interwar years also saw the rise of other social welfare policies such as the UK's Unemployment Insurance Act of 1920, which offered insurance to approximately 20 million workers in an attempt to address the dysfunctions of the market.[10]

The assistance offered to refugees at the time parallels domestic welfare trends in its minimalism: rather than the international humanitarian community supporting refugees through 'hand-outs' for months or years before transitioning them to self-reliance assistance – what in later eras would become known as development support – the interwar years offered the latter form of support almost immediately, and at times proffered it simultaneously with or even instead of emergency relief. This state- and internationally-funded assistance, which was limited and designated as 'no-charity', therefore reflected the tenets of state non-interference regarding citizen welfare and the nascent welfare state systems at the time. Although the British welfare state, for example, saw an expansion compared to the years leading up to the First World War, the relationship between unemployment and the need for healthcare as well as for other 'basic necessities' went largely unrecognized.[11] Indeed, the types and aims of the provision of refugee assistance in the interwar years suggest an era where emergency relief was quickly replaced with assistance intended to help refugees get out of states' pockets and onto their pay rolls.

The focus on assistance to enable employment was widely evident within the League; the High Commission, renamed the Nansen International Office for Refugees in the 1930s, had a strict 'no-charity' philosophy and conceptualized refugees as an economic and 'technical' problem with economic solutions.[12] As Dr Fridtjof Nansen, the High Commissioner for Refugees, stated in 1923, 'The guiding principle was not indiscriminate charity which tends to the degeneration of the refugees, but to encourage them to work for themselves and thus become producers of wealth and independent citizens as soon as possible.'[13] This was enabled through the common naturalization of refugees at the time, which significantly reduced barriers to accessing work. The provision of material assistance to refugees was innovative for the time and 'League initiatives in helping refugees achieve

[10] Garside, W. R. (2002) *British Unemployment 1919–1939: A study in public policy*. Cambridge: Cambridge University Press, p 37.

[11] Thanes, P. (1988) 'The British welfare state: its origin and character'. *Refresh* 6(Spring): 5–8.

[12] ILO (1928) 'Refugee problems and their solution'. *International Labour Review*, 1768–1785.

[13] LN (1923) 'Near East refugees, Western Thrace refugee settlement'. Report by Dr Nansen, High Commissioner for Refugees, to League of Nations, Communicated to the Council. Geneva, 22 April 1923.

self-sufficiency were a dramatic departure from the past'.[14] The League's overall doctrine of refugee self-reliance persisted into the 1930s, reflecting the tenets of state non-interference regarding citizen welfare.

The no-charity philosophy of the League also stemmed from the Commission's own financial constraints and its mandate to coordinate rather than implement programmes. Refugees were originally assumed to be an ephemeral phenomenon, and the Commission was only meant to be temporary.[15] The High Commission, and later Nansen Office, had to fight to remain in existence up to the start of the Second World War.[16] Indeed, both offices rarely received more than one per cent of the League's budget[17] and thus faced a challenging lack of funding. Due to this and a dearth of prior experience, the League's refugee relief efforts were largely ad hoc trials,[18] which became increasingly orchestrated in the late 1930s. The initial provisional nature of assistance facilitated accommodating policies regarding refugee livelihoods and self-sufficiency in rehabilitation and settlement efforts.

Due to social and political trends, internal funding constraints, and a lack of prior experience in refugee assistance, League assistance strategies emphasized bottom-up methods (those sourced from refugees themselves) and refugees' capacity to contribute to independent national commissions and rehabilitation through their own expertise as well as financial means. The promotion of refugee self-sufficiency and professional skills meant that refugees became employed in settlement commissions, served as delegates of the High Commission and even funded other refugees' settlements through micro-finance loans. However, they were also subjects of material and conceptual instrumentalization by states, co-opted nationally and internationally for political, social, and economic gains.

Self-reliance assistance in interwar Greece

After the break-up of the German, Russian, Austro-Hungarian, and Ottoman empires, nationalism became one of the main items on the agenda

---

[14] Skran, C. (1985) 'The Refugee Problem in Interwar Europe, 1919–1939', MPhil thesis. Oxford: University of Oxford, p 113.

[15] LN (1934) 'Human welfare and the League'. League of Nations Union, O.LNU/1934(13), p 66.

[16] Hansson, M. (1938) 'The Refugee Problem and the League of Nations'. Conference Given at the Nobel Institute Oslo on 7 January 1938. Geneva: Nansen International Office for Refugees.

[17] Johnson, T. F. (1938) *International Tramps: From chaos to permanent world peace*. London: Hutchinson, p 207.

[18] Housden, M. (2012) *The League of Nations and the Organization of Peace*. Harlow: Longman, p 59.

for the myriad minorities throughout Europe. Nationalist movements that had been brewing prior to the war found themselves able to legitimately form new nations, as nation-states were to be governed by the principle of self-determination based on US President Woodrow Wilson's Fourteen Points, an outline of principles for world peace set out during the peace negotiations to end the First World War.[19] The nation-state was conceived as a sovereign entity that presided over a homogeneous group of people of (ambiguously) shared language, religion, culture, and descent. With the creation of nine new nation-states, the Great War and its conclusion in the Treaty of Versailles marked the transition from the age of empire to the age of the nation-state. The interwar era formation of nation-states cannot be divorced from the human displacement that partially created new nations.[20] According to the guiding tenets of the modern nation-state system, peace could be maintained if people who 'belonged' within particular territories stayed there – even if they had to be moved there by force.

Despite the efforts to maintain peace, the formation of nation-states was anything but peaceful for the over two million people forcibly displaced after the war. In 1919, under the Treaty of Neuilly, Greeks from Bulgaria were 'exchanged' with Bulgarian inhabitants of Salinik (soon to become Salonika and later Thessaloniki).[21] While recorded in League documents and discussions by states as an 'exchange', this was of course forced migration on a massive scale.[22] The tens of thousands exchanged in 1919 soon swelled to even more. Although the Great War was over, the final chapter of the life of the Ottoman Empire was the Greco-Turkish war, which spanned 1919–1922 and led to the forced – and condoned – displacement of approximately 1.5 million people. Approximately one million ethnic Greek refugees and 500,000 ethnic Turkish refugees were the object of a population transfer between Turkey and Greece that began in 1922 and became compulsory in 1923.

The Greek-Turkish population exchange was a monumental and tragic affair. The exchange itself is well documented and has been the evidence for the interwar years constituting the first international refugee regime[23]

19 Wilson, W. (1918) 'President Woodrow Wilson's Fourteen Points'. 8 January. Available at: http://avalon.law.yale.edu/20th_century/wilson14.asp (accessed 1 September 2017).

20 Zolberg, A. (1983) 'The formation of new states as a refugee-generating process'. *Annals of the American Academy of Political and Social Science*, 467: 24.

21 Mazower, M. (1992) 'The refugees, the economic crisis and the collapse of Venizelist hegemony, 1929–1932'. *Deltion Kentrou Mikrasiatikon Spoudon [Bulletin of the Centre of Asia Minor Studies]* 9: 119–134.

22 As mentioned in the introduction, I have chosen to retain as far as possible the terminology used from the time periods researched.

23 Skran, C. (1995) *Refugees in Inter-war Europe: The emergence of a regime*. Oxford: Clarendon Press.

and as a paradigmatic case of forced migration and population exchanges in the 20th century.[24] It even became a model for later forced transfers, including never-implemented plans by the British in 1930s' Palestine to settle the Jewish-Arab 'dispute'.[25] Bolstered by the 'success' of the Greek-Turkish population exchange, this concept of exchanges began to be perceived as a way to settle minority conflicts as well as international problems, and retained broad acceptance through and beyond the Second World War.[26]

Comparatively less examined is the long-term assistance provided to refugees in Greece during this time by the League of Nations-sponsored assistance body and humanitarian agencies. Its primary aim of self-reliance and how this assistance compares to long-term refugee assistance in later years has been hitherto neglected despite the important precedent it set in refugee assistance.

Refugee self-reliance assistance practices

In 1922, in the destination port city of Salonika, the products of the population exchange were the refugees in Dr Parmelee's hands. Despite their vast emergency needs, Dr Parmelee quickly realized other needs as well. In a 1922 report documenting the work of the AWH in Salonica in the first few months after her arrival, she writes,

> When trying to look into the actual condition of these Refugees it is natural to think of their physical needs, for at a glance hunger, nakedness, lack of shelter and sickness are visible even to the casual observer. But there are other kinds of suffering that cannot be known to the relief worker, who is doing his work in a wholesale manner. It is only through individual talks with individuals that the heart-ache can be known … Contractors, artisans, manufacturers, professional men, small merchants and farmers were obliged to flee empty handed and leave their all behind; the same with the home-makers. … No business, no work, no homes! Such is the destitute conditions of the refugees in Salonica! … The one great cry among these refugees is for work! So often it is said: "We do not want charity bread; we want to earn it!" The Missionary Relief Committee heartily agrees that

[24] Zetter, R. (2012) *Lands of No Return, Population Exchange and Forced Displacement in the 20th Century*. Athens: Anemon Productions.

[25] Katz, Y. (1992) 'Transfer of population as a solution to international disputes'. *Political Geography* 11(1): 55–72.

[26] Katz, 'Transfer of population', pp 55–56.

> the most constructive relief work is that, given through some form of industrial work; and along these lines most strenuous efforts for relief are now being made.[27]

In a report written only ten months later, Dr Parmelee[28] discusses the 'Industrial Relief' she has helped to organize, including loans to refugee workers and the opening of a lace factory run by and employing refugee women. The rapid speed in the construction of this work is striking, and suggests that the contemporary strong distinction between emergency relief and development had not yet emerged in the interwar years.

Dr Parmelee and the AWHs were not alone in their relief and development efforts. Echoing the League's overall approach to assistance, the Greek Refugee Settlement Commission (GRSC) was formed in 1923 with the sole and immediate aim of settling and fostering the self-reliance of the Greek refugees. The League of Nations repeatedly stated that the most crucial need for refugees was work and, like later programmes implemented in the 1920s and 1930s, the Commission was forbidden to use funds on relief. The GRSC maintained a close connection to the national government, almost all GRSC staff were Greek and Henry Morgenthau, the first chairman and former ambassador to the Ottoman Empire during the First World War, stipulated that all posts should be given to Greek refugees.[29] Due to its success, the GRSC became a model for refugee settlements, replicated in further refugee crises in Bulgaria, Syria, and Lebanon. In Bulgaria between 1926 and 1933, for example, approximately 125,000 refugees were settled by a national commission through rural development that included building roads, clearing land, and providing refugee farmers with tools and seeds.[30]

The following sections outline the main refugee self-reliance assistance practices undertaken in the interwar years by assistance agencies such as the GRSC, ILO, and private charities like AWH. Although practices from Greece are highlighted, due to its status as a model form of settlement, larger European efforts to foster refugee self-reliance are also discussed. These practices are important to highlight as further chapters compare and contrast these initial methods, which were first used in the 1920s as part of international assistance to refugees.

---

27 Parmelee, 'Letter to family and friends'.

28 Parmelee, R. (1923) 'Refugee work in Salonica, Greece'. AWH Report No. 2, May 1923. Ruth A. Parmelee Papers, Box 3, Folder 3.12 Work Files, AWH 1922–1932. Hoover Institution Archives.

29 Skran, 'The Refugee Problem', p 179.

30 Skran, 'The Refugee Problem', p 49.

Agricultural settlement

Refugees created by population exchanges often entered states that perceived them as simultaneous economic burdens and opportunities.[31] Agricultural settlement was the dominant means of self-reliance assistance at the time and in Greece refugees were pivotal to economic growth, for they provided a cheap workforce as well as a domestic market. And the GRSC, in turn, was pivotal in helping refugees undertake labour at all. Indeed, of the Greek refugees, a 1929 Foreign Affairs article reads,

> The imported agriculturalists … often are better workmen then the indigenous ones, and the standard of Greek agriculture is already being raised by the competition and example of the newcomers … [T]obacco production of Macedonia has been doubled and cereal production greatly increased. … In consequence, the large adverse trade balance characteristic of Greek commerce is gradually being reduced. The Commission wisely followed the aim of getting as many of the refugees as possible into productive work on the land, and refused to attract them into the already overcrowded cities by building dwellings for them there. Roughly six-sevenths of the persons 'settled' by the Commission have been put on the land.[32]

This shows that Greece was able to improve exports and trade relations in part through the agricultural settlement of the majority of Greek refugees. This was supported through the work of the GRSC, which was tasked with placing as many refugees as possible into 'productive work'. However, the placing of refugees into work was heavily influenced by national and international demands for labour.

Having had to decide the post-war path to economic growth, Greece continued with agriculture instead of industrialization, which would have been difficult for the largely agrarian society to quickly achieve, and employed a mixture of import substitution and export.[33] As industrialization fell behind agriculture, refugees offered a cheap agrarian workforce and influenced political decisions leading to land reform. Formerly private land became government property and was then passed on to the GRSC to be reallocated

---

31 Howland, C. P. (1926) 'Greece and her refugees'. *Foreign Affairs* 4(4): 613–623.

32 Armstrong, H. (1929) 'Venizelos again supreme in Greece'. *Foreign Affairs* 8(1): 120–129, pp 122–123.

33 Mazower, M. (1992) 'The Messiah and the bourgeoisie: Venizelos and politics in Greece, 1909–1912'. *The Historical Journal* 35(4): 885–904, p 119.

accordingly.[34] Refugee self-reliance assistance through agricultural settlement was central to the attainment of both political and economic aims, as land reform was undertaken in order to provide the GRSC with enough land upon which to settle refugees. The Greek government sped up land reform in late 1924 in order to provide the GRSC with more land upon which to settle refugees, thereby deepening a linkage between the Commission's work and the reform.[35] In turn, the GRSC settled refugees on this newly available land, using most of their funds to settle refugees in rural rather than urban areas. Through the work of the GRSC, over 500,000 refugees were settled in rural areas, mainly in the north of Greece.[36] They contributed enormously to the Greek economy as an agrarian workforce.

By 1931, 650,000 people had been settled and 2,000 agricultural colonies and urban quarters had been built around Greece.[37] For homesteading families, the Commission provided tools, animals, and seeds for one year, as well as created infrastructure such as schools, hospitals, and model farms that also assisted local Greeks.[38] A 1933 League pamphlet discusses a colony of 15 villages created to settle 15,000 refugees, mainly farmers.[39] Refugees lived in tents until material to build huts was provided. In addition to farms, cottage industries such as charcoal burning and carpet weaving were set up and, by the end of the first year after resettlement, the majority of refugees had become entirely self-reliant.[40]

Figures documenting the results of the land reform also suggest the significance of refugees' agricultural contribution to the Greek economy, as the rate of cultivation grew fastest in the new territories where the refugees were settled, mainly Macedonia and Thrace. Between 1922 and 1931, Macedonia's cultivated area expanded from 275,000 to 550,000 hectares and in Thrace from 72,000 to 148,000.[41] This was strikingly large compared to areas of central Greece sparsely populated with refugees, where cultivated land rose only from 260,000 to 330,000.[42] Tobacco exports accordingly soared, further suggesting the agricultural benefit of refugees to the economy.

---

34 As Mazower explains, 'The Greek state shifted the costs of expropriation into the former owners of the land, freeing large areas which were eventually handed over to the Refugee Settlement Commission'. 'The Messiah and the bourgeoisie', p 120.

35 Mazower, M. (1991) *Greece and the Inter-war Economic Crisis*. Oxford: OUP Catalogue, pp 77, 79–80.

36 Mazower, *Greece and the Inter-war Economic Crisis*.

37 Skran, 'The Refugee Problem', p 48.

38 Skran, C. (1989) 'The International Refugee Regime and the Refugee Problem in Interwar Europe', DPhil dissertation. Oxford: University of Oxford, p 178.

39 LN (1933) 'Human welfare and the League'. League of Nations Union, January 1933, No. 155. O.LNU/1933(8), pp 72–73.

40 LN, 'Human welfare and the League'.

41 Mazower, *Greece and the Inter-war Economic Crisis*, pp 79–80.

42 Mazower, *Greece and the Inter-war Economic Crisis*, pp 79–80.

However, the main impetus for pursuing the land reform was not to promote refugee self-reliance but to prevent the radicalization of peasants and prevent political uprisings. As Mazower states,

> [Greek Prime Minister] Venizelos realized that the creation of a large class of peasant smallholders might defuse peasant radicalism, prevent the formation of a peasant-worker bloc, and do much to secure the social stability of the Republic. This was the thinking which lay behind the land reform of the 1920s, which benefited refugee and indigenous farmers alike, and which provided a cause in which the League of Nations and the Greek authorities combined to provide a notable instance of a decisive and far-reaching reshaping of the economy.[43]

As this quote demonstrates, and similar to the struggle to separate economies from states, it is difficult to parse out political from economic – and humanitarian – aims. Both a political and economic impulse underlay many of the decisions targeting refugees, and the government's concern at quelling potential unrest by refugees through employment in rural settings.

In addition to providing economic support to the country, the agricultural settlement of refugees became a means to use this population to claim land and populate newly gained territories after the First World War. For example, in this period Macedonia was an important crossroads for trading that was sought after by Bulgaria, Serbia, Romania, Greece, and Turkey, all of which believed they had claim to part or all of the region.[44] Greece used newly arrived refugees to 'colonize' the newly acquired territories of Macedonia – heavily facilitated by the GRSC and other refugee assistance. Between 1924 and 1929, the GRSC was provided 812,592 acres of land upon which to settle more than half a million refugees primarily in the northern provinces of 'New Greece'; 90 per cent of refugees were settled there, mainly in Macedonia and Thrace.[45] One report states that

> *The Government colonization scheme in Macedonia* is providing land, draught animals, housing, seed and a limited amount of food for the refugees that are being settled in New Greece. The scheme is to provide the refugees with land heretofore not cultivated by the owner

[43] Mazower, *Greece and the Inter-war Economic Crisis*, p 75.

[44] Psomas A. (1974) 'The Nation, the State and the International System: The case of Modern Greece'. Thesis. Proquest Dissertation Publishing, p 158.

[45] Pentzopoulos, D. (2002) *The Balkan Exchange of Minorities and Its Impact on Greece*. London: Hurst & Co, p 107.

> and to assist a refugee to settle himself on the land and become self-supporting.[46] [emphasis added]

In this way we see that the result of refugees becoming 'self-supporting' was multi-pronged – not only were refugees meant to live independently from relief aid through agricultural production, and thereby act as a beneficial workforce feeding the Greek economy, but in so doing help to 'colonize' Macedonia, the territory Greece so fervently sought to claim. Refugees were therefore drawn into the economics of statecraft not only through forced displacement but through their so-called 'rehabilitation' in their new homeland. In large part, this process occurred due to the Greek government, agencies, and commissions that led refugee assistance at the time and, as previously discussed, preferred rural settlement. Refugee self-reliance occurred in line with the Greek government's aim to increase agricultural production while refugees served an additional purpose as bodies physically occupying the territory of New Greece.[47]

The emphasis on land for refugees also served a further purpose. Greek Prime Minister Venizelos, who served several terms from 1910 to 1920 and from 1928 to 1933, sought to 'modernize' Greece through economic and constitutional reforms in part by providing land for refugees to farm on. In addition to physical labour provided by refugees, development occurred through the Commission's provision of new tools and agricultural methods. Of Greece, Mears writes:

> Better breeds of livestock are being introduced, and nomadic shepherds are being replaced by stock breeders who raise forage crops on their own land. Fallowing has given place to artificial fertilization, and new tools supplied by the Refugee Settlement Commission are gradually causing the peasants to discard antiquated methods of agriculture.[48]

---

46 Salmon, B. P. (1924) 'The Report', Folder 1, Writings, 1923–1924. Brainerd P. Salmon Papers, Hoover Institution Archives, p 3.

47 The utilization of refugees as labourers and as means to occupy territory also occurred in other countries during the interwar years. In Bulgaria, national authorities '"used" their immigrants and refugees in the same way as did the other Balkan nations – namely, to populate deserted or economically important areas, or to change the ethnic composition of the population of certain areas in order to create an overwhelming Bulgarian majority, especially in precarious border areas'. Source: Detrez, R. (2015) 'Refugees as Tools of Irredentist Policies in Interwar Bulgaria', in H. Vermeulen, M. Baldwin-Edwards, and R. van Boeschoten (eds) *Migration in the Southern Balkans*. Cham: Springer International Publishing, pp 47–62 (p 53).

48 Mears, E. G. (1929) *Greece Today: The aftermath of the refugee impact*. Stanford, CA: Stanford University Press, p 279. Eliot Mears was a well-respected Stanford professor known for his work on modern Greece and Turkey. He spent 1916–1920 in the Middle East, 'in the service of the United States Department of Commerce and of economic missions to

Simultaneously Venizelos instrumentalized refugees as a political platform and used refugees' productive power to uphold the ruling political elites through economic growth largely spurred on by the refugees. He also pushed through the naturalization of refugees due to their support for him and his belief that they would support him politically if they were to become citizens – which served to smoothly enable not only their right to work but also their right to vote.[49]

While agricultural settlement was the preferred option by the GRSC and Greek government for settlement, self-reliance through agriculture was not assured. Tobacco had long been an important export for Greece, and one which continued to flourish as Greek refugees took over the agricultural plots that ethnic Turks had been forced to leave behind. In the early 1920s when the GRSC was settling refugees, tobacco prices were high. It was in demand by the Americans at the time due to the cigarette industry, and the US was the main importer.[50] By the mid-1920s tobacco had become the key commodity of Greece and accounted for over half of Greece's export earnings.[51] Given the success of selling tobacco, it was not a problem that refugees were often settled on plots so small that only cash crop cultivation made economic sense. Indeed, to keep up with the demand, the Greek National Bank made loans to refugee farmers with the aim of incentivizing them to expand their cultivation of cash crops. In 1929 it was estimated that 100 out of 131 refugee settlements in the Kavalla region of northern Greece were dependent on tobacco crops as their livelihood.[52] However, in the late 1920s, prices dropped and refugees found themselves unable to earn enough to buy food. Neither the loan assistance provided nor the encouragement from the GRSC to mainly cultivate cash crops seemed as helpful as it once had. Wheat production also failed to support farmer self-sufficiency and in 1930 Greek Minister of Parliament F. Sarantis stated, "[W]heat growing is on the lowest rung of incomes and the shortage of large agricultural

---

countries in Asia Minor'. His writings were well respected and he was a trusted voice on international trade. Source: *Yearbook of the Association of Pacific Coast Geographers* (1947) Eliot Grinnell Mears, 1889–1946. University of Hawai'i Press, vol 9, p 30.

49 Kritikos, G. (2005) 'The agricultural settlement of refugees: a source of productive work and stability in Greece, 1923–1930'. *Agricultural History* 79(3): 321–346.

50 Morgenthau, H. (1930) 'I was sent to Athens'. *Journal of Hellenic Studies* 50: 167 (pp 256, 259, 275).

51 LN (1925) 'Financial situation in Greece. Letter and note from the representative of the Greek Government'. Geneva, 3 September, League Greek Delegation, No. 2935. 10/46055/26389; Mazower, *Greece and the Inter-war Economic Crisis*, p 87.

52 Altsitzoglou, F. (1941) *Oi giakades kai o kampos tis Xanthis*. Athens. Cited in Mazower, *Greece and the Inter-war Economic Crisis*, p 87.

ownerships renders problematic the survival of the farmers who insist on wheat cultivation".[53]

Starvation became a real fear, and the GRSC was accused of financially exploiting refugee farmers 'in the interests of foreign bondholders'.[54] As Mazower writes, 'By 1930 local bank managers were extremely worried at prevailing levels of indebtedness: credit was being spent on consumer goods, or wage labour, at levels which could only be sustained so long as the boom kept prices high'.[55] As prices dropped, refugee farmers became unable to pay their loans – and were unable to be self-sufficient, as their plots had not been cultivated for subsistence. Refugees' loss of livelihoods therefore appears to be in part due to the very encouragement to borrow loans and grow cash crops from the assistance agencies that sought to foster their self-reliance.

A handwritten letter by a Greek refugee named Ignatios Tsakalopoulos to the League of Nations, written on 17 November 1926, further demonstrates the need to critically examine who benefited from refugee assistance and in which ways (Figure 2.1). In documenting the state of refugee assistance in Cavalla, Greece, he both confirms and refutes institutional accounts of assistance. Tsakalopoulos writes:

> [I] was poorly received and was installed by the Greek Government in the warehouse of the tobacco factories in the hope that within a month at least we should be transferred to some suitable dwelling of those which had been abandoned by the exchanged Moslems, but for 18, for 36 months we have waited in vain … Even at present there are still quite a large number of warehouses and tents full of refugees. After so many years of suffering no arrangements have yet been made to house them and protect them from suffering, overcrowding and particularly the lack of water. Almost one half the families have died, the deceased including my mother-in-law and aunt.
>
> Both personally and on behalf of a large number of families of my acquaintance, I feel bound to inform you regarding the woeful condition of the refugees and ask you, nay pray you, to send me some reply. So many thousands of human beings have been exchanged. … They have been deceived, are without work and are seeking charity … In view of the appalling conditions among the refugees I beg you in God's name to consider our case and send representatives to verify for themselves the conditions of the refugees in order that your sacred aims may be attained by loan … I beg of you not to grant any subsidies or

[53] Efimeris ton Syzitiseon (1930) 38th Session, Feb. 17, 1930, 650–65, 626, Library of the Greek Parliament in Athens. Cited in Kritikos, 'The agricultural settlement of refugees', p 323.

[54] Mazower, *Greece and the Inter-war Economic Crisis*, p 125.

[55] Mazower, *Greece and the Inter-war Economic Crisis*, p 124.

> loans for the establishment of refugees if the money is to be wasted in the merry-making and entertainment of those who receive it, instead of the object for which it is intended.[56]

The descriptions in this letter contrast with much of the positive rhetoric about refugees' living and working conditions present in institutional documents from the time. Through the overt request for a loan to only be provided for actual refugee assistance, this letter illuminates a sense of distrust of Greek authorities as well as a keen awareness of some of the financial activities related to refugee settlement, discussed below.

Urban refugee settlements

The predominant focus of the GRSC on rural development assistance to refugees can be seen through the fact that just a quarter of the initial budget was devoted to urban settlements. Despite the varied success of this approach in Greece, settling refugees in both urban and rural areas became the norm in countries such as Bulgaria and Lebanon. The economic reasoning behind the notably reduced support to urban refugees as compared to those settled in rural areas is clear: in 1924 the Greek Minister of Agriculture posited that it was easier to settle refugees in rural areas than urban ones, stating, 'Because a small piece of land, a small rural dwelling and a few essential tools would not only improve the lot of the peasants, *they would also have an immediate effect in terms of the State Treasury. This is the class that produces faster yields*' [emphasis added].[57]

Where urban resettlement was an option, relocated urban dwellers had increased opportunities to continue their past professions and utilize financial and trading skills.[58] Refugees constituted 90 per cent of the labour force for constructing houses in urban areas.[59] In addition to providing temporary jobs in construction, urban support occurred through the modest provision of housing, small loans, and some effort to help skilled refugees who sought to continue their trade as a group in urban areas.[60] A League report recalling the Greek refugees stated, 'The famous

[56] Tsakalopoulos, I. (1926) [Letter from a Refugee] By Ignatios Tsakalopoulos (an exchanged person), Cavalla, 17 November 1926. To the President of the Council of the League of Nations, Geneva. 10/55542X/263891.

[57] Protonotarios, A. B. (1924) To Prosfygiko Provlima apo Istorikis, Nomikis kai Kratikis Apopseos, 88; Efimeris ton Syzitiseon, 65th Session, 24 June 1924, 458. Cited in Kritikos, 'The agricultural settlement of refugees', p 343.

[58] Housden, *The League of Nations and the Organization of Peace*, p 70.

[59] Skran, 'The Refugee Problem', p 179.

[60] Giannuli, D. (1995) 'Greeks or "strangers at home": the experiences of Ottoman Greek refugees during their exodus to Greece, 1922–1923'. *Journal of Modern Greek Studies* 13(2): 271–287, p 280.

Figure 2.1: Letter by Ignatios Tsakalopoulos

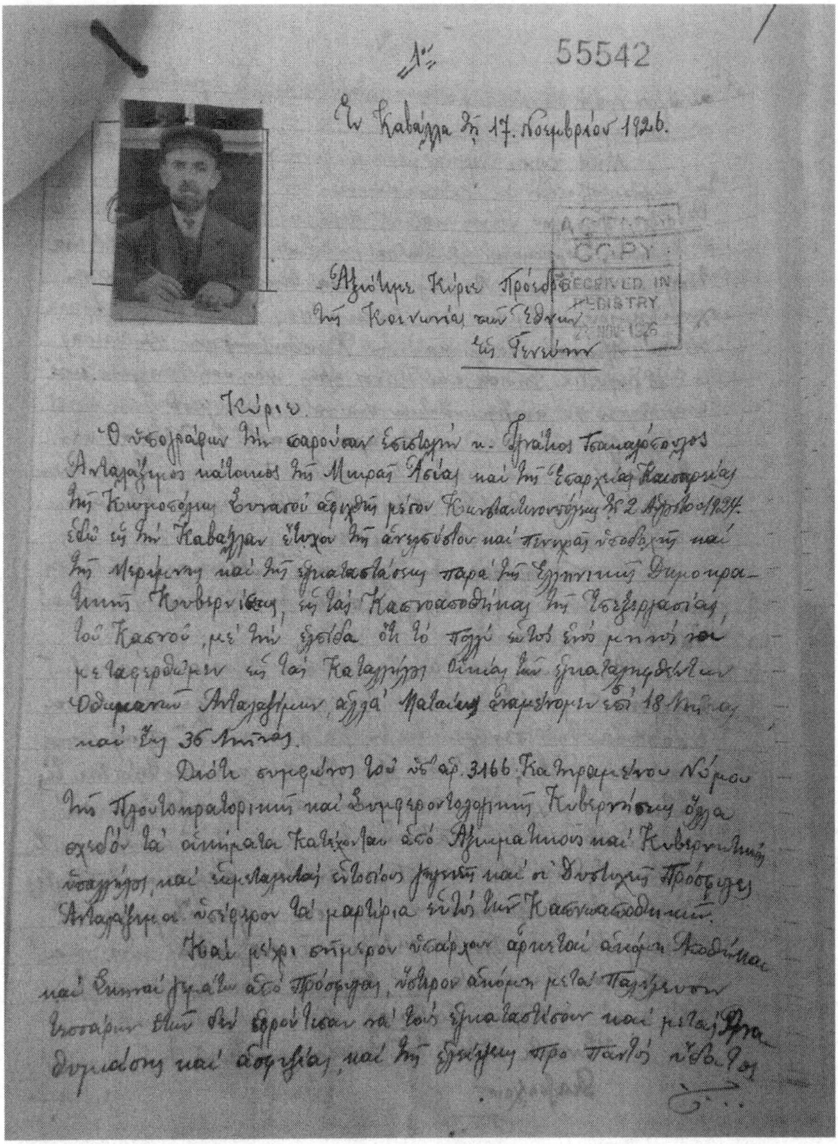
55542

Ἐν Καβάλλᾳ τῇ 17. Νοεμβρίου 1926.

Ἀξιότιμε Κύριε Πρόεδρε
τῆς Κοινωνίας τῶν Ἐθνῶν
εἰς Γενεύην

COPY
RECEIVED IN REGISTRY
23 NOV 1926

Κύριε.

Source: United Nations Archives at Geneva. 10/55542X/263891

Smyrna carpet industry has now moved bodily, with the men who used to practice it, from Smyrna to the Piraeus'.[61] However, there are accounts of economic exploitation and mistreatment by native Greeks, and evidence of some Greeks moving from city to city in efforts to escape exploitative employers.[62] Urban refugees' living situations were often deplorable; over two-thirds of homes that the GRSC visited in 1929 were temporary dwellings that were often overcrowded and squalid.[63] The prewar urban housing crisis was exacerbated by the refugee influx, but complicated rights of tenure and political promises by the government that were never fulfilled affected the Greek refugees for decades.[64]

In the 1920s, one of the largest urban refugee quarters in Greece was the district of Kokkina near Piraeus, which had a refugee population of over 70,000 and an AWH hospital that Dr Parmelee took charge of in 1925.[65] In the 1970s, anthropologist Dr Renée Hirschon undertook a study[66] on the social life of refugees in Yerania, a neighbourhood in Kokkina and the last to be provided with housing by the GRSC. This work reveals longstanding social and economic exclusion stemming from the treatment of urban refugees after the population exchange. In addition to refugees and their children living in overcrowded conditions in poverty, often in areas lacking central sewerage systems, she writes, 'The existence of a separate sense of identity through five to six decades is notable since the original refugees and the host population, metropolitan Greeks, shared most social and cultural characteristics. The refugees were all Orthodox Christians, culturally and physically identifiable as Greeks, and the overwhelming majority were Greek-speaking.'[67] Despite ostensible similarities, the Greek refugees were still isolated and marginalized over 50 years after the population exchange, thus calling into question the extent of the 'success' of urban refugee settlement and the exchange itself.

---

61 LN (1934) 'Human welfare and the League'. League of Nations Union, O.LNU/1934(13), p 74.

62 Giannuli, 'Greeks or "strangers at home"'.

63 Morgenthau, 'I was sent to Athens', p 243.

64 Hirschon, R. (1998) *Heirs of the Greek Catastrophe: The social life of Asia Minor refugees in Piraeus*. Oxford: Berghahn Books.

65 AWH (American Women's Hospitals) (1923) AWH Bulletin 1923. Folder 3.13, Work Files AWH 1923–1952, Ruth A. Palmeree Papers, Hoover Institution Archives; Palmeree, R. (1952) 'Dedication Piraeus Hospital', 1923. Folder 3.13, Work Files AWH 1923–1952, Ruth A. Palmeree Papers, Hoover Institution Archives.

66 This is one of the few studies in English that focuses on this population. Regrettably, due to time and language constraints, local and national Greek archives were not included in this research.

67 Hirschon, R. (1998) *Heirs of the Greek Catastrophe: The social life of Asia Minor refugees in Piraeus*. Oxford: Berghahn Books, p 5.

Loans for refugees and the refugee-led revolving fund

Although settlement primarily occurred in rural areas, the GRSC did advocate for refugees to start their own businesses in urban areas, and the government enabled loans to be taken out from the Greek National Bank. Loans were also offered through humanitarian organizations such as the AWH. In 1923, Dr Parmelee wrote in a report that 'time loans' amounting to $1500.00 USD had been provided to refugees. Two loans enabled refugees to open factories where over 150 men, women, and girls were employed to weave cloth, card and spin wool, and make rugs. She expressed hope that more funds would enable the factories to double in size. Multiple smaller loans offered craftsmen such as street vendors and shoemakers to open their own businesses, which enabled more than 75 refugees to be 'taken from the Charity Roll'.[68]

In addition to receiving loans, refugees also contributed financially to other refugees' settlement. By the late 1930s, the main source of income for the Nansen Office was provided by refugees themselves through a fee of five gold francs for the Nansen passport, the identity travel document for refugees designed by Nansen in 1922. With these fees, the so-called Nansen Stamp Fund was created – a revolving fund providing loans to refugees that were repaid as they established themselves.[69] This ultimately 'formed a nucleus of a humanitarian fund large enough to help refugees become self-supporting'.[70] The system of revolving funds was integral to creating Armenian settlements in Syria and Lebanon, and money donated to the settlements was loaned to refugees with a high success rate of repayment.[71] In the 1930s, small loans to establish businesses such as restaurants and shops were also granted to refugees through the revolving fund. In this way, refugees' successful livelihoods creation enabled through the Nansen Stamp Fund provided the funding for further refugee rehabilitation. Through offering loans to refugees in urban areas, refugees contributed to local urban economies as well as supported each other in becoming settled.

As earlier discussed, however, granting loans to refugees was a risky means of embedding them in the market economy, as the success of the livelihoods they sought to create was not assured. It was also not purely altruistic. Loan provision to both refugee farmers and entrepreneurs at the national level also addressed the national and indeed international perceived threat of radical socialist ideology; in 1925, the National Bank stated that its lending

[68] Palmeree, R. (1923) Untitled private letter. Folder 3.13, Work Files AWH 1923–1952, Ruth A. Palmeree Papers, Hoover Institution Archives.

[69] LN (1934) 'Human welfare and the League'. League of Nations Union, O.LNU/1934(13), p 69.

[70] Skran, 'The International Refugee Regime', p 206.

[71] Skran, 'Refugees in Interwar Europe', pp 181–182.

had 'led tens of thousands of petty bourgeois refugees into production and regular life, creating from this passive element autonomous tiny economic units, rather than falling inevitably and fatefully victims of diverse subversive propaganda whose end result would be grievous constitutional and social disturbances, if not uprisings'.[72]

The alignment of Greece's financial system with liberal international standards, therefore, offered the opportunity for refugees' individual prosperity through loans and the creation of enterprises, and in this way fostered a preference of the free market over socialism.[73]

Vocational training and small-scale industries

The vocational training of refugees and the creation of small-scale industries also took place through both the GRSC and independent charities and agencies such as the AWH. Skills ranged from carpentry to sewing to skills in various cottage industries. In the year after the mass arrival of refugees to Greece, the High Commissariat of the League of Nations placed considerable effort into creating small-scale industries for refugees, including brick-making and road-making. The charcoal burning industry in Gumuldjina, a district of Western Thrace, was placed under the control of the High Commissariat and became one such self-supporting industry that employed some of the 611 refugees that had found jobs in industries supported by the League.[74] A League report from 1923 on the subject stated:

> While the reconstruction work undertaken by the High Commissariat is very small in comparison with the vastness of the Greek Refugee problem, it must be remembered that our object has been to set an example of what can and should be done on a very much larger scale, if a terrible catastrophe is to be avoided … some 11,000 refugees will have become self-supporting members of the community by July next, at an approximate cost to the League of 1 GBP per head.[75]

[72] Dritsa, M. (1990) *Βιομηχανία καί τράπεζες στήν Ἑλλάδα τοῦ μεσοπολέμου*. Athens: Educational Institution of the National Bank, p 336. Cited in Mazower, 'The refugees, the economic crisis and the collapse of Venizelist hegemony, 1929–1932', p 122.

[73] Kritikos, 'The agricultural settlement of refugees', p 337.

[74] Nansen, F. (1923) 'Near East refugees, Western Thrace refugee settlement'. Report by Dr Nansen, High Commissioner for Refugees, to League of Nations, Communicated to the Council. Geneva, 22 April 1923. R395 League of Nations Archive, Registry Files, 1919–1927, Section: No. 10 Series 25480 to 26389 Files 42710 to 27191.

[75] Nansen, 'Near East refugees, Western Thrace refugee settlement', p 6.

This focus on reconstruction and cost-effective support to refugees, in turn, helps explains the GRSC's own mandate when it was formed in 1923 – to provide refugees with permanent, productive labour. For those living in urban areas, particularly, training or retraining offered a means to lead them into wage labour, which in turn offered a way to support local economies as both employees and entrepreneurs.

In 1923, Dr Parmelee reported on the positive developments of a lace industry for refugees in Salonica. That April, the number of female refugees employed in the industry had risen to 127, and a training component for others had been added:

> A refugee Armenian girl from Marsovan, Turkey – an only child, whose widowed mother was deported in 1915 and never heard from again – has now been called to assist in this Department. She is giving daily instructions to about 20 girls in the art of needle work; besides assisting in supervising the women mentioned above who are regularly employed. It is hoped these girls now under instruction will soon be added to our list of bread winners.[76]

Near Athens, the Near East Relief created an orphanage that gave vocational training to over 7,000 youth, including industrial and 'home-making' skills.[77] Greek women's organizations were created, which sought to rehabilitate refugee women through training as well as fight for women's rights, such as the right to vote.[78] This trend of vocational training for refugees extended beyond Greece to other European countries, and included Jewish organizations across Europe that provided employment training for refugees and those seeking to emigrate to Palestine.[79]

Dr Parmelee also trained refugees as nurses and doctors to work in AWH across Greece. In so doing she followed the League's habit of employing refugees in assistance efforts, creating a nursing training school for refugees and employing them in AWH hospitals across Greece. 'There were two aims in this training,' she wrote in a speech given decades later,

76 Parmelee, 'Untitled Private Letter'.

77 Barton, J. (1930) *Story of Near East Relief (1915–1930): An interpretation*. New York: Macmillan; Skran, 'The Refugee Problem', p 88.

78 These included the Christianiki Enosi Neanidon (XEN) (Christian Union for Young Women) in 1922, and Enosi Ellinidon Epistimonon (Union of Greek Women Graduates) in 1924. Source: Lazaridis, G. (1994) 'The feminist movement in Greece: an overview'. *Journal of Gender Studies* 3(2): 205–209 (p 206).

79 Moore, B. (1990) 'Jewish refugee entrepreneurs and the Dutch economy in the 1930s'. *Immigrants & Minorities* 9(1): 46–63.

Figure 2.2: 'Sister Sarra's busy day'. Nurse Sarra, an Armenian refugee in Greece

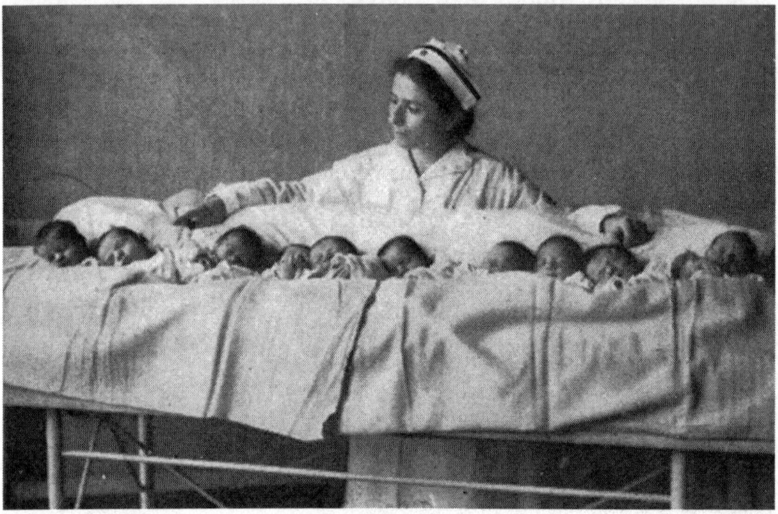

Source: American Women's Hospital Bulletin 1925, Hoover Institution Library and Archives, Stanford University.

> [First] to assure better nursing care for our patients; and [secondly] to give a practical education to young refugee women which would make them useful in the future. … As soon as possible, we reorganized the school of nursing which had been opened in the Salonica American Women's Hospital on January 23, 1923 and carried on the course leading to the full diploma in nursing, eventually graduating three classes. Emphasis was placed on training both in obstetrical nursing and midwifery, also in public health.[80]

One refugee who received this training and of whom Dr Parmelee often wrote was 'Sister Sarra', a Christian refugee from Asia Minor. She worked under Dr Parmelee for months, being trained and eventually graduating as a nurse. She then went on to run the maternity ward of the AWH in Salonica, and is pictured in Figure 2.2.

AWH bulletins and reports, from which these pictures are reproduced (see Figure 2.3), provide a positive portrayal of productive refugees providing desperately needed medical care for fellow refugees. This sentiment was vociferously echoed by Dr Parmelee in letters to family and friends and official AWH reports during her decades in Greece, painting a picture of a

[80] Palmeree, 'Dedication Piraeus Hospital'.

situation in which trained medical professionals were few and far between and an era where refugees were encouraged to be 'productive' in a variety of ways. More broadly, these efforts by the League and the AWH speak to the nascent public welfare system at the time, which was unable to provide long-term humanitarian assistance and the resulting necessity for people to support themselves.

These industries and vocational training centres in Greece are notable for several reasons. First, many of these trainings and industries were led by refugees for refugees. They were made possible by loans from organizations as well as by refugees themselves through the Nansen Stamp Fund and

Figure 2.3: AWH Bulletin, 1923–1924

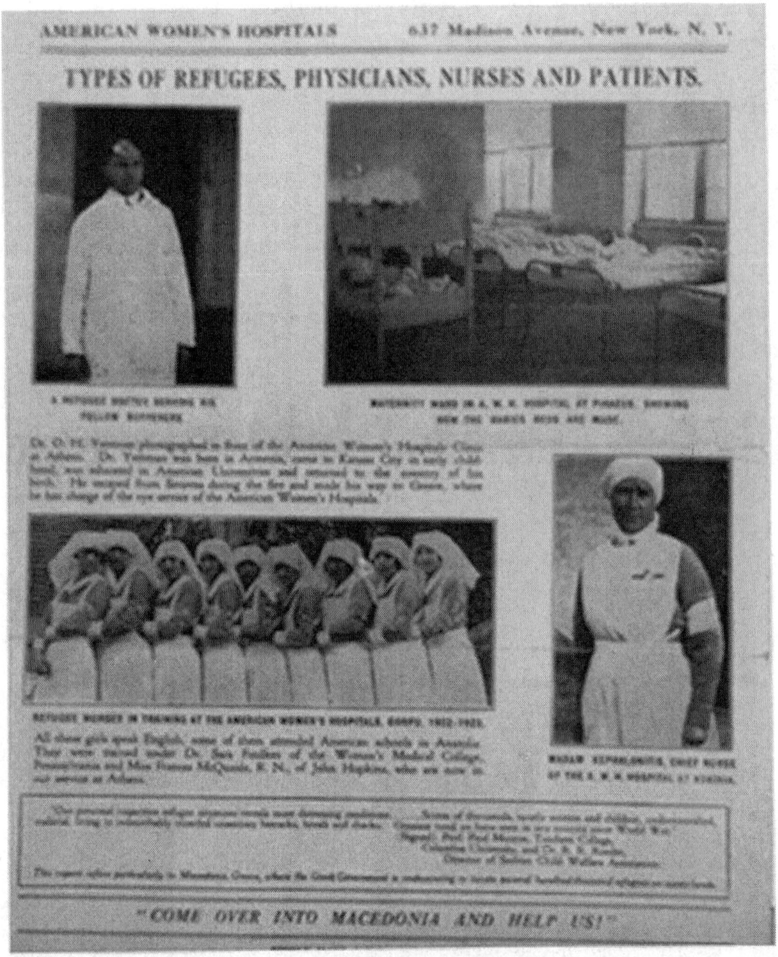

Source: Ruth A. Parmelee Papers, Folder 3.13, Work Files AWH 1923–1952, Box 3. Hoover Institution Library and Archives.

demonstrate the extent of refugees' embeddedness in refugee assistance. Second, the fact that these trainings and industries were in many instances created just months after refugees arrived demonstrates the commitment of humanitarianism at the time to offer both what we currently define as emergency *and* development assistance. In December 1922, hardly two months after she and many refugees had arrived in Salonica, Dr Parmelee had already written of plans for the lace industry for refugee women. In 1925, she wrote:

> One of our [nursing] pupils is now district nurse for her refugee village near Ekaterini. Another is serving the 'Patriotic League' in the city of Salonica in child welfare work and visiting in the homes. Two have gone to London to take the full hospital course in nurse's training. Others have served other hospitals of the organization in Greece as head-nurses.[81]

Refugee employment and ILO's employment-matching scheme

Although the Greek settlement was considered a success, refugees in countries like Lebanon and Syria struggled to find employment.[82] By 1924, it had become clear that the refugee 'problem' was not a temporary one and that 'in the main their problem was to find work, or have it found for them'.[83] In response, the ILO was incorporated into refugee relief and rehabilitation efforts to address 'the employment, emigration and settlement of refugees'.[84] On 25 September 1924, 'the technical work still to be accomplished on behalf of Russian and Armenian refugees' was transferred from the High Commissioner, Fridtjof Nansen, to the ILO.[85] From 1925 to 1929, ILO facilitated the technical aspects of refugee emigration, including transportation. Its efforts in refugee settlement illustrate the centrality of refugees' existing livelihoods in assistance strategies, and the dominant perception of refugees as individual workers with specific skills.

---

81 Palmeree, R. (1925) 'American Women's Hospital for women and children'. Salonica, Greece. Report. Ruth A. Parmelee Papers, Box 3, Folder 3.12, Work Files, AWH 1922–1932. Hoover Institution Archives.

82 Migliorino, N. (2008) *(Re)Constructing Armenia in Lebanon and Syria: Ethno-cultural diversity and the state in the aftermath of a refugee crisis*. Oxford: Berghahn, pp 75–77.

83 LN (1933) 'Human welfare and the League'. League of Nations Union, January 1933, No. 155. O.LNU/1933(8), p 67.

84 ILO, 'Refugee problems and their solution', p 1768.

85 ILO (1926) 'Refugees and labour conditions in Bulgaria'. International Labour Organization Report. Geneva: International Labour Office.

Between 1925 and 1929, ILO initiated a successful 'employment-matching scheme' which included refugee censuses, identifying labour shortages in European countries, and then 'matching' skilled refugees, largely based on their existing livelihoods, into suitable positions. ILO, as well as charities, provided oversight in the resettlement process in an effort to prevent the exploitation of refugees. Fifty thousand refugees, mainly from China and European countries, found employment through this endeavour, which proved both cost-effective and successful in enabling refugee self-reliance.[86] During the first half of 1925, over 15,000 Russian refugees and 2,600 Armenian refugees had been brought into employment by the ILO.[87] By 1929, ILO had achieved a reduction in the number of able-bodied refugees seeking employment from 400,000 to 200,000.[88]

Such means of assistance suggest the haphazard reliance of humanitarian organizations on the economic system to support refugees in both urban and rural areas. In particular urban areas, we see how refugees were successfully incorporated into national economies as much-needed labourers – and that this employment-matching took place as a major form of assistance. The majority of refugees that benefited from this scheme, for example, were placed in France, which was desirous of able-bodied labourers due to the heavy losses it had suffered during the First World War. In rural areas, the majority of refugees were encouraged to move beyond agricultural subsistence and expand to cash crop farming, which also led to a reliance on the market economy. When it took place, subsistence farming seems to have been largely successful, but cash crop schemes, as we saw earlier, presented challenges that ultimately constrained refugees' ability to become self-reliant. While temporary funding could be secured to train refugees in vocational activities, the end aim of such training was not self-reliance in the sense of personal subsistence, but instead refugees' reliance on the market economy through securing employment, commercial farming, or becoming an entrepreneur. GRSC and League documents from the time depict a domestic and international humanitarian system strained by a lack of funds. This perhaps helps to explain the emphasis on agricultural subsistence and farming, which promised a quicker way to get refugees off the GRSC's payroll than more costly urban settlement. Despite the predominant emphasis of assistance through employment or productive work, the cost of refugee assistance was, in fact, too high for Greece to finance on its own.

86 ILO, 'Refugee problems and their solution', pp 84–85.

87 ILO, 'Refugees and labour conditions in Bulgaria'.

88 Skran, 'The Refugee Problem', p 205.

The Refugee Loan

Between 1923 and 1928, the League helped issue nine loans to European countries. As the League had no funding pool for loans itself, it acted mainly as a guarantor for countries that were too unstable to receive loans through other forms of recourse. As one report stated, countries that received loans from the League would 'have found it impossible to borrow abroad by any other method'.[89] After the Great War, many countries had residual debts that impeded their ability to easily borrow new loans in international capital markets. At the same time, the disruption in international trade meant that these same countries faced challenges in economic recovery. While the League loans have been criticized for their failure to prevent the economic depression of the 1930s, they have also been lauded for the support they provided to countries like Greece to 'reestablish the productive basis of their economies'.[90]

While most of these so-called 'League loans' were for reconstruction and currency stabilization, loans provided to Greece and Bulgaria were also intended for refugee settlement. Greece had lost credibility in international capital markets after the Smyrna invasion but the country's creditworthiness improved from 1923, thus enabling the so-called 'Refugee Loan' as well as a later one in 1927. In 1924, a 10 million GBP bond loan was issued in London and New York at 88 per cent and provided to the GRSC. It was to be repaid with a 7 per cent interest rate over 40 years. The loan provided the financial means to provide settlement, with rural settlement heavily preferred. At the beginning of 1929, £9,117,362 had been used for the agricultural settlement of refugees and only £1,302,734 for urban settlement.[91]

However, the loan also embedded Greece in the international economy through its heavy regulation.[92] It seems that foreign investors provided loans to the Greek government in the 19th and 20th centuries, including during the 1920s, only in cases 'in which the latter credibly committed itself to the drachma's participation in the international monetary system'.[93] The reliance of Greece on other countries in the interwar years made it necessary to adhere to loan standards and stipulations:

---

89 Royal Institute of International Affairs (1937) *The Problem of International Investment: A report by a study group of members of the Royal Institute of International Affairs*. London, New York: Oxford University Press.

90 Myers, M. G. (1945) 'The League Loans'. *Political Science Quarterly* 60(4): 492–526 (p 505).

91 Kritikos, 'The agricultural settlement of refugees'.

92 The loan to Bulgaria was similarly heavily regulated.

93 Lazaretou, S. (2005) The drachma, foreign creditors, and the international monetary system: tales of a currency during the 19th and the early 20th centuries. *Explorations in Economic History*, *42*(2), 202–236, (p 232).

> [A] major issue concerned the integration of these new countries into the world economy by fostering international trade on the one hand and by creating access to capital markets on the other. Most of those countries had to build up their productive activities and set up stable monetary and fiscal systems, for which foreign investment was necessary.[94]

This generally occurred through adhering to the gold standard in order to receive better lending rates, due to a lower risk of default. This is seen in a further international loan issued to the Greek government in 1927 for 9 million GBP at 91 per cent. The conditions of this second loan evidence the ways in which refugees' livelihoods and self-reliance were integral to obtaining it. As M. Caphandaris, the Minister of Finance of Greece, wrote in a letter to the Secretary-General of the League, 'It would be impossible to continue the refugee settlement work with any hope of rapid and successful completion without concluding a supplementary loan abroad, and thus make it possible to adopt a far-reaching plan of systematic reform.' He went on to request a 'single loan intended to finish the settlement work, stabilize the currency and liquidate the deficits'.[95]

Interestingly, despite such assertions, only 3 million pounds went toward refugee settlement while the remaining 6 million was divided evenly between 'budget arrears' and 'strengthening the Bank'. This was explained through a report by the Financial Committee on the loan proposal to the League, which stated:

> It is obvious that, as indicated in the Committee's last report, the possibilities of raising a new loan for this purpose under satisfactory conditions depend very largely indeed upon the general financial position in Greece – *upon the prospects of the stability of the currency and the equilibrium of the budget.* The Committee is therefore glad to learn that the Greek Government has asked the Council of the League for its assistance in connection with *a comprehensive scheme designed to secure financial stabilization and reform as well as to meet the needs of the refugee work.*[96] [emphasis added]

---

94 Flores, J. and Decorzant, Y. (2012) 'Public borrowing in harsh times: the League of Nations loans revisited'. Department of Economics Working Paper Series No. 2091. Geneva: University of Geneva, p 7.

95 Flores and Decorzant, 'Public borrowing in harsh times', p 7.

96 LN (1927) 'Settlement of Greek Refugees. Report of the Financial Committee'. C.322.1927.II.F.410. Geneva, 14 June 1927. R397, 10, 60557, 26389.

It was agreed that the Greek government and National Bank would stabilize the drachma on a gold exchange rate and undertake comprehensive 'monetary and banking reorganization' as part of the loan agreement.[97]

Both refugees' assets and their assistance from the GRSC were used as loan security. This collateral was determined in a meeting of the League of Nations Council as comprising:

i. property belonging to the 'exchangables' which have been definitely transferred to the RSC [Greek Refugee Settlement Commission];
ii. cultivable land in the definite possession of the RSC;
iii. buildings and lots of land for building purposes of urban settlements ceded to the RSC;
iv. collection in cash by the RSC from refugees' debts.[98]

Through this we see that refugee self-reliance settlement was intricately bound up in Greece's financial reform, driven from both within and outside the country. By sparking the initial need for such a loan, refugee assistance contributed to the expansion of the modern capitalist system in Greece, which was forced to undertake financial reform according to monetary loan stipulations and in this way become assimilated into the post-war international economy. Loans justified as constituting refugee assistance thereby instrumentalized the objective of refugee self-reliance in order to further embed Greece in the international capitalist system through the reforms and measures that dictated their financial growth.

Refugees' contribution to agricultural production in Greece further benefited the international market economy through the increased export and import of cash crops. One way that refugees were meant to help repay the international Refugee Loan was through agricultural outputs such as tobacco. However, as we saw, the drop in tobacco prices not only impoverished refugees, who found themselves unable to repay loans, but strained refugee assistance, which counted on refugees' repayment in order to repay the Refugee Loan. Partial agreements were eventually reached, such as the Greek government taking on a large portion of the cost of settlement, yet tensions continued into the 1930s.

[97] Caphandaris, M. (1927) 'Annex. Letter from M. Caphandaris, Minister of Finance of Greece, to the Secretary-General of the League'. Geneva, 14 June 1927. League of Nations Archives, R397.

[98] LN Council (1927) Extract from Process Verbal of 6th Meeting of 45th Session of the Council, 17 June 1927. Work of the Greek [RSC] 10.60185.26389.

This struggle demonstrates the questionable nature of fostering refugee self-reliance alongside meeting other goals. Refugees' self-reliance as well as their property, labour, and capital became risky collateral in a loan intended not merely to support refugee settlement but instead to undertake a far-reaching and systematic financial reform of Greece. The danger of this collateral for the self-reliance of refugees themselves appeared to have been an afterthought not taken into consideration.

The interwar years saw the beginning of a growing trend to incorporate refugees into the capitalist workforce. At this point in history most refugee self-reliance assistance was concentrated in rural areas, reflecting the rural focus and economic development course of Greece and other countries in this period. While most refugees were resettled in agricultural settlements in Greece and continued their farming, many of them transitioned from being subsistence farmers to commercial farmers, with the support and, indeed, the urging of both the GSRC and the Greek government which offered seeds, land, new agricultural methods, and readily accessible bank loans. Yet the growing of cash crops such as tobacco eventually impinged upon refugees' self-reliance as they found themselves unable to repay loans from their commercial activities and without enough subsistence crops to survive. Regardless of where they found work, it is notable that for refugees this process of expansion into the modern economy was largely facilitated by refugee assistance agencies themselves, which sought to create self-supporting populations that were capable of contributing to host countries.

The Great Depression and refugee settlement

Unfortunately, despite the limited agency some refugees felt already, the Great Depression and ensuing austerity beginning in the late 1920s and continuing into the 1930s had the effect of further constraining it through reducing settlement options. France's stance on receiving refugees became more restrictive in the 1930s due to the economic recession. Other countries throughout Europe became more restrictionist as well and no longer viewed refugees as valuable sources of labour. Instead, fears of rising unemployment and the economic burden of refugee settlement became paramount. Lamenting refugees' lack of opportunity for employment, in 1938 the president of the Nansen Office stated, 'Under these changed conditions it has proved impossible to solve the refugee problem which, to a large extent, is an economic problem'.[99] The League had striven to remain apolitical in refugee affairs, and continued to construe refugees as an economic problem

[99] Hansson, 'The Refugee Problem', pp 15–16.

with an economic solution, even in the face of the discriminatory causes of German Jewish displacement.[100]

The recession also reduced employment positions for refugees within the Nansen Office. In contrast to the 1920s, refugees in the 1930s were gradually excluded from holding decision-making or operational roles in settlement implementation. In 1938, Michael Hansson, president of the Nansen Office, discussed replacing refugee workers with foreign employees, likely due to the difficulties that non-refugees now also experienced in finding work. He stated:

> There is no denying the great advantage that has been derived from the employment of refugees themselves as collaborators in the countries where the Nansen Office has been obliged to maintain representatives. … But should it prove necessary, or desirable, there is no reason why non-refugees should not be employed as widely as possible, wherever of course people be found who are willing to devote themselves to this work.[101]

To combat virulent European restrictionism toward both German Jews and other refugee groups, the League also proposed 'solutions' to refugee settlement outside of Europe. We therefore see refugee self-reliance through employment or homesteading redirected to non-European countries with labour opportunities. Plans included a League resettlement scheme in Latin and South American countries with sufficient employment opportunities, to be partially coordinated by the ILO.[102] In Paraguay, for example, 'a Colony bearing Nansen's name [was] established with the support of the Government and under the supervision of a Swiss landowner'.[103] Although few such schemes were ever implemented, a 1939 review of suitable countries included Brazil, Venezuela, and Chile due to their vast land resources. Rural 'pioneering' was proffered for refugees with agricultural backgrounds to combat population rise in already overcrowded cities:

> Take a great part of the interior of Brazil, Venezuela, Colombia, or some other suitable section; move in with modern machinery and medicine; clear off the land, drain the swamps, bridge the streams;

[100] McDonald, J. G., Breitman, R., Stewart, B. M., and Hochberg, S. (eds) (2007) *Advocate for the Doomed: The diaries and papers of James G. McDonald, 1932–1935*. Vol 1. Bloomington: Indiana University Press.

[101] Hansson, 'The Refugee Problem', pp 25–26.

[102] ILO, 'Refugee problems and their solution'; Inman, S. G. (1939) 'Refugee settlement in Latin America'. *Annals of the American Academy of Political and Social Science*, 203: 183–193.

[103] Hansson, 'The Refugee Problem', p 9.

> build settlements, initiate farming, cattle raising, and industrial activities. Let hardy refugees themselves … be important participants in the enterprise. The remarkable accomplishments of Henry Ford in building a modern industrial community away up in the interior of Brazil in the Amazon jungle shows the possibility of such a dream.[104]

The proposed plans for refugee settlement in South America exemplify the broader intellectual and institutional shifts that began even before the Second World War and greatly influenced conceptions of and support for refugee assistance. The suggestion of a 'made to order' community[105] demonstrates a heightened regard for science, technology, and planning in language that prefigures the post-war discourse of development. The creativity of these plans only thinly disguises their 'outsourcing' nature, foreshadowing as well the treatment of refugees not as labourers or even victims, but rather as 'surplus' to be used or discarded.

Shifting conceptions of refugees as workers

The interwar years saw the emergence of, despite their ad hoc nature, not only the first international refugee regime, but a participatory assistance regime with the joint aims of refugee self-reliance and host country and international economic development. In the words of Katy Long, '[R]efugee protection was constructed around the twin facets of migration – movement and employment – in the first decades of the international refugee regime'.[106] League-sponsored resettlement commissions in the 1920s and 1930s are powerful examples of the first international bodies attempting to foster self-reliance 'systematically, and along international lines' with displaced populations.[107] Innovative rehabilitation strategies included material assistance while emphasizing refugees' ability to contribute through their own skills, expertise, and financial means.

Rural settlements in the 1920s were the first attempts to undertake integrated development programmes that targeted locals as well as refugees, which became known in the 1980s as 'Refugee Aid and Development' and in the 2000s as 'Development Assistance for Refugees'. What remains noteworthy, however, for those aware of the longstanding 'humanitarian-development gap' in refugee assistance, is the relatively immediate nature

[104] Inman, 'Refugee settlement in Latin America', p 193.

[105] Inman, 'Refugee settlement in Latin America', p 193.

[106] Long, K. (2013) 'When refugees stopped being migrants: movement, labour and humanitarian protection'. *Migration Studies* 1(1): 4–26 (p 8).

[107] Macartney, C. A. (1930) *Refugees: The work of the League*. London: League of Nations Union, p 5.

of interwar self-reliance assistance. While refugees did receive food and emergency medical care, assistance addressed their 'rehabilitation' through the fostering of self-reliance rather than the mere perpetuation of survival. Dr Parmelee began working on opening factories and vocational training centres for refugees in the months directly after their arrival in Greece, at the same time as she combated bouts of typhoid, malaria, and other diseases. Similarly, the GRSC offered tools and loans alongside food, expecting refugees to become self-sufficient soon after a successful harvest. In this way, the notion of so-called 'refugee dependency' was not even a potential outcome of assistance, in stark contrast to the protracted refugee situations of today.

Understanding the large extent to which self-reliance assistance was integrated into the refugee response challenges the contemporary notion of refugees as mainly humanitarian subjects as well as the purported division between emergency and development assistance. During the interwar years, refugees were largely viewed as an economic and technical problem with economic solutions,[108] construed as labourers and members of a surplus population waiting to be integrated into national economies. Correspondingly, they were considered labour migrants rather than subjects – or masses – of humanitarian need. Rehabilitation efforts corresponded to states' growing but still limited perception of responsibility toward both nationals and refugees, but largely on the basis of their perceived capability for work rather than their assumed right to protection. Largely congruent with this construction was the nature of the assistance offered to them, which sought to quickly place them into employment or help them become 'productive'. This construction makes sense due to host country aims, as countries recovering from the First World War were often in need of labour (at least up until the recession).

Yet, just as striking as the construction of refugees as workers at this time is the determined lack of discussion surrounding the relationship between politics and refugees in League of Nations and GRSC documents. The construction of refugees as economic and technical problems perpetuated their identity as apolitical labourers – although their labour itself was used for political ends. The political relationship between refugees and the nation-state in the interwar years also goes beyond just the displacer and the displaced. '[R]efugees and returnees were not merely passive objects of policy, but often themselves participated in nationalist and state-building projects and in negotiating their status in the new collectives.'[109] The construction of

[108] ILO, 'Refugee problems and their solution'.

[109] Baron, N. and Gatrell, P. (2003) 'Population displacement, state-building, and social identity in the lands of the former Russian Empire, 1917–23'. *Kritika: Explorations in Russian and Eurasian History* 4(1): 51–100 (p 52).

refugees in this period as workers rather than victims also, whether intended or otherwise, fits into the dominant idea of refugees 'rightfully' moved to their 'homeland' and able to contribute to it as naturalized citizens. In this way, the culpability of states is elided as is acknowledgement of the victims that refugees also became through the redrawing of state lines.

Overall, the Greek refugee response sheds light on the ways that both refugee assistance and refugee self-reliance were instrumentalized in the interwar years. Refugee self-reliance assistance served multiple ends, not only 'rehabilitating' refugees but populating territories and creating economic gain at both the national and international levels. This occurred through the means and type of assistance designed to foster refugee self-reliance, and through the actions of refugees themselves, who became members of the wage-labour economy. Refugee self-reliance assistance instrumentalized refugees' efforts toward self-reliance in ways that largely benefited states and the elites within them. The result was the incorporation of both refugees and host states such as Greece into the modern capitalist economy and the nation-state system that arose alongside it, showing refugee self-reliance assistance to be an arm of this modern system, and refugees as economic and political pawns who were used to support it. During this time, refugees were a largely agrarian workforce that produced cash crops to boost the Greek economy and contribute to the rekindling of international trade. To a limited extent, refugees were individually drawn into the capitalist market system through loans to become entrepreneurs and grow cash crops, which for some led to a market dependence that threatened their self-reliance.

Refugee self-reliance assistance at this time was more inclusive than in later eras, with refugees employed in various assistance positions. A variety of factors contributed to this inclusive approach, including the League's own funding constraints, the common host state policy of naturalizing refugees, and an overall context of limited government welfare intervention. Refugees were also largely conceptualized as economic immigrants, which at different times enabled and hindered the support they received. The fluctuating assistance that refugees received, such as resettlement based on employment opportunities and support for urban or agricultural work at different times, demonstrates the importance of exogenous factors such as changing global economic contexts in achieving resettlement and refugee self-sufficiency.

The conception of refugees as workers began to change in the 1930s as refugee settlement was cast as a humanitarian imperative toward vulnerable groups. Partly in response to restrictionism, humanitarianism in the late 1930s shifted from serving groups defined by their identity to offering aid based on need to vulnerable populations.[110] This shift occurred alongside

[110] Barnett, *Empire of Humanity*, p 94.

the professionalization of humanitarianism and growing technocratic and top-down means of rehabilitating refugees. The result, as we shall see in the following chapter, was the gradual surpassing of the role of refugees in their own relief by foreign employees within increasingly planned settlement schemes.

The interwar years also incubated practices that defined the following era; throughout this period the League, the ILO, and assistance agencies gained important experience that was built upon after the Second World War. The start of the war in 1939 brought a virtual halt to refugee resettlement and large-scale assistance efforts, yet amid these changes, refugee self-reliance assistance did continue. Dr Parmelee, for instance, opened a training school for nurses, and then another. She supported Greeks suffering under German occupation, and undertook medical work that was later taken over by the United Nations Relief and Rehabilitation Administration (UNRRA). From Greece she went to Palestine, using the knowledge she had gained during the interwar years – much as the international refugee regime did – to support other refugees in other places in the aftermath of war.

3

Socialism and Self-Reliance: Refugee Self-Reliance Assistance in Post-Colonial East Africa

Introduction

After the Second World War ended, and throughout the rest of the 1940s and early 1950s, the Allies concentrated efforts on repatriating or resettling the 10 to 12 million displaced persons scattered across Europe. Both the successes and the failures of the League of Nations, which dissolved in 1946, paved the way for the United Nations (UN), an international institution more structured, influential, and broader in scope than the League had ever been. In 1951, UNHCR superseded the International Refugee Organisation and UNRRA, which had originally addressed war-related European displacement.[1] With the Second World War nearly two decades behind them, and the 'Clear the Camps'[2] campaign freshly closed, the international refugee regime moved from Europe to Africa. A contemporary of Dr Ruth Parmelee, a man named Tristam Frederick Betts began working

[1] In-progress research on the role of UNRRA in the 'rehabilitation' of refugees suggests that vocational training and other interwar years' self-reliance practices continued in Europe after the Second World War and may have influenced later self-reliance practices, as well. However, it was beyond the scope of this book to cover this work in detail. For more information, see: UNRRA (1946) *UNRRA: structure and operations*. London; UNRRA (1950) *UNRRA: the history of the United Nations Relief and Rehabilitation Administration*. New York: Columbia University Press; Pettiss, S. (2004) *After the Shooting Stopped: The story of an UNRRA welfare worker in Germany 1945–1947*. Victoria, BC: Trafford.

[2] 1959–1960 was designated as 'World Refugee Year' by the United Nations and was the year in which the displaced persons camps in Europe were to be closed.

in Africa just as the wider international refugee regime did. He spent much of his time both prior to and after decolonization in Tanzania, the focus of this chapter.

Only a certain type of person eschews the title of 'scholar' and nods in approval at the description of 'gadfly'.[3] Yet box upon grey box in Oxford's Refugee Studies Centre archives detail Betts' work, a man who, friends and colleagues agree, would rather have had the latter title. 'Despite a somewhat crusty exterior,' a journal dedication reads, 'the humanitarianism in his heart was not easily disguised, and motivated all his best work.'[4] Betts became the Oxfam Field Director for East and Southern Africa in 1962, thereby beginning two decades of work in refugee resettlement. Vociferous, critical, and adamantly honest, Betts wrote scathing reviews of ill-conceived rural development plans, multiple papers for international conferences pertaining to refugees, and reams of refugee settlement reports. Together, the papers comprising the T. F. Betts Collection paint a strikingly thorough picture of refugee assistance in Africa from the 1960s to the 1980s. Pointillism of sorts, the collection reveals the mundane inner workings of settlement administration as well as provides an overarching analysis of trends in refugee assistance (including repeatedly unaddressed problems) that most other relevant archives lack. It is this collection, along with UNHCR and ILO archives, that form the empirical basis of this chapter.

This chapter focuses on refugee self-reliance assistance in East Africa from the 1960s to the late 1970s. The assistance provided to refugees and the reasons behind it are examined, as are the partners of UNHCR (including ILO and the World Bank), and the national and international agendas that influenced the nature of self-reliance assistance.

Refugee policy in Africa at this time cannot be divorced either from the colonial history that freshly preceded it or from the global capitalist expansion encompassed within the post-war 'development project'. Parallels and continuities between colonial practices, development, and the refugee self-reliance assistance that later took place on the continent are presented through a case study of dominant refugee self-reliance assistance practices in Tanzania between 1964 and 1979. The changing role of UNHCR and other agencies in refugee assistance are sketched and the dominant assistance approaches in Africa outlined. The discussion provides more information on the colonial

[3] The Oxford English Dictionary defines a 'gadfly' as 'A person who annoys or criticizes others in order to provoke them into action'. Source: OED (Oxford English Dictionary) (2017) Definition: Gadfly. Oxford: Oxford University Press.

[4] Hawley, E. (1984) 'Dedication to Tristram F. (Jimmy) Betts (1908–1983) scholar, humanitarian, gadfly'. *Africa Today, Refugees and Integrated Rural Development in Africa* 31(1): 3–5.

precedents of these practices and their linkages to wider development aims. These practices are then analyzed alongside larger macrostructural and historical factors to help explain refugee self-reliance assistance at the time.

Decolonization and the advent of refugee assistance in Africa

Although war in Europe had come to an end, the so-called 'post-war' period was not reflected across the globe. Instead, beginning in the 1940s and increasing in the 1950s and 1960s, wars for independence from colonial rule raged across Africa. From Algeria to Mozambique, independence movements sought to claim control of their country, often leading to violent civil conflicts that created mass refugee flows. The number of African refugees rose steadily throughout the 1960s and 1970s. This contributed to the adoption of the 1967 Protocol Relating to the Status of Refugees, which expanded the definition of refugees beyond Europe, and led the Organisation of African Unity (OAU)[5] to state in 1968:

> one of the most acute refugee problems today is to be found on the African continent. Judging from the great numbers involved, the extent of the economic and social misery and dislocation, and the consequent human tragedy it has generated, the problems certainly constitutes 'one of the most agonising and complex problems from which African society is suffering'.[6]

Refugee assistance in Africa remained similar to assistance provided during the interwar years through a focus on self-reliance through agricultural production. In the early 1960s, as UNHCR began operating in Africa, a policy of material assistance was instated which superseded the agency's emphasis on legal protection. Although disputed internally, UNHCR's funding was initially so limited that material assistance programmes were highly limited in content and scale, and mainly viewed as emergency rather than long-term relief.[7] Initially, UNHCR programmes targeted refugee

[5] An examination of the OAU's engagement with refugees is beyond the scope of this book. For an overview of this history, see for example: Sharpe, M. (2011) 'Engaging with refugee protection? The Organization of African Unity and African Union since 1963'. UNHCR New Issues in Refugee Research, Research Paper No. 226. Geneva: UNHCR.

[6] OAU (1978) Organization of African Unity: Final Report: Conference on the Legal, Economic and Social Aspects of African Refugee Problems, 9–18 October 1967, December 1978, p 7.

[7] Loescher, G. (2001) *The UNHCR and World Politics: A perilous path*. New York: Oxford University Press, p 118.

self-reliance by offering land, tools, and seeds – a strategy known as basic minimal assistance. In instances where food aid was provided, the agency aimed to cut it off as soon as possible. Programmes were initially hands-off and, in this way, further emulated those implemented by the League. However, this assistance rarely led to economic self-sufficiency,[8] and, as we shall see, the programmes that replaced it provided both more support and more regulation.

UNHCR's objectives for African refugees in the first half of the 1960s are reflected in statements by then UNHCR High Commissioner Schnyder, such as in the 1964 opening statement to the Executive Committee of the High Commissioner's Programme:

> It will soon be possible to discontinue the distribution of foodstuffs to all [Rwandan] refugees whom we have been trying to settle in their country of asylum. *The main objective – which is to enable these refugees to provide for themselves as soon as possible* – is now well on the way towards being achieved. … Another equally encouraging fact is that … the countries of asylum have also recognized the value of these additional human resources. *The attitude adopted by Tanganyika, for instance, and by other countries of asylum shows that Governments reali[s]e that these refugees, so far from being a long-term burden, are rather a valuable asset for the future economic and social development of their countries.*[9] [emphasis added]

In contrast to the interwar years, refugees were no longer settled in urban or rural areas best suited to their background and skills, but instead

---

[8] Stein, B. (1990) 'Refugee integration and older refugee settlements in Africa'. Paper presented at the 1990 meeting of the American Anthropological Association. New Orleans: Michigan State University, p 13; Loescher, *The UNHCR and World Politics*, p 122.

[9] Schnyder, F. (1964) 'Opening Statement by Mr Felix Schnyder, United Nations High Commissioner for Refugees, to the Executive Committee of the High Commissioner's Programme, second special session, 28 January 1964'. Available at: www.unhcr.org/uk/admin/hcspeeches/49f81111e/opening-statement-mr-felix-schnyder-united-nations-high-commissioner-refugees.html. Such assertions of aiming to foster refugee self-reliance are repeated in further statements, such as: 'what we have to do is to enable these refugees to become self supporting as soon as possible, and to make a useful contribution to the economic and social life of their country of asylum'. Schnyder, F. (1964) 'Statement by Mr Felix Schnyder, United Nations High Commissioner for Refugees, to the Thirty-seventh Session of the United Nations Economic and Social Council (ECOSOC), 1 May'. Available at: www.unhcr.org/uk/admin/hcspeeches/3ae68fb81c/statement-mr-felix-schnyder-united-nations-high-commissioner-refugees-thirty.html.

were expected to live in settlements. UNHCR's mandate at the time was to only protect and provide assistance to these refugees unless a host government specifically requested otherwise, a policy which led to criticism.[10] Although 'self-settlement' or 'spontaneous settlement'[11] was acknowledged as one form of land settlement for African refugees – and an estimated 60 per cent of African refugees were self-settled[12] – refugees in cases were forcibly removed from the 'spontaneous' settlements they had created and instead brought to organized, planned settlements. However, due in part to harsh prohibitions and regulations, a common strategy of refugees included leaving settlements to find work elsewhere.[13] A 1970 International Council of Voluntary Agencies (ICVA) report cites a growing 'exodus of refugees from the settlements' in Eastern Africa, noting with concern that this was occurring for reasons including internal politics, poor agricultural conditions, and high taxation.[14] Many of the settlements that eventually became self-sufficient, defined as no longer needing food aid due to successful subsistence farming, experienced a dramatic decline in population before becoming stable.[15]

---

[10] Coat, P. (1978) 'Material assistance: some policy problems reviewed in the light of Robert Chambers' evaluation reports'. Geneva: UNHCR.

[11] This was defined in the 1967 African Conference as:

> A process whereby a group of refugees settles down in the country of asylum either in existing villages or by establishing new villages, in or near the area of arrival, which is usually inhabited by a population of similar ethnic origin, by arrangement with the local chiefs and other leaders of the local population, as well as with representatives of the central government, but only with ancillary material assistance from the outside.

Source: Betts Collection (1967) 'Conference on the Legal, Economic and Social Aspects of African Refugee Problems Addis Ababa', 9–18 October 1967. Betts Collection, Bodleian Social Science Library, University of Oxford: Box No. 15, General Work: 12, p 14.

[12] Betts Collection, 'Conference on the Legal, Economic and Social Aspects of African Refugee Problems, p 14.

[13] Betts, T. F. (1969) 'Sudanese refugees in Uganda: the position in May 1969'. Report of Advice on Zonal Rural Development, Oxfam, 13 May; UNHCR (1970) 'Report of the United Nations High Commissioner for Refugees, UNHCR Reports to General Assembly'. 1 January. United Nations General Assembly Official Records: Twenty-Fourth Session. Supplement No. 12 (A/7612). Geneva: UNHCR.

[14] ICVA (1970) 'ICVA Working Group on Integrated Rural Development: Summary Record of the Third Meeting International Council of Voluntary Agencies, January 6'. Betts Collection: A10.13.(33a), Rural Development Background, Box No. 13, p 2.

[15] RPG (Refugee Policy Group) (1985) 'Older refugee settlements in Africa: final report'. Washington, DC: Refugee Policy Group; Stein, 'Refugee integration'.

Zonal development and refugee self-reliance

Although agricultural production was predominant in the 1960s, UNHCR proponents of greater assistance, such as High Commissioner Schnyder, also advocated for a comprehensive development approach that included local host communities and contributed to host country economies. Known as 'zonal development' or 'integrated rural development', this was in essence a repackaging of self-reliance programmes from the interwar years. The ambit of refugee assistance and self-sufficiency therefore began to include infrastructure development for entire areas hosting refugee settlements, now modelled partly on the World Bank's integrated rural development settlements.[16] Zonal development targeted both refugee and host populations, and included the building of roads, schools, and health facilities in addition to agricultural production. As early as 1962, UNHCR focused on integrated rural settlement as a form of development. Writing of such settlements in Togo, a UNHCR report stated:

> The aim of such a development plan would be the creation of one or several series of new settlements. To make these settlements really self-supporting the plan would have to include road-building, irrigation and/or drainage and would have to be completed (as soon as the first income is earned by the refugees) by building adequate accommodation for the settlers. In each of the larger settlements a primary school would need to be established, and in each group of settlements a dispensary, a small vocational training center, and if possible a community center should be set up. The new settlements would thus become the centers of development for the whole area.[17]

As this quote demonstrates, integrated zonal development sought to 'develop' both refugees and locals and in this way contribute to both national and international development. Although this passage refers to one country in particular, it in fact succinctly summarizes reports from across Africa which sought to implement similar development plans in the 1960s and 1970s, thereby demonstrating a 'roll-out' of similar methods of development across the continent.[18]

---

16 Loescher, *The UNHCR and World Politics*, p 122.

17 UNHCR (1962) 'Summary Report on the Refugee Problem in the Republic of Togo'. HCR/RS/23IRev.1, p 5.

18 Betts Collection (1971–1976) 'Compiled Reports and Reviews of East African Refugee Settlement Schemes (Burundi, Rwanda, Tanzania, 1971–1976)'. Betts Collection: General Box 1.

In part due to varied experiences in zonal development, organizations working in Africa sought to establish best practices for refugee settlement. As part of this aim, in 1967 the Conference on the Legal, Economic and Social Aspects of African Refugee Problems was convened in Addis Ababa (the Addis Ababa Conference). As Betts writes,

> The Conference accepted that refugee self-sufficiency at mere subsistence levels could not be considered as conclusive. *Zonal development was required both to consolidate the refugee settlements and to integrate them into the local economic and social system.* Furthermore, such development prompted by the refugee presence should contribute effectively to the overall development of the country of asylum; thus the surrounding population must be ensured an equal share of the advantages accruing.[19] [emphasis added]

The 'development project' and refugee agency

UNHCR's African refugee settlements became embedded in the larger 'development project' in myriad ways, such as zonal development, thereby embodying both national and international development plans. Western development aid increased in the 1960s, in part as developing countries such as the Group of 77 became more strident in advocating for it;[20] refugee assistance was also overtly premised on development rather than just emergency relief during this time. Indeed, through zonal development, refugee settlements acted as focal points for international development schemes that influenced host societies, as well. In such projects, public services and infrastructure were improved in large part *in order* to increase agricultural outputs of export crops such as tea and tobacco.[21] Through the production of cash crops, national economies were to be improved and international trade was envisioned to increase. In this way, both 'underdeveloped' countries and those residing within them could be further integrated into the international capitalist economy.

---

[19] Betts, T. F. (1984) 'Evolution and promotion of the integrated rural development approach to refugee policy in Africa'. *Africa Today* 31(1): 7–24 (p 12).

[20] The Group of 77 is the 'largest intergovernmental organization of developing countries in the United Nations which provides the means for the countries of the South to articulate and promote their collective economic interests and enhance their joint negotiating capacity on all major international economic issues within the United Nations system, and promote South-South cooperation for development.' Source: Group of 77 (2017) Webpage. Available at: www.g77.org/doc/ (accessed 3 November 2017).

[21] Lele, U. (1975) *The Design of Rural Development: Lessons from Africa*. London: Johns Hopkins University Press, p 12.

Through agricultural production in rural settlements, refugees provided an important source of labour in 'underdeveloped' areas of a host country while following a policy of containment within settlements. Main assistance practices, such as agricultural production and vocational training in settlements, continued, yet occurred with little emphasis on accommodating or promoting the existing livelihoods strategies of refugees. The utilization of refugee labour through assistance intended to foster their self-reliance therefore remained similar to that provided in countries such as Greece and Bulgaria during the interwar years – with the critical caveat of increased levels of the regulation and control of refugee agency.

A 1967 overview of the work of 20 organizations comprising the ICVA reveals little focus on livelihoods activities, and instead attention placed on food and medicine and the promotion of basic education.[22] Few micro-finance programmes were implemented; the funding of those that were came from international donors through aid agencies rather than from refugees themselves.[23] The few livelihood-focused projects invested in cash crops as the main means to self-sufficiency, demonstrating institutions' and host states' main focus on integrating refugees into national economies in this way.[24] Alternative settlement livelihoods schemes such as cooperative shops were largely run by camp staff and thus could not rightfully be seen as refugee enterprises.[25]

One reason partially accounting for this is the nearly exclusive Western control of the international refugee regime. By the late 1960s in East Africa, foreign workers were almost solely directing and implementing refugee rehabilitation, in stark contrast to the former role of European refugees and host country nationals in these matters. Africans were not employed within UNHCR in the 1960s and the agency's organizational partners had little prior experience in Africa.[26] In Tanzania, major refugee projects were undertaken throughout the country, yet it was mainly donors who decided which projects would be implemented, meaning that the Tanzanian

[22] ICVA (International Council of Voluntary Agencies) (1967) 'Assistance to African Refugees by Voluntary Organizations Conference on the Legal, Economic and Social Aspects of African Refugee Problems'. Addis Ababa, 9–18 October. Afr/Ref/Conf. 1967/No. 13, Betts Collection, Box No. 15, General Work.

[23] IORD (International Organization for Rural Development) (1971) 'International Organization for Rural Development: Annual Report 1970'. March, Brussels, Betts Collections: Background, Box 13: 37.

[24] ICVA, 'Assistance to African Refugees'.

[25] Morsink (1971) 'Report on training and employment (TRE)'. Betts Collection: Compiled Reports and Reviews of East African Refugee Settlement Schemes (Burundi, Rwanda, Tanzania, 1971–1976)'. Betts Collection: General Box 1, p 5.

[26] Loescher, *The UNHCR and World Politics*, p 119.

government provided only their final approval. Individual refugee suggestions or requests were rarely taken into consideration; in one isolated case in the early 1960s UNHCR and another assistance agency approved refugees' requests for roofing material for settlement churches.[27] However, later requests for the same were denied.

Paradoxically, very little research was undertaken on those refugees not involved in any form of international assistance – that is, refugees who truly *were* self-reliant. There existed little information beyond rough estimates of those outside UNHCR's ambit. Chambers criticizes UNHCR for this oversight, stating that the needs of 'self-settled refugees' and those in non-institutionally planned 'spontaneous settlements' were overlooked.[28] This lack of research, he writes, 'presents an arena for broad prejudices and convenient rationalizations [by] problem-minimizing bureaucrats who might argue that "no news is good news" [and] dyed-in-the-wool do-gooders who might argue that "no news is bad news." The simple fact, however, is that usually no one knows. No news is no news.'[29]

One result of this lack of research was an ongoing focus on refugees in settlements, who were helped by a bevy of international assistance actors according to their own beliefs of what appropriate assistance constituted. Until 1972 local integration was the 'major policy objective' of UNHCR with approximately three-quarters of UNHCR's material assistance efforts funded through UNHCR's General Programme.[30] However, in contrast to contemporary understandings of the term, local integration mainly referred to the creation of self-reliant refugee settlements, or barring that, the mere acceptance of refugees in host countries of the Global South. As Daley writes of the period, 'In the final analysis, Africa's refugee policy is not really a reflection of foreign policy choices or even of domestic policy, but of the prevailing interest of the major donors to the United Nations. It is therefore not surprising that in a neo-colonial age, African states have no independent refugee policy.'[31]

A variety of social and economic factors account for this institutional structure. Just as the recession in the 1930s led to the engagement of more foreign non-refugee employees in refugee relief, the 1960 recession affected the refugee regime similarly. Indeed, a report from the Addis Ababa Conference stated 'every State is anxious to safeguard its employment

27 Daley, P. (1989) 'Refugees and Underdevelopment in Africa: The case of Barundi Refugees in Tanzania'. DPhil Thesis. Oxford: University of Oxford, p 133.

28 Chambers, R. (1976) *Rural Refugees after Arusha*. Mimeographed. Geneva: UNHCR.

29 Chambers, *Rural Refugees after Arusha*, p 7.

30 Pitterman, S. (1984) 'A comparative survey of two decades of international assistance to refugees in Africa'. *Africa Today* 31(1): 25–54 (p 29).

31 Daley, 'Refugees and Underdevelopment', pp 106–107.

market. ... As a result, states have been known to employ European expatriate staff on contract basis, rather than African refugees'.[32] Eriksson, Melander and Nobel echoed this, noting that African governments preferred to employ foreign experts instead of refugees, as their salaries were frequently paid through development assistance programmes instead of their own national budgets.[33]

The 1967 Addis Ababa Conference explicitly recommended foreign NGOs as implementing agencies due to the purported lack of skilled African development staff.[34] In addition to barring refugees from employment, the implementation of this recommendation meant that host country national governments were in many cases effectively precluded from controlling aid policies. Western donor funds went, in most cases, through Western intergovernmental agencies or NGOs employing mainly Westerners. This structure and the outcomes it contributed to can be further seen through the case study of Tanzanian refugee settlements.

Refugee self-reliance assistance in post-colonial Tanzania

A UN Trust Territory since 1947, Tanzania's path toward independence occurred mainly through political negotiation[35] and a notably peaceful process led it to become an independent country on 9 December 1961. Julius Nyerere, the charismatic leader of the Tanganyika African National Union (TANU), became president and furthered a unique agenda of African socialism known as *ujamaa* (roughly translated from Swahili as 'brotherhood' or 'extended family'). Although definitions varied across countries and leaders, African socialism was premised on sharing resources in a communitarian way based on culture and tribal communities. Countries involved in this project included Mali, Senegal, Ghana, and Guinea in addition to Tanzania. Three main themes of African socialism were broadly consistent across countries: economic development, African identity, and class formation. Nyerere, a vanguard of the concept, sought to use African socialism as a basis for economic development in the aftermath of colonial rule through a focus on communal land ownership, cooperative agriculture,

[32] Betts Collection, 'Conference on the Legal, Economic and Social Aspects of African Refugee Problems', p 12.

[33] Eriksson, L. G., Melander, G., and Nobel, P. (eds) (1981) *An Analysing Account of the Conference on the African Refugee Problem, Arusha, May 1979*. Uppsala: Nordic Africa Institute, p 29.

[34] Betts Collection, 'Conference on the Legal, Economic and Social Aspects of African Refugee Problems', Recommendation 8.

[35] Lohrmann, U. (2007) *Voices from Tanganyika: Great Britain, The United Nations and the decolonization of a Trust Territory, 1946–1961*. Berlin: Lit Verlag.

and a large public sector. This manifested largely as village-level development, culminating in *ujamaa* villages.

Refugee policy was influenced by *ujamaa* as the basis of national development, including by the nationalization of factories and plantations, collective villages for agricultural production, and an economic, political, and social emphasis on self-reliance. In addition to its practical influence on the design of refugee assistance, the ideology of *ujamaa* also played a role in refugees' initial welcome into the country. In this way Tanzania presents a unique context of strong nationalism in addition to international involvement through refugee self-reliance assistance, often embedded within national development assistance.

Self-reliance assistance to refugees in East Africa during this time upheld agricultural production for international export. In Tanzania, this aligned with and benefited the country's national development plan. As Nyerere stated in the 1967 Arusha Declaration, widely known as the marker of the beginning of the country's focus on socialism, 'From now on we shall stand upright and walk forward on our feet rather than look at this problem upside down. Industries will come and money will come but their foundation is the people and their hard work, especially in AGRICULTURE. This is the meaning of self-reliance'[36] [emphasis in text].

The backdrop of Tanzania's focus on agriculture was import substitution industrialization, which began in the 1960s and continued until the country's neoliberal shift to Structural Adjustment Programmes (SAPs) in the mid-1980s.[37] Emblematic of the development strategies of African countries in the 1960s, Tanzania sought to nationally produce the goods they had once been forced to import. Profits from agriculture were to go toward the financing of national industries, which in turn would further develop the country.[38] In this way, the economic, political, and social value of refugees intertwined, as their agricultural labour embodied Nyerere's emphasis on 'the land and agriculture; people; [and] the policy of socialism and self-reliance'.[39] This focus was anti-colonial and anti-exploitative in nature, premised on creating a self-reliant Tanzania and an independent Africa unshackled by foreign capital. Refugees were a component of this, as through *ujamaa* 'utilization of refugee labour was intentionally part of Tanzanian development strategy'.[40]

---

36 Nyerere, J. (1967) 'The Arusha Declaration. Section: "Hard Work is the Root of Development"'. Available at: www.marxists.org/subject/africa/nyerere/1967/arusha-declaration.htm (accessed 1 November 1).

37 Mendes, A. P. F., Bertella, M. A., and Teixeira, R. F. (2014) 'Industrialization in sub-Saharan Africa and import substitution policy'. *Revista de Economia Política* 34(1): 120–138.

38 Nyerere, 'The Arusha Declaration. Section: "Hard Work is the Root of Development"'.

39 Nyerere, 'The Arusha Declaration. Section: "Hard Work is the Root of Development"'.

40 Daley, 'Refugees and Underdevelopment in Africa', p 79.

Despite having avoided violent conflicts of its own, shortly after independence in 1961, Tanzania had several significant refugee influxes that lasted up to the 1980s. It became known as a generous host country, and one of the first African countries to naturalize refugees on a large scale, due in large part to Nyerere's commitment to a refugee policy founded on humanist principles and Pan-Africanism.[41] During the 1960s and 1970s, approximately 45,000 Mozambican refugees were settled in five camps in the southern regions of Lindi and Ruvuma. The majority repatriated in 1974 following Mozambique's independence, and international aid focused on the Western border regions along Rwanda, Burundi, Uganda, Zaire, and Zambia. Altogether, an estimated 200,500 refugees from these countries arrived in Tanzania at different times.[42] By 1987, 90 per cent of the refugees in Tanzania were concentrated in the Kigoma, Tabora, and Rukwa regions.[43]

Starting in 1964, the Lutheran World Federation (LWF), through its local partner, the Tanganyika Christian Refugee Service (TCRS) implemented most refugee projects in Tanzania through tripartite agreements between the Government of Tanzania (GoT), UNHCR, and LWF/TCRS. After agreements were signed, UNHCR coordinated the provision of basic assistance such as food, medicine, and transport through the World Food Programme and UNICEF.[44] Through these partnerships, TCRS became the sole operational agency for UNHCR-financed projects;[45] in this way it became what implementing partners are to UNHCR today. However, across Tanzania, settlements became sites for community and rural development projects led by myriad international organizations including ILO, the United Nations Development Programme (UNDP), and members of ICVA, which often worked in tandem to achieve their aims. Jointly led programmes by UNHCR, Oxfam, UNDP, the World Bank, and host country governments were also undertaken in different regions across Africa including the Mwese Highlands refugee settlement in Tanzania and the Canguzo area of Burundi.[46]

41 Nyerere, J. (1968) *Ujamaa: Essays on Socialism*. Nairobi: Oxford University Press, p 103.

42 Refugees from Rwanda arrived between 1959 and 1964, from Zaire in 1964 and onwards, from Burundi in 1972 and onwards, and from Uganda between 1971 and 1985. Source: Daley, 'Refugees and Underdevelopment in Africa', p 142.

43 Daley, 'Refugees and Underdevelopment in Africa', p 140.

44 Daley, 'Refugees and Underdevelopment in Africa', p 128.

45 TCRS (Tanganyika Christian Refugee Service) (1971) 'Annual Report 1971'. Betts Collection, Bodleian Social Science Library, University of Oxford: Box 53. Tanzania: Rural Settlement Planning [394], p 3.

46 Betts, T. F. (1969) 'Sudanese refugees in Uganda', p 150.

Refugee self-reliance assistance practices

Like the majority of refugees in Africa at the time, refugees in Tanzania were encouraged to create or join agricultural settlements, through which they were meant to become self-reliant. These settlements were generally embedded within larger development projects. However, unlike refugees in other countries, Tanzanian refugee settlements acted as prototypes for – and in some cases became – the *ujamaa* villages that were the hallmark of African socialism.[47] Refugee settlements initially for Tutsi refugees from Rwanda and Mozambican refugees built in the mid-1960s are considered examples for the *ujamaa* villages of the following decade and in this way profoundly influenced Tanzanian national development.[48] After refugee groups such as the Mozambicans returned home in 1974, settlements housing them were turned over to the Tanzanian government and then became official *ujamaa* villages. As Tague notes, '[D]espite the fact that *ujamaa* has been seen as a distinctly Tanzanian endeavor, these villages were built not by Tanzanians, but rather through Mozambican refugee labor'.[49]

Self-reliance assistance in the Mwese refugee settlement

Ujamaa and refugee settlements further merged through integrated zonal development. The Mwese refugee settlement in Western Tanzania for Rwandan refugees exemplifies the dominant zonal development assistance model at the time. The settlement was envisioned as a model for further refugee settlements in Tanzania's undeveloped rural areas and became a site where local, national, and international development aims converged through integrated rural development. Refugee labour was at the crux of this and served both national and international ends.

Although Tanzania was – to a more and lesser disputed extent – a socialist country until the 1980s, this in no way made it a site of capitalist exception. Instead, the World Bank was involved with financial structuring beginning in the 1960s, nearly two decades before its heavy involvement in stipulating SAPs. The World Bank was also involved in recommending projects for refugee settlements, as in the case of the Mwese Settlement.

47 Tague, J. (2012) 'A War to Build the Nation: Mozambican Refugees, Rural Development, and State Sovereignty in Tanzania, 1964–1975'. Dissertation. University of California, Davis.

48 Tague, 'A War to Build the Nation'.

49 Tague, 'A War to Build the Nation', p 4.

Other international entities such as the ILO also presented plans for vocational centres and other activities in line with the socialist vision of the country, demonstrating a larger international acceptance of Tanzanian policy while retaining a focus on private, market-based activities. Based on project proposals and reports targeting refugees as well as just Tanzanians, these 'international experts'' aim of capitalist accumulation did not seem impeded by the macro-socialist vision of the country.

Reports on refugees from the era are littered with the same statistics and projections of income and capital surplus as broader development plans at the time, as well as similar visions of modernization and the need for expertise.[50] Strategies promoting refugee self-reliance became infused with the broader political and intellectual thought of a post-war development order focused on 'progress', defined by Gross Domestic Product (GDP) and the introduction of new populations into liberal economies. Through offering an agricultural workforce that provided targeted value to national host governments and Western countries promoting development, refugee assistance at this time retained the interwar years' emphasis on subsistence farming and cash crops. However, we also begin to see an increased importance placed on refugees' involvement in a cash-based economy. The ILO and World Bank appear to be the strongest proponents of this, discussing the need for refugees to sell products from within settlements and for the creation of refugee cooperatives and marketing societies.[51]

---

50 As one 1969 ILO report on rural settlement stated:

> This document stresses the fact that Tanzania has to face realities: [it is] an economy based on agriculture with insufficient capital to invest in factories or modern machinery and an inadequate number of skilled and experienced workers, but with land in abundance and people willing to work hard for improving their living conditions … The main barrier to its agricultural progress lies in the fact that farmers do not possess sufficient knowledge and technical training. The rural young people are not attracted by farming but by urban life and as a result there is a general exodus that creates social and economic problems of great importance. It is as urgent to train villages as it is to raise the general standard of the rural population.

Source: ILO (1969) 'Tanzania: Rural Prevocational and Vocational Training in Tanzania'. Betts Collection: Box 53 [399], pp 7, 10.

51 Oxfam (1968) 'Tanzania: A Pilot Scheme of Agricultural Development for the Mwese Highlands in Tanzania'. Betts Collection, Refugee Research Project – Tanzania, Box 53A.; ILO, 'Tanzania: Rural Prevocational and Vocational Training'; TCRS (1972) 'Annual Report'. Betts Collection, Bodleian Social Science Library, University of Oxford: Box 53. Tanzania: Rural Settlement Planning [394].

In 1964, the Mwese refugee settlement was the site of the first tripartite agreement between UNHCR, the GoT, and TCRS, with financial support from Oxfam. Villages meant to accommodate 100 families were built across a 100-acre site on the Mwese Highlands which offered one acre of cultivation adjacent to families' houses and two further acres near the village. A hospital was built, which was meant to serve 10,000 people, and an existing building was converted into a police station.[52] Although originally envisaged to house 10,000 refugees, by 1968 only 3,000 had settled there. Refugees were initially provided with free food, clothing, and medical services, but the aim of the settlement was to produce enough food for the refugees to become self-reliant, defined at the time as meeting their own subsistence requirements. Given this aim, a gradual process of withdrawing free rations and clothing was instituted, and by late 1966 and 1967 the majority of families – far below the number envisioned to live in the settlement – were able to produce enough food for themselves. A small number had even managed to produce surplus to sell.[53]

In 1968, when the refugees in Mwese were largely considered self-reliant, grander international plans were created for the settlement: in the name of increasing their level of self-reliance, the World Bank stepped in. The Bank had long been involved in Tanzania's agricultural development, including promoting the concept of integrated development programmes and supporting them through a 'combination of inputs and extension to increase crop production with an arsenal of supporting infrastructural and social service investments (marketing, education, water supply, road maintenance, etc.)'.[54] Regarding the Bank's plans with refugees, one archival report prepared by the World Bank and funded by Oxfam noted in a segment entitled 'Future Orientation':

> *The settlement of a group of alien refugees, inexperienced and not necessarily inclined towards agriculture, in a remote and wholly undeveloped location, inevitably presents great difficulties.* All things considered, the progress made so far at Mwese is quite creditable. The point has now been reached, however, where Government feels that the people of the area, including the settlers and a few previous residents, should be able with appropriate assistance to lift themselves above bare subsistence level and *to become more self-reliant and productive farmers. To this end, the Government requested the Agricultural Development Service of the World*

52 Oxfam, 'Tanzania: A Pilot Scheme'.
53 Oxfam, 'Tanzania: A Pilot Scheme'.
54 Payer, C. (1983) 'Tanzania and the World Bank'. *Third World Quarterly* 5(4): 791–813 (p 797).

> *Bank to assist* in the preparation of a pilot project for development of the Mwese area.[55] [emphasis added]

This pilot project aimed to create surplus agricultural output and thereafter an organized marketing system. According to Tanzanian government policy at the time, all agricultural produce sales were made through primary cooperative societies, in which members pooled resources and labour for agricultural production. It was envisioned that a new primary society would be created at Mwese to enable the sale of surplus maize and beans.[56] Refugee farmers would receive in-kind loans in seeds, fertilizer and other material instead of cash, and would 'repay' these loans through adequate levels of produce, which they would then hand over to the development officer of the scheme. The main benefits of the scheme were perceived as follows:

- a previously unutilized 10,000 acres of land would be 'harnessed for production';
- agricultural production to stimulate the national economy;
- revenue to central and local government, thereby 'ensuring that refugees do not remain a permanent burden to Government';
- integration of refugee and 'local Tanzanian settlers';
- small cash surplus for refugees awaiting settlement, who would be employed by the scheme;
- the training of local staff in the 'development of simple planned agriculture which is an essential ingredient of sound agricultural development elsewhere in Tanzania' [what we would today likely term agricultural extension officers];
- the scheme would act as a pilot for the development of up to 100,000 acres in the region.[57]

In this way we see the planned integration of refugee labour and agricultural outputs into the national system of production. As the report stated, 'In the past the investment in refugee settlement schemes has normally produced only a subsistence type agriculture which has made little contribution to the national economy and has not raised the low state of morale among the participants. This scheme is planned to overcome these problems.'[58] Just as refugees in Greece were encouraged and assisted to become farmers in order

55 Oxfam, 'Tanzania: A Pilot Scheme', p 3.
56 Oxfam, 'Tanzania: A Pilot Scheme', p 8.
57 Oxfam, 'Tanzania: A Pilot Scheme', p 12.
58 Oxfam, 'Tanzania: A Pilot Scheme', p 12.

to meet their own subsistence needs and produce cash crops for their host country's economy, so were refugees across Africa encouraged to do the same.

This pilot project by the Bank illustrates how refugee settlements became the sites of larger plans to integrate African countries further into the international economy through initiatives encouraging refugee populations to enter cash economies. The World Bank and the ILO became involved in not only improving agricultural production but setting up marketing societies and increasing refugees' circulation of small amounts of capital. These strategies were explicitly defined as targeting the self-sufficiency of refugees. One 1971 UNHCR evaluation report on Tanzanian and other East African settlements, for example, criticizes measures taken to restrict the livelihood initiatives of fishermen, tailors, and craftsmen who did not want to farm – not because of the restriction of refugees' rights but because it was considered a 'misconceived' policy for accruing profit

> based on the false assumption that the agricultural self-sufficiency of *each* refugee is the best way of reaching overall goals of economic viability. Considerable cash incomes can be achieved even within the very restricted market along the lake shore. The cash returns to labour time spent fishing are many times more than the returns from growing crops. If substantial cash surpluses were earned they could be used for purchasing grain from other areas and for encouraging the development of more commercialized local food production.[59] [emphasis in text]

Through this logic we see the criticism of forced farming due to its economic inefficiency, and the advocacy for diversified (and self-chosen) livelihoods arising due to the potential for cash surplus rather than out of respect for refugees' agency. Ultimately, the report concludes, 'The key to all these activities is the development of cash surpluses which can form the basis of circulation for exchange. In the long run a cash based farm economy is needed for a balanced and viable socio-economic system in the refugee settlements.'[60] This report echoes much of the 1960s and 1970s development discourse on modernization, and in so doing suggests the strong degree to which refugee assistance was embedded in visions of the international economic integration of the so-called Third World.

[59] Feldman, D. (1971) 'Report in Dependence/Initiative Section—1'. Betts Collection: Compiled Reports and Reviews of East African Refugee Settlement Schemes (Burundi, Rwanda, Tanzania, 1971–1976), Betts Collection: General Box 1, p 41.

[60] Feldman, 1971, 'Report in Dependence', p 58; Feldman, D. 'Appraisal of the economic viability of four refugee settlements in Southern Tanzania confidential (final draft) report – for internal use only'. Neldner Archives, Bodleian Social Science Library, University of Oxford: RSP/NELD/LT 59.44 FEL.

What these shifting self-reliance practices also demonstrate is a larger shift of rural 'undeveloped' populations moving from agricultural subsistence to a dependence on markets and, ultimately, on wage labour. This period of refugee assistance paralleled larger development processes occurring around the globe after the Second World War. As industrialization began to be favoured over agricultural production, peasants – both voluntarily and by force – became wage labourers. Refugees were not exempt from this process. As such, the definition of refugee self-reliance – previously perceived as agricultural subsistence – began to both expand and contract, illustrating the dynamism of the concept.

Although agricultural production was widely promoted and perceived as the predominant aim of integrated rural development projects, there was also criticism of these large-scale, capital-intensive schemes. Writing in the 1980s but reflecting on the decades prior, Betts discussed the need for refugee censuses, particularly identifying refugees' skills, in order to offer 'opportunities for alternative employment beyond the drudgery of cash crop production'.[61] He also advocated a different policy approach that involved 'placing greater reliance on the creation of comparatively small peasant communities, unified and supported by cooperatives, covering agricultural credit, marketing and supply. Governments should be persuaded to give high priority to cooperative training and organization.'[62] Discussing the problem of low rural wages in East Africa, he conceded that raising wages could pose a problem for major agricultural schemes essentially built on cheap labour but suggested nonetheless an income target for the chosen areas of development, calculated from both the national average and a percentage that would be gained from the advanced development to come. He writes, '[P]resent policies of low seasonal wage rates for migrant seasonal labor drawn from more poverty-stricken areas and otherwise dependent on a marginal subsistence existence is scarcely consistent with the surge of national development to which it is hoped that the new development-oriented program will make a significant contribution'.[63]

This statement exemplifies the issues of many development schemes at the time, both those 'integrated' ones as well as those solely designed for local populations. The purported aim of such projects was the development of regions in order to move the populations within them from 'dependency' or subsistence self-sufficiency to what could be considered 'surplus self-sufficiency', at which point refugees would be able to participate in a cash

[61] Betts, T. F. and Pitterman, S. (1984) 'Evolution and promotion of the Integrated Rural Development approach to refugee policy in Africa'. *Africa Today* 31(1): 7–24 (p 18).

[62] Betts and Pitterman, 'Evolution and promotion', p 15.

[63] Betts and Pitterman, 'Evolution and promotion', p 15.

economy. However, the actual practices involved were often little more than the exploitation of impoverished Africans, refugee and local alike. Refugees filled an important gap in rural labour, such as with Mozambican refugees in Tanzania, many of whom had followed a rural migration route established by colonial powers.[64] Elsewhere in the 1970s, an influx of Angolan refugees into Zaire replaced the labourers who had moved to Kinshasa, the new capital, thereby enabling agricultural expansion and the provision of food to new urban areas.[65] Similar examples of refugees filling agricultural labour shortages and contributing to vital food production is also documented in Zambia, Tanzania, and Sudan.[66] Yet despite this significant contribution of labour to 'development', wage payment for refugees was not guaranteed.

The structure of refugee self-reliance assistance

In contrast to the largely hands-off settlement approach of the League in the interwar years, overwhelmingly negative reports of East African refugee settlements in Tanzania, Burundi, and Rwanda between 1971 and 1976 cite a highly authoritarian administration that restricted refugees' self-reliance strategies and the overall effectiveness of rural development plans.[67] Refugees were not employees or delegates of organizations such as UNHCR but instead mere 'beneficiaries'. They were not only discouraged, but actively punished for having any livelihood other than an institutionally mandated one – usually farming.

Vocational programmes and settlement classes, ostensibly to teach skills to enable self-reliance, ultimately contributed to perpetuating power disparities between refugees and settlement staff. Foreign-led 'Settlement Community Development Programmes' were instituted to teach and train refugees according to designated methods. At the Rutamba Settlement in Tanzania, established in 1965, these programmes included: '[O]fficial urging … to engage in certain types of agriculture and in block farming, or to introduce certain kinds of crops; "softer" methods used include "classes" and "clubs" for women and youth and to a lesser extent demonstrations, for instance, of food preparation.'[68]

64 Tague, 'A War to Build the Nation'.

65 Betts and Pitterman, 'Evolution and promotion', p 16.

66 Betts and Pitterman, 'Evolution and promotion', p 16.

67 Betts Collection, 'Compiled Reports and Reviews'.

68 Trappe, P. (1971) 'Social change and development institutions in a refugee population: development from below as an alternative: the case of the Nakapiripirit Settlement Scheme in Uganda'. Geneva: United Nations Research Institute for Social Development.

Such directive programmes occurred in conjunction with stringent regulations surrounding refugees' own self-reliance practices. Some of these rules were host country policies, such as a policy shift that prohibited refugee marketing organizations in Tanzania. This resulted in a dependency on outside cooperative societies to buy refugees' crops and an attendant lack of refugee ownership over their own source of income; as one settlement impact assessor remarked, 'As the refugee farmers were not able to join these societies so they were unable to exert any pressure on the societies to provide them with an adequate service.'[69]

Many other harmful policies came from within the settlements themselves.[70] Supported by UNHCR and the LWF, in 1967, the Rutamba settlement held 8,000 refugees struggling to become self-sufficient.[71] Refugees were originally intended to grow cashew nuts as the main cash crop, but this expanded to others in an effort to raise refugees above the subsistence level. However:

> Most [refugee] farmers questioned said they were prevented by the settlement authorities from extending their fishing activities. The main rationale behind discouraging fishing is the desire to maximise the cultivated area of the settlement. *Fishing … is tolerated only if it does not interfere with the agricultural projects. The use of coercion is considered normal, and refugees are put into prison if they fail to provide expected labour requirements for projects* such as the establishment this year of 400 acres of block farms to grow more rice, beans and cassava.[72] [emphasis added]

In some instances this coercion seemed to occur out of paternalism, as demonstrated through a private letter from the TCRS Agricultural Programme Supervisor to Mr Neldner, the TCRS director, in response to a damning UNHCR evaluation report of Tanzanian refugee settlements. 'The [report] writer indicates that the settlement management says that non-agricultural enterprises should not interfere with the agricultural work,' he starts out, 'I agree that it should be like that, but it is very easy to get a society of non-agricultural workers looking down upon agricultural workers. It is also a security for the refugees to grow enough food for themselves.'[73] Through this excerpt we see both an awareness of and a disregard for refugee

69 Morsink, 'Report on training and employment', p 5.

70 RPG, 'Older refugee settlements'.

71 ICVA, 'Assistance to African Refugees'.

72 Trappe, 'Social change and development institutions', p 10.

73 Jernaes, J. (1971) 'Letter to Mr. Neldner, regarding Mr. Feldman's report 25th September'. Neldner Archives, Bodleian Social Science Library, University of Oxford. RSP/NELD/LT 59.44 FEL.

agency, and particularly that of refugees who previously held professions other than farming. The letter continues:

> It is serious that people are put in prison if they don't work on the communal farm, but it is a fact that people along the lake mainly grow cassava and *they have to be pushed to change this.* As said before there should be done something to improve the fishing in Lundo but *fishing does not need to be increased in the cultivating time, but mainly in the dry season.*[74] [emphasis added]

Here we find a similar contempt for refugees' own self-reliance strategies, with the agricultural programme supervisor tacitly accepting the use of imprisonment as a means to change the livelihoods activities of refugees. It is clear that fishing, if tolerated at all, is not conceived as an appropriate activity when cultivating could instead be taking place. Further control is evident from the general conclusions of the programme supervisor from the UNHCR report: 'The people who have made the comments have talked much about the negative aspects in the settlements and not talked enough about the positive sides. This is a very important thing and the field staff should be told that they have to be careful about making negative remarks.'[75]

The dearth of refugees and local experts involved in settlement structures drastically impacted the mandated self-reliance practices employed, and led to a variety of social and practical problems.[76] As Betts repeatedly called out in reports and speeches, due to ignorance and a lack of site planning, plots were often too small for more than subsistence farming and officials disregarded both important preliminary soil quality surveys and necessary planting times.[77] Innovative and ultimately destructive technologies such as bulldozers impeded successful crop production through scraping away rich topsoil, leading only cassava to grow in some Tanzanian settlements.[78] Despite multiple reports of 'land exhaustion'[79] in various settlements, a main focus remained on cultivating cash crops such as tobacco and improving means of agricultural production. A 1971 assessment of Tanzanian settlements states:

---

74 Jernaes, 'Letter to Mr. Neldner'.

75 Jernaes, 'Letter to Mr. Neldner'.

76 ICVA (1969) 'Zonal Development Planning in Africa: Summary Record of an ICVA Ad Hoc Meeting, March 20', Betts Collection: J10.13(33r), Rural Development Background, Box No. 13, p 1; Betts Collection, 'Compiled Reports and Reviews'; RPG, 'Older Refugee Settlements', p 99.

77 Betts Collection, 'Compiled Reports and Reviews'.

78 Feldman, 'Report in Dependence', p 2.

79 IORD, 'International Organization for Rural Development', p 11.

> The more general conclusion is that the potential of the agricultural infrastructure has not been effectively utilised. *This is mainly because of a lack of experience of those controlling them*, and the inadequate information provided … In retrospect, it does appear that a large amount of the settlements' infrastructure and therefore *the 'cost' of settling the refugees, can be primarily explained in terms of the capital support needed to maintain project staff. Their limited technical expertise, and their limited access to technical information available locally has meant that there have been few long term benefits from such expenditures.*[80] [emphasis added]

This top-down authority and lack of expertise was accompanied by an absence of communication with refugees and locals and the virtual suppression of refugee agency from decision-making and implementation roles as well as from the aforementioned undertaking of livelihoods. The administration of the Rutamba settlement is representative of top-down post-war refugee self-reliance assistance. Although refugee settlement leaders were elected, they wielded no true power. Of Rutamba, Trappe writes: 'There is no participation by refugees in the management of the Settlement. The sixty-five "leaders" play only a rather passive role in the organisation … The Settlement Commandant and his staff … adopt the system of pure direction from above.'[81]

In part through descriptions such as these, settlement reports, budgets, and critiques can reveal much about the inner workings of refugee settlements and their relationship with outside donors and international organizations, but often fail to describe refugees' own attitudes and strategies toward the policies and situations imposed upon them. Although the period of analysis here is restricted to the 1960s and 1970s, ethnographic research and oral histories undertaken with refugees in Tanzania by scholars such as Liisa Malkki and Patricia Daley in the 1980s provide useful information on the perspectives of refugees in settlements still structured similarly to the time period examined here. Malkki's ethnography of Hutu refugees from Burundi in the Mishamo Refugee Settlement and Kigoma Township in Western Tanzania between 1985 and 1986, for example, deals with many of the same issues relating to agricultural production and coercion noted in earlier settlement reports.[82] Quotes from two informants in particular illustrate how some refugees experienced the settlement administration and the agricultural production expected of them:

> There exist different kinds of camps. There are military camps. In these military camps there are Commandants, those who command

[80] Feldman, 'Report in Dependence', p 5.

[81] Trappe, 'Social change and development institutions', p 2.

[82] Malkki, L. H. (1995) *Purity and Exile: Violence, memory, and national consciousness among Hutu refugees in Tanzania*. Chicago, IL: University of Chicago.

> the soldiers. Then there are refugee camps and settlements. A military camp is commanded, but a refugee camp is not. But I ask you: Who has the Commandant? It is we, refugees, here. Elsewhere, for example in the refugee settlements of Rwanda and Zambia, there are no Commandants. It is the refugees themselves who direct the affairs of the settlement, with the United Nations High Commissioner for Refugees. So, here this is not a settlement. This is a camp which has a Tanzanian Commandant. It is he who controls what happens in the camp. It is he who – in the name of the government – controls cultural, economic, and political affairs. It is the Commandant who decides. So, in our opinion, this is a camp. But UNHCR and TCRS do not want to say *camp* because the word has bad connotations … army, all that. They always want to say *settlement*.[83]

> And we left Burundi for this? Nothing has changed … we cultivate for the whole country. … We are the granaries of the Tanzanians. If we have a sack of beans, we cannot sell it to our friend. The government says to us that it is to be sold at two and a half [shillings] to the cooperative shop of the village. Same with the maize. Then the trucks of the NMC come to buy them. We, we do not go to Mpanda to sell them. They come here. … We are qualified workers, and they know it. … They do not want us to leave their country. We cultivate a lot, they eat a lot. We feed all the poor regions of Tanzania. From the big stores in Mpanda, food is taken to all regions of Tanzania. Now they say that we are nothing but immigrants who came in search of new, good land to cultivate, but it is not true. We have become their slaves. We have been given a pet name here, 'the tractors.' They benefit by us. This is the wherefore that they do not want us to leave here. They tell you that the refugee will say, 'I am a refugee of hunger because I did not have enough land to cultivate [in Burundi].' Lies![84]

These quotes, although not representative of all refugees in Tanzanian settlements, are striking in the parallels they present to UNHCR evaluation reports from over a decade earlier, where discussions of the use of coercion by settlement administration to grow crops are cited at multiple settlements. The first quote in particular alludes to the authority of the settlement administration, and the Commandant in particular. Both quotes illuminate a sense of anger over refugees' seeming inability in the settlement to make

[83] Hutu Refugee informant, quoted in: Malkki, *Purity and Exile*, p 117. It should also be noted that Tanzania's refugee policy became notably more stringent following the 1978–1979 Uganda–Tanzania war.

[84] Quoted in: Malkki, *Purity and Exile*, p 120.

decisions for themselves and take control over their own livelihoods. However, the cultural specificity of both assertions must also be taken into account, as Malkki notes the longstanding issue of slavery as central to the Hutu–Tutsi relationship in Burundi.[85] It is also notable that at this point in time refugee settlements in Tanzania had largely been 'handed over' to the Tanzanian government; however, as the above quote depicts, it seems that this transfer of administrative power had done little to change the previously existing unequal power relations between settlement staff and inhabitants.

Evaluating the outcomes of settlement self-reliance

Were such refugees truly becoming self-reliant through the process of agricultural production – meaning in this context at least growing enough crops for subsistence and potentially even producing surplus to sell? This, after all, was the stated aim of such initiatives, alongside regional development, and where the bulk of funding was placed. Settlement reports paint a bleak picture. Out of the 117 settlements established in Africa, UNHCR declared only 30 of these self-sufficient between 1966 and 1982.[86] Of these, 21 received renewed aid in this period, and eight enough aid to make their true self-sufficiency debatable.[87]

The combination of increased refugee numbers without corresponding rates of repatriation, as well as increased Western restrictionism, led to the convening of the first of multiple international conferences addressing refugees, development, and self-reliance in 1979. The Pan-African Conference on the Situation of Refugees in Africa (Arusha Conference) discussed the refugee 'problem' in Africa and promoted African-based solutions for it. Agricultural production and vocational training in refugee settlements were recommended as a way to attain 'self-sufficiency' and contribute to a region's overall development.[88] These self-reliance initiatives remained in line with host country national development aims, as demonstrated through a conference report stating that 'integration should include vocational training related to the planned manpower needs of the Government', and that integrated settlements would enable 'payment of tax by refugees on [the] same basis as for locals'.[89] While still

[85] Quoted in: Malkki, *Purity and Exile*, p 120.

[86] Stein, 'Refugee integration', p 3.

[87] Stein, 'Refugee integration', p 3; RPG, 'Older Refugee Settlements'.

[88] Regional Refugee Instruments and Related (1979) 'Recommendations from the Pan-African Conference on the Situation of Refugees in Africa'. Arusha (Tanzania). 17 May 1979. Available at: www.refworld.org/docid/3ae6b37214.html (accessed 26 September 2018).

[89] Regional Refugee Instruments and Related, 'Recommendations'.

supporting national development, two further conferences in the 1980s, the International Conferences on Assistance to Refugees in Africa (ICARA I and II), brought refugee self-reliance to the forefront of global discussions on international burden-sharing.[90] While voluntary repatriation remained the preferred durable solution – 'the ideal, best, preferred, most desirable solution'[91] – local integration as the second most desirable option remained clear, echoing the conclusions of the 1967 Conference. Achieving refugee self-reliance remained a key part of this aim.

Despite the failings of many settlements and the documented deleterious effects of authoritarian administrations, the main recommendations of the Arusha Conference were for agricultural development programmes and vocational training according to the needs of the host government.[92] The 'effective involvement of refugees in the integration and development process'[93] was recommended, yet it was the 'officials administering refugee affairs' who were encouraged to develop best practices for refugee self-reliance.[94] These recommendations, therefore, were simply reiterations of practices already in place and did not acknowledge the role that those 'officials' played in the emerging status quo of settlement dependency. They furthermore served as a basis for the livelihoods programmes encompassed within Refugee Aid and Development (RAD) and later initiatives to be discussed. It is in this restrictive way that refugee self-reliance assistance continued to be conceived in programmes and settlements led by main institutions such as UNHCR, ILO, and UNDP in the decades following.

Refugee self-reliance, politics, exploitation

Drawing and expanding on the history documented above, this section discusses some of the wider premises that gave rise to the particular aims and practices of refugee self-reliance assistance in Eastern Africa in the 1960s and 1970s, with a focus on Tanzania. As we have seen in this chapter, the international refugee assistance that began in Africa in the 1960s carried over many of the interwar practices to foster refugee self-reliance. Similar to the League's High Commission, UNHCR fully advocated a policy of

---

90 Gorman, R. (1986) 'Beyond ICARA II: implementing refugee-related development assistance'. *International Migration Review* 20(2): 283–298; Gorman, R. (1987) 'Taking stock of the Second International Conference on Assistance to Refugees in Africa (ICARA II)'. *Journal of African Studies* 14(1): 4–11; ICARA I and II are discussed in more depth in the 'context' section of the following chapter.

91 Stein, B. N. (1986) 'Durable solutions for developing country refugees'. *International Migration Review* 20(2): 264–282 (p 269).

92 Regional Refugee Instruments and Related, 'Recommendations', paras 1b, 3c.

93 Regional Refugee Instruments and Related, 'Recommendations', para. 3d.

94 Regional Refugee Instruments and Related, 'Recommendations', para. 4.

self-reliance in these early years of post-war assistance to African refugees, seeking to help refugees become self-reliant mainly promoting agricultural productivity as demanded by dominant economic thought. In contrast to the interwar years, this assistance was provided without expectation of repayment and instead constituted a framework for the provision of hand-outs that is still associated with refugee assistance today. Like the interwar years, rural settlements were formed with the hopes of refugees becoming self-reliant through agricultural production, mainly through cash crops. Through zonal development, refugees also became involved in regional public works projects to 'develop' rural areas of host countries. Yet the structure of assistance changed significantly, excluding refugees from positions within organizations and bypassing their influence on the methods intended to foster self-reliance. The assistance practices most focused on individuals – micro finance loans and employment-matching or job placements – were also largely lost, as was the focus on settling refugees in urban areas or encouraging refugees to self-settle.

During this time the dominant perception of refugees changed from the migrant labourers of the interwar years to dependent refugees in need of external help to become self-reliant. This was influenced by broader changes in humanitarian assistance. Building on the trend that had emerged before the war, organizations increased humanitarian aid on the basis of need and protection, rather than identity and employable skills.[95] Long discusses this shifting conceptualization of refugee resettlement as concretized through those European refugees who did not meet migration criteria due to illness or age, and remained in displaced persons camps after the Second World War.[96] Indeed, by the time the so-called 'last million' European refugees were resettled in the 1950s, the resettlement of refugees as workers had become the exception rather than the norm.[97]

Starting at this time, Western states became more involved in citizens' welfare and economic well-being, as institutional and state assistance in general increased significantly after the war, furthering what Barnett depicts as a 'shift from state-as-night-watchman to the state-as-caretaker'.[98] In this way, the ambitions of refugee self-reliance assistance rose alongside that of the post-war Western 'welfare state', which promoted access to social as well as civil and political rights through state programmes within an amalgam of democracy, capitalism, and welfare.[99] Wider international assistance reflected

[95] Barnett, M. N. (2011) *Empire of Humanity: A history of humanitarianism*. Ithaca, NY: Cornell.

[96] Long, 'When refugees stopped being migrants', pp 13–15.

[97] Long, 'When refugees stopped being migrants', pp 13–15.

[98] Barnett, *Empire of Humanity*, p 99.

[99] Marshall defined the social component as the right to 'a modicum of economic welfare and security to the right to share to the full in the social heritage and to live the life of a

heightened 'international responsibility' and states' focus on a 'common humanity' and 'international community',[100] with the aim of advancing international cooperation based on mutual interests. The well-being of those beyond the boundaries of nation-states increased in importance, reflected in the rise of the 'development project'.

Refugee assistance targeted *collective* refugee self-reliance in the 1960s and 1970s, and focused on settlement self-reliance rather than individual self-reliance. At this time, refugee assistance and broader development assistance was informed by US internationalists within the UN, ILO and elsewhere, who – by both broad thought and tangible donor funding – advocated economic growth and mass prosperity over social reform and individual social welfare.[101] Strategies to foster refugee self-reliance therefore aligned with the dominant development focus on mass well-being and a primary interest in the development of countries as opposed to the individuals within them.

Relatedly, the ruling post-war economic theory, Keynesianism, advocated strong government intervention in order to improve citizens' welfare; during this time, refugee assistance through integrated rural development provided social services to whole regions, thereby utilizing this 'international welfare' for refugees and citizens alike. In turn, refugee assistance sought to 'modernize' not only refugees but the entire regions they lived within; in Tanzania, refugees tested new forms of hybrid maize, distributed as a form of refugee assistance through TCRS, and received health education from Community Development Workers that emphasized 'village hygiene and improved food preparation methods'.[102] We therefore see an instrumentalization of both the concept and practice of refugee self-reliance by Western governments and international organizations, which used the ostensible goal of self-reliance as an entry point to enact 'progress' in regions housing refugees and local Africans alike.

Yet a passive refugee identity persisted in African refugee assistance. Indeed, the contrast in depictions of the Greek refugees of the interwar years to the Tanzanian refugees of post-colonial Africa is striking. Despite the agricultural provenance of the majority of both populations, post-Second World War settlement documents focus on the need to 'develop', to 'teach', to 'train'

civilized being' (Marshall, T. H. (1950) *Citizenship and Social Class*. Cambridge: Cambridge University Press, p 69).

100 Barnett, *Empire of Humanity*.

101 Jensen, J. (2013) 'US New Deal Social Policy Experts and the ILO, 1948–1954', in S. Kott and J. Droux (eds) *Globalizing Social Rights: The International Labour Organization and beyond*. Basingstoke: Palgrave Macmillan, pp 172–189 (p 185).

102 TCRS (1967) 'Annual Report 1967'. Betts Collection, Bodleian Social Science Library, University of Oxford: Box 53. Tanzania: Rural Settlement Planning [394], p 3.

African refugees, whereas the general resilience of Greek refugees during the interwar years was emphasized in similar organizational reports.[103]

The inherent contradiction of this construction of African refugees was that these supposedly dependent beneficiaries were also treated as labourers who were expected to work and become self-reliant. This appears to have been resolved through an understanding by assistance agencies and host and donor governments that trainings and carefully prescribed livelihoods would help refugees achieve self-reliance. This stance therefore demanded external 'experts' to help refugees learn how to become self-reliant, thereby justifying the suppression of refugees' own strategies to do so.

Refugee self-reliance in Tanzania

As discussed earlier in the chapter, refugee settlements have been called the 'prototype' for *ujamaa*, the collective villagization that became the basis of agrarian change in Tanzania in the 1960s and 1970s.[104] These agricultural settlements and the locus they constituted for integrated rural development embedded the means and aims of refugee self-reliance within a larger national and Pan-African project of self-reliance. *Ujamaa* itself represents a complex convergence of national, regional, and international aims. As Lal writes:

> Rather than amounting to a circumscribed exercise in nation building, *the Tanzanian project significantly overlapped and intersected with larger global dynamics surrounding the end of empire and the attempted imposition of a bipolar world order.* … The Tanzanian emphasis on the village, preoccupation with family as a metaphor and basis for political community, promotion of self-reliance, and anxiety about security were all multivalent conceptual features that responded to changing domestic and international conditions, built on indigenous political thought, and drew from a range of outside sources.[105] [emphasis added]

Modes of refugee assistance in the country reflected this convergence of influences, as well. While refugee settlement projects may have been acceptable to Tanzania's vision of collective rural agricultural development, they also fed international aims of capitalist accumulation, often along

[103] See, as a comparison, reports from the Betts Collection, 1971–1976, with the Palmeree Documents and reports from High Commissioner Fridtjof Nansen.

[104] Tague, 'A War to Build the Nation'.

[105] Lal, P. (2017) *African Socialism in Postcolonial Tanzania: Between the village and the world.* Cambridge: Cambridge University Press, pp 28–29.

colonial lines. The US and UK were among those countries eager to 'develop' Africa according to their vision of an international economy, maintain allies against Communism, and ensure the continuity of export and import relations. The crops grown in settlements were mainly cashew nuts, tobacco, and sisal, which corresponded to the country's previous and ongoing international exports. In 1969, Tanzania's principal export market was the UK, which received 30 per cent of all exports while the countries of the European Economic Community received 20 per cent and North America 10 per cent,[106] reflecting a continuity in colonial trade relations. Many East African refugee self-reliance settlements' promotion of mono-crop cultivation for national exportation in the 1960s and 1970s can therefore be attributed to both colonial economic legacy and wider international economic aims. In cases, as earlier discussed, refugees were forced to forgo alternative means of self-reliance in favour of growing these cash crops, illustrating a heavy-handed coercion and paternalism arguably at odds with the concept of fostering self-reliance.

Yet this self-reliance assistance helped refugees engage in production in ways useful to host countries and thus served to alleviate worries that hosting refugees would 'burden' societies. The conditionality of productivity with which refugees were often received by African host countries is evident in a confidential note by the UNHCR High Commissioner regarding a meeting with the Kenyan Secretary of Foreign Affairs in 1966:

> He [the Secretary] expressed concern over the fact that a great many of these refugees did not appear to want to work. This was the main reason why Kenya had been reluctant to admit them. Dar es Salaam [for example] was fast becoming a town of beggars, since many of the refugees preferred to receive hand-outs so as to continue to lead an idle life, rather than get a job. This created a social and economic problem which could easily get out of control in the large urban centers of East Africa.[107]

The increase of development aid in the 1960s sought to address the 'social and economic problem' that refugees' lack of employment constituted, and contributed to refugee assistance becoming more overtly premised on self-reliance rather than just emergency relief. This extended refugee assistance into broader arenas of societies and economies such as their integration into

[106] ILO, 'Tanzania: Rural Prevocational and Vocational Training'.

[107] UNHCR (1966) 'Saddrudin Aga Khan. Note for the File (Confidential)'. 4 August 1966. UNHCR Archives, [Sadruddin Aga Khan (Deputy High Commissioner)] Archives. 11/1–1/7/43. Fonds 11/Series 1/Box 69 ARC-2/A40.

cash economies, illustrating its longer-term aims. These strategies also sought to satisfy donor countries unwilling to provide everlasting emergency relief.

The longer history of integrated rural development programmes

Integrated rural development programmes, also called zonal development, encompassing refugee self-reliance assistance illustrate how self-reliance assistance for refugees reflected and furthered social and economic agendas of the time. As we have seen, these programmes were based in part on World Bank projects and supported national and international development ideals in various ways, such as focusing on 'progress' through capital circulation, and targeting entire populations rather than individuals. However, it is little known that many assistance initiatives for African refugees were borne out of social security and social development programmes premised alternately on anti-Communist efforts and colonial humanitarianism, and often focused on the issue of labour.[108] These welfare-driven community development programmes had roots in the US in the 1930s and development efforts in Africa by the British Colonial Office.[109] As Lacroix writes,

> The community development concept was seen, both by the United States and the United Nations as a democratic means to bring about economic, social and political developments. … It was designed to encourage self-help efforts to raise standards of living and to create self-reliant communities with an assured sense of social and political responsibility.[110]

In 1960, over 60 countries in Africa, Latin America, and Asia had national community development programmes, which emphasized social cohesion and welfare, with economic development considered secondary. The importance initially laid on 'social and political responsibility' came in large part as a reaction to the threat of Communism and the destabilization it posed; in this way community development programmes served a larger purpose than just self-reliance – for communities within the US and those around the world embedded in Cold War politics by proxy.

Whereas community development was driven by a desire for community cohesion in the face of Communism, by 1965 these programmes were discontinued in favour of an integrated rural development approach that

---

[108] Cooper, F. (1996) *Decolonization and African Society: The labor question in French and British Africa*. Cambridge: Cambridge University Press.

[109] Lacroix, R. L. (1985) *Integrated Rural Development in Latin America* (Vol. 716). B. Mundial (ed). Washington, DC: World Bank, p 8.

[110] Lacroix, *Integrated Rural Development*, p 8.

was seen 'as a means to foster economic growth among the rural poor and a way to achieve a more equitable distribution of the fruits of economic development'.[111] In this way we see rural development shift from a predominantly political strategy for fighting Communism to a politico-economic one aiming to combat Communism by increasing wealth and prosperity through economic growth. Indeed, this strategy was employed internationally as well as domestically. As early as 1961, when Tanzania became independent and was created through merging Zanzibar and Tanganyika, the US offered support to the country: the US Ambassador in Tanzania reported to Washington that 'Nyerere's United Republic has given us the initial political framework with which we can work' and therefore urged the US State Department to offer Nyerere 'the maximum quiet support from the beginning'.[112] Despite being a socialist-oriented state allied with the Soviet Union during the Cold War, Overseas Development Assistance funding to Tanzania rose from zero per cent of GNP to 22 per cent between 1975 and 1997.[113] Refugees and their self-reliance were implicated in this funding as particular African host countries received Western development aid intended for refugees in exchange for aligning with the West in ideological proxy Cold Wars.[114] In turn, most of this funding was channelled to settlements, themselves designed to foster refugee self-reliance.

Colonialism and refugee self-reliance

Ideological battles were not the only factor impacting refugee self-reliance assistance in Africa in the 1960s and 1970s. In Tanzania, assistance was shaped not only by international and national aims but by the colonial history and enduring colonial mentality of practices and processes in African countries at the time.[115] Much has been written about neo-colonialism in Africa but much less about the impact of colonial practices on assistance

[111] Lacroix, '*Integrated Rural Development*', p 10.

[112] Quoted in: Mentan, T. (2017). *Africa in the Colonial Ages of Empire: Slavery, capitalism, racism, colonialism, decolonization, independence as recolonization, and beyond.* Bamenda: Langaa RPCIG, p 274.

[113] Dunning, T. (2004) 'Conditioning the effects of aid: Cold War politics, donor credibility, and democracy in Africa. *International Organization* 58(2): 409–423, p 416.

[114] Loescher, *The UNHCR and World Politics*.

[115] It is beyond the scope of this book to conduct the thorough process of tracing and excavation of colonial archives that would be required to provide extensive primary evidence for this claim. I therefore rely primarily on secondary literature and make connections to information in the archives and their parallels to colonial actions and behaviour. Although this is not the main focus of this book, the role that the history of colonialism, and by extension racism, played in African refugee assistance at the time should not be overlooked and deserves to be the focus of future research.

to African refugees. It is of course hard to distinguish the remnants left behind *by* the colonial period from the colonial mindset and practices that aid and development organizations brought *to* Africa. However, three particular aspects of colonial rule in Tanzania remained hallmarks of development assistance for both refugees and citizens in Africa. First, cash crop production and cooperatives were part of an *economic* system of production, which colonial immigration policies had previously sought to uphold through control: 'Population influxes, if managed and redistributed like transferable commodities to suit agricultural need, were the panacea to perennial labour shortages.'[116] After the Second World War, the British faced a high demand for labour on sisal and rubber estates in then-Tanganyika and therefore created refugee camps near migration routes – a 'conditioning camp system' – with the aim of drawing refugees in as labourers.[117] While Nyerere's refugee policies were welcoming and humanistic, they also sought to make use of refugee labour in a similar way; Chaulia writes of Tanzania at the time: 'Arguably, development policies of a freely administered nationalistic government were quite different from crude extraction and transfer of wealth under the colonial yoke, but the utilitarian intentions of hosting immigrant labour were more or less consonant with those of the pre-independence era.'[118]

Second, *political* governance structures involved embedding local Africans, including refugees, into hollow administrative structures and committees reminiscent of the colonial period. This connected to, third, *social* attitudes and perceptions of African refugees which alternated between and merged into a racist paternalism and ideals of self-governance that justified not only the pre-independence colonial rule but intervention in the name of development assistance thereafter.[119] Deutsch writes of the public

[116] Chaulia, S. S. (2003) 'The politics of refugee hosting in Tanzania: from open door to unsustainability, insecurity and receding receptivity'. *Journal of Refugee Studies* 16(2): 147–166 (p 151).

[117] Orde-Browne, J. (1946) *Labour Conditions in East Africa*. London: HMSO, p 49.

[118] Chaulia, 'The politics of refugee hosting in Tanzania', p 156.

[119] Chaulia writes that, '[T]he British considered themselves the most liberal, humane and enlightened empire-builders, who were helping the natives attain self-governance through indirect rule and delegation of local authority to natives, as opposed to the Belgians and the French who were only interested in exploitation'. In: Chaulia, 'The politics of refugee hosting in Tanzania'. This position was summarized in 1929 by Jan Smuts, British war cabinet member and South African Prime Minister,

> The British Empire does not stand for the assimilation of its peoples into a common type, it does not stand for standardization, but for the fullest freest development of its people along their own specific lines. … We will preserve Africa's unity with her own past and build her future progress and civilization on specifically African foundations.

sphere in Tanzania under colonial rule as an integral site for the creation of colonial consent by Tanzanians, which was achieved in part through the 'repetitive display of power' that formal public meetings and local councils comprised.[120]

Similar displays of ceremony and hollow power were created through the formation of Refugee Councils in refugee settlements in the 1960s and 1970s. As Deutsch writes of colonial authorities, 'The government knew that in order to be recognized as a legitimate authority, colonial rule had to be rooted, at least to some extent, in the everyday life of both rulers and subjects alike.'[121] In refugee settlements this took the form of meetings between refugee leaders and settlement administration, but with little effect of equalizing power relations. As discussed in the chapter, livelihoods and educational trainings led by international agencies provided an avenue to 'teach' refugees everything from farm skills to cooking, and in this way asserted a paternalistic dominance over everyday activities. The paradox of this 'assistance' to foster self-reliance through the virtual suppression of refugees' own agency is evident, and led to a further disempowerment of refugees from the very work intended to lead to their independence.

Conclusion

By 1980 Africa hosted more than 4 million refugees – a third of the world's refugee population. However, only $70 million USD of UNHCR's budget was earmarked for the continent compared to $105 million USD for the one million South East Asian refugees, suggesting a limited regard for these protracted African refugee populations.[122] More broadly, the impacts of the 1973–1975 global recession led to a 'deep capitalist crisis' that was

> first and foremost a reflection of the inability of world capitalism as instituted under US hegemony to deliver on the promises of a Global New Deal. This led to 'a liquidation of the labour-friendly and development-friendly international regime of the preceding thirty years

Source: Mamdani, M. (1996) *Citizen and Subject: Contemporary Africa and the legacy of late colonialism*. Princeton, NJ: Princeton University Press, p 5.

[120] Deutsch, J. G. (2002) 'Celebrating power in everyday life: the administration of law and the public sphere in colonial Tanzania, 1890–1914'. *Journal of African Cultural Studies* 15(1): 93–103 (p 101).

[121] Deutsch, 'Celebrating power in everyday life', p 95.

[122] However, this number was still notably higher than the funding refugees had been allotted two decades prior when assistance in Africa began; D'Souza, F. (1980) 'The Refugee Dilemma: International Recognition and Acceptance'. Report No. 43. London: Minority Rights Group, p 7.

> in favour of a capital-friendly regime. … Under the new regime, the crisis of capitalism quickly turned into a crisis of organized labour and of the welfare state in rich countries, and of the crisis of Communism and of the developmental state in poorer countries'.[123]

By the 1980s Tanzania itself had largely abandoned its aim of national self-reliance, and liberalization measures undertaken by the World Bank in the mid-1980s stripped the country of many forms of collective welfare. SAPs are seen as having influenced Tanzania's change to a restrictive refugee policy and having negatively impacted refugees' livelihoods through economic reform policies including a 'two-acre policy' which sought to consolidate land.[124] Overall, the effect of SAPs on Tanzania is summarized well in the following exchange between Nyerere and the head of the World Bank and staff:

> 'Why have you (Tanzanians) made such a mess of things?' he was asked by the Bank's experts who were alluding to the economic situation in Tanzania. Nyerere replied: 'The British Empire left us a country with 85% illiteracy, two engineers and twelve doctors. When I left government, we had 9% illiteracy, and thousands of engineers and doctors. I left government 13 years ago. At that time our per capita income was double what it is today. [Now] [w]e have a third of children who lack schooling, while health and public services are in ruins. During those 13 years, Tanzania did everything that World Bank and the IMF demanded of it.' And Nyerere returned the question to the experts: 'Why have you made such a mess of things?' [125]

The treatment of refugees was one of many outcomes of this. A 'renegotiation of the state's obligation to and contact with displaced populations' and more restrictive refugee policies ensued.[126] Caught between competing local, national, and international economic and social interests, it is therefore perhaps not surprising that by the late 1970s refugee settlements in Tanzania and elsewhere in Eastern Africa were failing in their self-reliance aims, and

[123] Silver, B. and Arrighi, G. (2000) 'Workers North and South', in L. Panitch and C. Leys (eds) *The Socialist Register 2001* (Vol 37). London: Merlin Press, pp 53–76 (p 56).

[124] As Daley (1992: 144) wrote, 'The economic welfare of refugees is threatened by the liberalization process'. Source: Daley, P. (1992) 'The Politics of the Refugee Crisis in Tanzania', in H. Campbell and H. Stein (eds) *Tanzania and the IMF*. London: Routledge, pp 125–146.

[125] Quoted in: Caplan, P. (2007) 'Between Socialism and Neo-Liberalism: Mafia Island, Tanzania, 1965–2004'. *Review of African Political Economy* 34(114): 679–694 (p 680).

[126] Hyndman, J. (2000) *Managing Displacement: Refugees and the politics of humanitarianism*. London: University of Minnesota Press, p 182.

the majority of encamped refugees remained at least partially dependent on foreign assistance.[127] A combination of poor soil, a policy of encampment that restricted refugees' access to local economies, and ill-trained authoritarian settlement administrators all acted as contributing factors to the widespread failure of institutionally planned refugee self-reliance.[128] By this point *ujamaa* as a policy had also failed, and integrated rural development programmes were criticized by the World Bank and other donors for their ill-planned structure and implementation – despite having been largely guided by these same actors.[129]

For refugees in particular, despite increased assistance and more funding for UNHCR programmes than ever before, there was limited successful refugee self-reliance fostered by refugee agencies in the Global South. The seeds, tools, housing, and training refugees had received, meant to foster their reintegration (or, in many cases, integration for the first time) into agricultural production and the market economy, instead largely acted as a guise for the exploitation of refugees as workers. Unpaid and trapped in settlements, refugees in Tanzania and elsewhere in East Africa appear to have been subordinate to an assistance focused on 'modernization' and 'development' and instrumentalized for economic aims far grander than that of their own self-reliance.

---

127 RPG, 'Older Refugee Settlements'.

128 Easton-Calabria, E. (2015) 'From bottom-up to top-down: the "pre-history" of refugee livelihoods assistance from 1919–1979'. *Journal of Refugee Studies* 28(3): 412–436.

129 As Payer writes,

> There is one very curious aspect of the World Bank's criticisms of Tanzanian agricultural policy which cannot be emphasised too strongly. This is that Tanzanian agricultural strategies over the past decade, and many of the particular policies and projects singled out for criticism … were not only financed by the World Bank but, according to insiders' accounts, in many cases were shaped by World Bank advice and conditionality.

Source: Payer, 'Tanzania and the World Bank', p 803.

4

Warriors of Self-Reliance: Refugee Self-Reliance Assistance in Cold War Pakistan

Introduction

Just a few months into his tenure in 1986, UN High Commissioner for Refugees Jean-Pierre Hocké made a trip to refugee-hosting regions of Pakistan. He stated:

> UNHCR must proceed along two major lines of action. First, we must react to existing and new refugee crises with a three-pronged approach that combines effective emergency response, the prompt establishment of basic services, and early action in respect of income-generating activities that will quickly put the refugees back on their feet. Second, and almost simultaneously, we must embark on a systematic and dynamic search for solutions to end the problem, so that the refugees need not be refugees indefinitely.[1]

In the same speech, Hocké cited a UNHCR/World Bank project in Pakistan for Afghan refugees as a model of development assistance, and succinctly outlined the advantages of merging refugee self-reliance with national development:

[1] Hocké, J. (1986) 'Statement by Mr. Jean-Pierre Hocké, United Nations High Commissioner for Refugees, at the Informal Meeting of Permanent Representatives in Geneva of States Members of the Executive Committee of the High Commissioner's Programme (ExCom), 13 June'. Geneva: UNHCR.

> Where such projects can be successfully implemented in the context of the host country's national development plans, they achieve a triple benefit: they maintain the refugees' self-respect and sustaining their will to return home; they offer development opportunities to the local population; and they permit the host country to limit the damage caused by large influxes and to inherit, wherever possible, a tangible legacy when the refugees leave their soil.[2]

In essence, Hocké's statement outlines the League of Nations' approach to refugee assistance; a combination of emergency relief and development assistance at the beginning of displacement. A familiar 'triple bottom line' of refugee self-reliance assistance is also presented – its potential to support refugees in supporting themselves while helping local hosts and the development of their host country as a whole. It is a long journey from Tanzania to Pakistan, but evidently the concept of refugee self-reliance made the trip.

The linkage of self-reliance with development – at least on paper – continued throughout the decade.[3] However, similar to other discursive shifts we have already seen, the language of the often similar assistance programmes to foster refugee self-reliance changed yet again. In the 1980s, no longer was 'integrated rural development' or 'zonal development' cited as a goal; instead, the aim was refugees' 'income generation' and 'economic self-reliance'[4] in ways that also targeted 'national development' or 'economic development'. As the concept changed continents it therefore also shifted focus, becoming more centred on urban areas and market-based assistance than the predominantly agricultural assistance in East Africa and Europe. It furthermore became actively militarized, set in a context of Cold War proxy conflict on which the previous chapter did not focus. In Afghanistan, for example, refugee camps consequently

2 Hocké, 'Statement by Mr. Jean-Pierre Hocké'.

3 See speeches and statements by UNHCR High Commissioners Poul Hartling and Jean-Pierre Hocké, available on the UNHCR website at: https://tinyurl.com/yd9fzyul [Poul Hartling] and https://tinyurl.com/ycpb3kbp [Jean-Pierre Hocké].

4 Economic self-reliance is 'the capacity of refugees to provide for their own economic support and the support of their families'. Source: Martin, S. F. and Copeland, E. (1988) *Making Ends Meet*. Washington, DC: Refugee Policy Group, p 1. The report provides various explanations for the increased emphasis on economic self-reliance for refugees:

> First, there is a perception that increased self-reliance will facilitate durable solutions. With greater capacity to provide for themselves, the refugees will be better prepared to return to their countries of origin if conditions permit, or integrate into the local society if settlement in the country of first asylum or a third country is possible.

became sites of sanctuary for both refugees and the Afghan resistance movement (often indiscernible from each other), and the concept and practices of refugee self-reliance assistance were deployed for new, often contentious, ends.

Assistance for Afghan refugees went through several distinct shifts throughout the 1980s and early 1990s before being significantly reduced in Pakistan. In particular, self-reliance assistance changed from an economic strategy to a tool of protection that simultaneously focused on the material and psychosocial well-being of 'vulnerable' Afghan refugees, primarily disabled people and single women. Four main phases of self-reliance assistance to Afghan refugees overlapped with different stages of more general NGO involvement with refugees. After an initial period focused on relief, the early 1980s marked a period of focus on income generation by UNHCR and other agencies, often through waged employment. The mid-1980s saw an increased recognition of 'refugee dependency syndrome' (a purported dependence on humanitarian aid), which led to a wider range of self-reliance strategies beyond waged employment. Familiar to those of us aware of the earlier history of refugee self-reliance, these practices included vocational training and micro-finance as well as production and marketing schemes, and environmental conservation efforts.[5] However, beginning in 1987 and more pronounced from 1989 onwards, there was a pivotal shift in refugee self-reliance assistance from aiming to support the economic independence of all Afghan refugees in refugee tentage villages (RTVs) to providing targeted assistance to vulnerable people, defined as those for whom self-reliance was harder to achieve. Then, as peace accords were signed at the end of the decade, refugee self-reliance expanded to include the 'Afghanization' of NGOs tasked with rebuilding their Afghanistan. This chapter reviews these phases of assistance in more depth, providing case studies to illustrate main practices, followed by a discussion of linkages to wider economic and social tenets of the era.

UNHCR's 'Refugee Aid and Development Strategy'

In the early 1980s, the predecessor of High Commissioner Hocké, UN High Commissioner for Refugees Poul Hartling, held meetings with UNHCR officials to define the agency's 'Refugee Aid and Development Strategy', a by-now familiar means of providing refugees with income generation through host country national development projects. However, it was presented as a new strategy arising out of vehement criticism by African states at the attention refugees from countries such as Afghanistan

5 Sinclair, M. (1993) 'NGO income generation programmes for Afghan refugees in Pakistan'. *Journal of International Development* 5(4): 391–399 (p 392).

received while African refugees – and the states that hosted them – were comparably neglected.[6]

This frustration on the part of African states about unequal burden-sharing led to two international conferences on refugees briefly referenced in the previous chapter: the 1981 and 1984 International Conferences on Assistance to Refugees in Africa (ICARA I and II) which sought to compensate African host states through greater international burden-sharing. During ICARA I, UNHCR introduced 'Refugee Aid and Development' (RAD) and proposals to facilitate refugee self-reliance through development assistance.[7] This discourse brought refugee self-reliance to the forefront of global discussions on international burden-sharing to combat constructions of refugees as 'dependent' and 'burdens'.[8] Self-reliance was promoted as an integral form of development to address protracted refugee situations, and emphasized in the RAD assistance strategy. The ICARA RAD strategy stipulates that it

> is development-oriented from the outset; enables refugees to self-sufficiency; move[s] towards self-reliance and helps least developed host countries to cope with the burden that refugees place on their social and economic structures; provides benefits to both refugees and to the local population in the areas where they have settled; and, is consistent with the national development plan of the host country.[9]

In this way, RAD aimed to benefit refugees, host states, and locals in refugee-hosting regions and self-reliance assistance to refugees was intended to align with host country national development plans. It therefore differed little from the aims of this assistance in previous decades. RAD gained some traction in the early 1980s, particularly during ICARA I and II, and was endorsed by the UNHCR Executive Committee in 1984.[10] However, it did not spread as a mainstream strategy, due in part to ICARA I and II's failure to achieve funding for development projects[11] and increase international

6 Loescher, G. (2001) *The UNHCR and World Politics: A perilous path*. New York: Oxford University Press, p 227.

7 Loescher, G., Betts, A., and Milner, J. (2008) *The United Nations High Commissioner for Refugees (UNHCR): The politics and practice of refugee protection into the 21st century*. London: Routledge.

8 Gorman, R. (1993) *Refugee Aid and Development: Theory and practice*. Westport, CT: Greenwood.

9 Cited in Stein, B. (1994) *Returnee aid and development*. United Nations High Commissioner for Refugees (UNHCR). Central Evaluation Section. Geneva: UNHCR.

10 Loescher et al, *UNHCR: Politics and practice*.

11 Although $570 million USD was pledged, the majority of ICARA funds was earmarked and not materialized. Loescher et al, *UNHCR: Politics and practice*, p 42.

burden-sharing.[12] Compassion fatigue alongside new emergency crises such as the Ethiopian famine left little attention for addressing the needs of protracted refugee situations and development assistance for refugees was placed behind the priority of emergency relief.

That is, in most of the world.

After the 1978 coup of the People's Democratic Party of Afghanistan and the 1979 Soviet invasion of Afghanistan, over three million Afghans fled to Pakistan.[13] By December of 1980, the number of Afghan refugees was estimated at 1.9 million, making it the largest single group of refugees in the world. Approximately 1.5 million others fled to Iran, living largely without international assistance. However, Pakistan quickly received millions in aid. This support stood in stark contrast to its previous international isolation, which had arisen in large part due to its negative human rights record and its nuclear weapons research. The assistance it gained can be partially attributed to its geopolitical significance – the 1979 fall of the Shah left the state increasingly vulnerable to Communist influence, and the US saw Pakistan's potential to provide assistance to curb Soviet expansion.

Indeed, the Soviet invasion of Afghanistan in 1979 and the resulting Afghan refugees in Pakistan proved to be an exceptional situation in terms of both funding for refugee assistance in general and self-reliance projects in particular. Despite repeated discussions on RAD at UNHCR, the UNHCR/World Bank project for income generation for Afghan refugees in Pakistan and a similar Bank project in Sudan were notable exceptions to a dominant refugee assistance approach that ultimately consisted of 'care and maintenance' in refugee camps. This can largely be attributed to Cold War politics, which saw Western states such as the US paradoxically utilizing Afghan refugees as both victims of Communism and as 'Cold War Warriors'.[14]

In the mid-1980s, discussions on RAD became more overt with the advent of Hocké as High Commissioner. Hocké was critical of UNHCR's previous assistance approaches which had left millions of refugees stuck in

[12] Gorman, R. F. (1986) 'Beyond ICARA II: implementing refugee-related development assistance'. *International Migration Review* 20(2): 283–298; Loescher et al, *UNHCR: Politics and Practice*; Betts, A. (2009) *Development Assistance and Refugees: Towards a North–South Grand Bargain?* Oxford: Refugee Studies Centre, Oxford Department of International Development.

[13] 400,000 Afghans had fled to Pakistan by December 1979 and another 200,000 to Iran. UNHCR (1997) 'The biggest caseload in the world. Afghanistan: the unending crisis'. *Refugees Magazine*, Issue 108. Available at: www.unhcr.org/en-us/publications/refugeemag/3b680fbfc/refugees-magazine-issue-108-afghanistan-unending-crisis-biggest-caseload.html.

[14] Loescher, *The UNHCR and World Politics*. Archival IRC documents in particular demonstrate Cold War ideology.

camps, and became determined to more closely link refugee assistance with development approaches.[15] This focus continued throughout his tenure. In a 1988 address to the UN Administrative Committee on Coordination, Hocké emphasized the integral link between refugees and development, stating, 'One cannot any longer deny the linkage between mass displacement and missed development. … Development is not an irrelevancy in refugee affairs: it is rapidly becoming the central factor in our ability to resolve refugee problems.'[16] He backed up his argument through citing the financial costs that could be reduced through a developmental focus, as well as the benefits that host countries could accrue. He also summarized a linkage between refugee self-reliance and development that became apparent in the late 1980s and constituted yet another phase of refugee self-reliance assistance: that of targeting self-reliance assistance to so-called vulnerable groups such as disabled refugees. Hocké stated:

> As we look toward a strategy for a new UN Development decade, we need the help of development agencies to ensure UNHCR does not remain a voice crying in the wilderness to include refugees in such a strategy. We are all aware of the priorities favouring the 'poorest of the poor' in development projects – women, children, the handicapped, the disadvantaged and the dispossessed. These very groups, most deserving of development assistance, are also UNHCR's concern. There is nothing vague or theoretical about them for us. This is where we labour every day. These are who the refugees are.[17]

One key 'vulnerable' group were women, who became a larger focus of assistance into the 1990s. This focus echoed a turning point in the 1990s in both the articulation and the operationalization of commitments toward gender equality internationally including the World Conference on Human Rights in 1993, the Vienna Declaration and Program of Action in 1993, the creation of the UN High Commissioner for Human Rights post in 1993, and the ways in which mass atrocities in Rwanda, Bosnia, and elsewhere drew international attention to the gendered manifestation of both violence and responses to it.[18] These conferences, declarations, and decisions caused programmatic shifts in international development and humanitarian action

[15] Hocké, 'Statement by Mr. Jean-Pierre Hocké'.

[16] Hocké, J. P. (1988) 'Speech by Mr. Jean-Pierre Hocké, United Nations High Commissioner for Refugees, to the United Nations Administrative Committee on Coordination', New York, 24 October. Geneva: UNHCR [np].

[17] Hocké, 'Speech by Mr. Jean-Pierre Hocké'.

[18] Also in 1993, the UN General Assembly adopted the Declaration on the Elimination of Violence Against Women. In 1994, the UN appointed a Special Rapporteur on Violence

with regard to gender and rights-based assistance approaches, which in turn became apparent in refugee assistance.

Refugee self-reliance assistance to Afghan refugees in Pakistan

Assistance to Afghan refugees in Pakistan was UNHCR's largest project for much of the 1980s, with programming both drawing on previous efforts and paving the way for those that would be implemented in the latter half of the 1990s and beyond. Several features of assistance to Afghan refugees have been widely analysed, including the geopolitical significance of the international assistance for both Western powers (mainly the US) and the Government of Pakistan,[19] as well as larger social and political projects of domination.[20] The militarization of refugee camps in Pakistan and the political instrumentalization of refugees have also been examined in detail.[21] Of Pakistan's instrumentalization of refugees, Terry writes,

> Pakistan was the first beneficiary of the legitimacy that often flows from international humanitarian action. As host to millions of refugees, the Pakistani government became pivotal as interlocutor between the international community and the refugees. The Pakistani president, General Zia, rapidly capitalized upon this. … Zia was turned by the refugee flow from an international pariah into a 'respectable' statesman … Pakistan's public image greatly improved as a result of its role as host to some three million refugees.[22]

Despite being critical of the strategic opportunity that refugees represented for Pakistan's politicians, much of this literature does not acknowledge the strategic, discursive, and practical role that self-reliance played in refugee assistance. The following sections review phases of this assistance in more depth, providing examples of the main practices employed at that time.

Against Women and in 1995, the UN Secretary General appointed a senior advisor on gender issues. The Fourth World Conference for Women was held in Beijing in 1995, which led to the Beijing Declaration and the Beijing Platform for Action, both of which list commitments toward women's empowerment and gender equality.

19 Khan, I. (1998) 'Afghanistan: a geopolitical study'. *Central Asian Survey* 17(3), 489–502.

20 Novak, P. (2011) 'The institutional incompleteness of empire'. *Central Asian Survey* 30(3–4): 389–406.

21 Zolberg, A. R., Suhrke, A., and Aguayo, S. (1992) *Escape from Violence: Conflict and the refugee crisis in the developing world*. Oxford: Oxford University Press; Terry, F. (2013) *Condemned to Repeat? The paradox of humanitarian action*. Ithaca, NY: Cornell University Press.

22 Terry, *Condemned to Repeat?*, p 66.

1979–1985: emergency relief and waged employment

Beginning in 1979, emergency assistance in the form of food, shelter, and healthcare was provided to Afghan refugees through NGOs and the Government of Pakistan (GoP).[23] Pakistan hosted three million Afghan refugees for over a decade yet never became a contracting party of the 1951 Refugee Convention. Instead, it developed and implemented its own refugee policy through the States and Frontier Regions Ministry (SAFRON), to which international agencies such as UNHCR had to adhere. This enabled Pakistan to retain elements of control over how – and to whom – assistance was given. UNHCR and other international agencies in coordination with provided emergency relief and self-reliance programmes. Assistance was mainly provided in the Baluchistan and Northwest Frontier Province (NWFP) regions, where most refugees were located.

Emergency assistance was provided throughout the duration of the refugee crisis, but many NGOs quickly began offering longer-term assistance designed to improve the lives of both Afghan refugees and, in some cases, the surrounding Pakistani populace. Save the Children, the International Rescue Committee (IRC), and UNHCR-funded projects offered income-generating activities of various sorts with a concentration on medical aid and training.[24] A pivotal ILO study published in 1983 entitled 'Tradition and dynamism among Afghan refugees: a report on income-generating activities for Afghan refugees in Pakistan' identified potential projects to enable refugees to 'rely on themselves in the long-term, thereby lessening the burden on the Government and the international community for their continued care and maintenance'.[25] The study found high levels of unemployment among the refugees despite their participation in a wide range of economic activities. Unemployment was attributed to limited markets, a dearth of suitable tools, and an unavailability of high-quality raw materials for production.

The ILO study proposed a variety of projects, including basic vocational and rural skills training, builder's teams, kitchen gardens, handicrafts marketing, activities to 'increase the self-reliance of refugee women in

[23] At this time, assistance was mainly relief and undertaken primarily through the UN and GoP with only limited NGO involvement. The organizations that were involved were largely those with an already established presence in the country, including Catholic Relief Services, Oxfam, and CARE. These organizations began health and income-generating programmes along the Pakistan-Afghan border in new refugee camps.

[24] Baitenmann, H. (1990) 'NGOs and the Afghan war: the politicisation of humanitarian aid'. *Third World Quarterly* 12(1): 62–85 (p 65).

[25] ILO (International Labour Organization) (1983) 'Tradition and dynamism among Afghan refugees: a report on income-generating activities for Afghan refugees in Pakistan'. Geneva: ILO.

fulfilling their basic needs', and small-scale industries such as carpentry to cover some percentage of material assistance for refugees that UNHCR and other assistance agencies imported internationally.[26] UNHCR's shifting emphasis from care and maintenance (essentially hand-outs of basic necessities to maintain rather than move beyond basic survival) to self-reliance after this point was largely attributed to the ILO report, which was credited with saving UNHCR funds: '[I]n 1983, the amount obligated was U.S. $85.5 million; in 1984, the amount allocated is estimated to be $75.3 million; the projected amount for 1985 is $61.5 million'.[27]

In this first period of self-reliance assistance, refugees were employed to construct stores, clinics, schools, and even produce relief goods such as bedding and clothing.[28] Public works programmes such as the World Bank scheme expanded on in the next section also offered a means to employ refugees while contributing to Pakistan's development.[29] One reason for this was that Afghan refugees in Pakistan were forbidden from purchasing and farming land. Arising from Pakistan's regulations, Afghan refugees were essentially force-fed into the wage-labour economy, aided in large part by self-reliance assistance led by INGOs. For many refugees – of whom one survey estimated almost 70 per cent were farmers[30] – this was noted as particularly devastating to both their self-reliance and their dignity. Men previously engaged in agriculture were forced to become unskilled casual labourers, and certain sectors, such as transport, came to be perceived as Afghan-dominated. One NGO described such shifts in profession as a 'radical change in lifestyle' as '[i]n the Pushtun value system, activities connected with agriculture rank considerably higher than [those of] crafts and commerce'.[31]

The UNHCR/World Bank project

One of the largest and most renowned income-generating programmes for Afghan refugees in Pakistan was a joint UNHCR/World Bank project

26 ILO, 'Tradition and dynamism among Afghan refugees', p 140.

27 US Committee for Refugees (1985) 'Afghan refugees: five years later'. RSC Boxes: FA/FP Afghanis in Pakistan, 1–36.1/9; FA/FP 30 USCR. P.10.

28 Sinclair, 'NGO income generation programmes for Afghan refugees', p 392.

29 Ullrich, W. (1993) 'Long-term aid: GTZ projects for Afghan refugees'. Focus Section, gate 3/93 [Magazine]. FA/FP 59.3 ULL D106904.

30 Christensen, H. and Scott, W. (1987) 'Survey of the social and economic conditions of Afghan refugees in Pakistan'. UNRISD. FA/FP 65 CHR in FA/FP 65–65.25.

31 Millwood, D. (1995) 'The Rädda Barnen Training Unit: community-based social work with Afghan refugees in Pakistan'. FA/FP 64.14 MIL in Box FA/FP Afghans in Pakistan, 59.3–64, p 10.

initiated in 1982, formally called the 'Income Generating Project for Refugee Areas'. Due to its meticulous monitoring, documentation, and feasibility studies implemented in line with World Bank practice, the project became recognized internationally as a model for refugee-hosting countries seeking to support refugees while contributing to national development. In 1988, UNHCR High Commissioner Hocké used the project as a 'classic example' of the benefits that development and refugee agencies could gain through collaboration: 'Here the combination of UNHCR, a respected development agency (the World Bank), and highly productive refugees working with local Pakistanis on environmental projects, among others, has produced a success formula that speaks to other development agencies, as well as to refugee situations in other parts of the world.'[32]

The three-year project sought to employ both Afghan refugees and Pakistanis in labour-intensive development activities that would benefit refugee-hosting regions of Pakistan.[33] An estimated 70 per cent of labour was provided by Afghan refugees with the costs of labour comprising 62 per cent of the project budget of $20 million USD.[34] The main areas of focus were reforestation, watershed management, and the building or upgrading of irrigation systems and roads. Each of these projects worked toward the long-term economic sustainability of regions, resource conservation, and the skill-building and employment of refugees.[35] As one report explained, the project:

> aimed at compensating the damage caused by the refugee presence as well as gradually reducing refugee dependency on external aid. The underlying concept here is multi-purpose; generating temporary employment, restoration of damage done to Pakistan's ecology and developing ecologically viable resources which will advance national development in the refugee areas.[36]

The importance of income generation for refugees through these projects is repeatedly stressed in project documents, such as a Bank appraisal report that estimated that over the period of the project Afghan refugees could

---

[32] UNHCR, 'Speech by Mr. Jean-Pierre Hocké'.

[33] Dupree, N. H. (1988) 'Demographic reporting on Afghan refugees'. *Modern Asian Studies* 22(4): 845–865.

[34] Dupree, 'Demographic reporting on Afghan refugees', p 857.

[35] UNHCR (1986) 'The first income generating project for refugees areas: project overview'. RSC Cardbox: FA/FP 65.1 WOR in FA/FAP 65–65.25.

[36] UNHCR (nd) 'UNHCR assistance programme for refugees in Pakistan'. Geneva: UNHCR. RSC Cardbox: FA/FP 59.3. UNHCR in FA/FP 59.3 A-Z.

increase their income by an estimated 25 per cent.[37] Quarterly reports were prepared for SAFRON and the Bank, 'which included specific data on the employment effects of the project. … The extent of refugee employment and the average wage earned from project works was assessed through sample surveys of laborers at worksites undertaken by UNHCR officers.'[38] As one UNHCR report positively states, 'Labour content and refugee participation rates continue to grow, and are high. … In brief, the objectives of these subprojects have been fully met and an improvement in the ecology is clearly visible.'[39] Indeed, apparently so successful was the initial three-year project that a second three-year phase was initiated with 91 sub-projects in October 1987, equalling over $40 million USD.[40]

The UNHCR/World Bank project is notable for several reasons. First is its apparent success, which by all accounts employed refugees, albeit on short-term contracts, and developed rural areas of Pakistan. Second, while the projects specifically targeted refugee-hosting regions of the country, the projects themselves often fell in line with the GoP's Five Year Plan, such as the increased funding provided for unpaved rural roads that aligned with the country's Sixth Five Year Plan.[41] Although this project was the Bank's first which focused on refugee employment, several other World Bank projects were already being implemented in Pakistan in the early 1980s, many of which targeted the same sectors as the UNHCR/World Bank project. In this way, both national and international plans for economic development merged – with refugees at the forefront of such undertakings. Third, the public works nature of the project emulated refugee assistance undertaken over half a century earlier in Europe, as the previous chapter illustrated, and to a lesser extent refugee self-reliance assistance after the Second World War in sub-Saharan Africa.[42]

Despite this longer history, many of these projects were perceived as UNHCR's first foray into development. One report states:

> The primary role of UNHCR in the Afghan refugee situation is to coordinate international aid and to oversee or supervise implementation of relief efforts; it does not have an operational role. Nevertheless, its *function has broadened in the past two years to include project activities that*

[37] WB (World Bank) (1983) 'Staff appraisal report, Pakistan: Income Generating Project for Refugee Areas'. World Bank, appraised on behalf of UNHCR. 6 December 1983. RSC Cardbox: FA/FP 65.1 WORLD BANK in FA/FP 65–65.25, p 35.

[38] UNHCR, 'The first income generating project for refugees areas', p 13.

[39] UNHCR, 'The first income generating project for refugees areas', p 13.

[40] UNHCR, 'Speech by Mr. Jean-Pierre Hocké'.

[41] World Bank, 'Staff appraisal report', Pakistan.

[42] Easton-Calabria, E. (2015) 'From bottom-up to top-down: the "pre-history" of refugee livelihoods assistance from 1919–1979'. *Journal of Refugee Studies* 28(3): 412–436.

> *fit more appropriately in the category of development assistance as distinct from refugee assistance.* In this respect, *the program in Pakistan presents new challenges, questions, and opportunities for UNHCR as it assesses the role it should take as the lead refugee agency in a changing and complex world.*[43] [emphasis added]

Despite similar aims and practices, prior experience does not seem to have been drawn upon for the UNHCR/World Bank and other refugee income-generating projects at the time; instead these newer projects were heralded as 'new models' for merging refugee assistance and national development programmes, thereby reflecting a longstanding lack of institutional memory in refugee assistance.

1986–1989: dependency syndrome and psychosocial support

In June 1985, an article published in *National Geographic* was accompanied by arguably the most iconic photograph of an Afghan circulated in Western discourse,[44] the eminent photograph of 'Afghan Girl'. The article states:

> There is a change in the air in Peshawar this year, and I sense a turning point. Pakistan is saturated with refugees, and compassion is drying up. Pakistanis, who opened their country in the name of Muslim hospitality and the Pashtun tradition of *panah*, or asylum, are now faced with the largest refugee population in the world.[45]

While reports prior to 1986 were often optimistic about Afghan refugees' transition 'from emergency toward self-reliance',[46] in the mid-1980s discussions of 'refugee dependency syndrome' arose alongside doubts of the effectiveness of self-reliance efforts. Replacing the original hospitality was an increasing frustration by Pakistanis in NWFP over the size of the refugee population, the length of their stay, and deteriorating security conditions due to an increased number of terrorist bombings.[47]

---

[43] US Committee for Refugees, 'Afghan refugees: five years later'.

[44] Schwartz-DuPre, R. L. (2010) 'Portraying the political: *National Geographic*'s 1985 Afghan Girl and a US alibi for aid'. *Critical Studies in Media Communication* 27(4): 336–356.

[45] Denker, D. (1985) 'Along Afghanistan's war-torn frontier'. *National Geographic Magazine*, June.

[46] Morton, J. (1992) 'The socio-economic status of Afghan refugees in Pakistan: an overview'. UNHCR Islamabad, May. RSC Cardbox: FA/FAP 65.1 MOR in FA/FP 65–65.25.

[47] Getler, M. (1987) 'For Afghan refugees in Pakistan, welcome mat is wearing thin'. *Washington Post*, 11 September. UNHCR, 100.PAK.AFG.

Throughout the decade, pathways to both social and economic participation were increasingly formed by efforts to help beneficiaries to meet their own needs. By the mid-1980s, refugees in Pakistan were encouraged to gain the skills needed to find or create jobs themselves, rather than have them offered directly. This marked the beginning of the second phase of refugee self-reliance assistance: a concentration on income-generating activities through entrepreneurship rather than waged employment to counter a fear of refugees' 'dependency' on international assistance[48] as well as to strengthen local markets in regions of high unemployment.

Many donors and organizations took issue with refugees' ongoing receipt of assistance. Emblematic of many reports on behavioural and physical symptoms of 'dependency syndrome', the US Committee for Refugees wrote:

> Recently, experts on Afghanistan who are studying the refugee population have reported that *the essence of Afghan character – their pride in being independent and self-sufficient – is in danger of being destroyed.* ... Another study reports that many of the refugees, especially those who are Pushtun, have developed the *psychosomatic symptoms associated with the psychological malaise known as 'dependency syndrome'* – various aches, coughs, unidentifiable fevers, hyperacidity, and digestive troubles. Pashtuns are particularly affected because agricultural or land-based pursuits – culturally so important to them – are, for the most part, not permitted to them in Pakistan.[49] [emphasis added]

The phenomenon of refugee dependency and the international humanitarian community's response to it demonstrates that refugees' unwillingness or inability to work was considered an ailment, with employment their panacea. In response to reports such as that excerpted above, increased efforts to foster refugee self-reliance through multifarious projects arose. In 1985, the IRC was requested by UNHCR to initiate self-reliance projects in RTVs. Following discussions with refugees on their ideas for income generation, a construction project began in 1986. Refugees built multiple health units, including replacing IRC tent clinics with permanent buildings, as well as dug wells and built diversion dykes. The project was followed by one for carpentry and welding, which built more than 10,000 school benches for refugee schools across the NWFP and then opened an automobile repair

[48] Discussions of 'refugee dependency' also occurred earlier in the decade, though not with as much prevalence as later. See: Boesen, I. (1983) 'From autonomy to dependency: aspects of the "dependency syndrome" among Afghan refugees'. Paper presented at the BIA (Bureau International d'Afghanistan) Conference on Afghan Refugees in Geneva, 4–6 November, 1983. RSC Cardbox: FA/FP 65 BOE in FA/FP 65–65.25.

[49] US Committee for Refugees, 'Afghan refugees: five years later', p 8.

shop.[50] Handicrafts centres for women were opened in several camps, though two centres were closed following disapproval by camp elders.

While many discussions on refugee dependency syndrome blamed refugees, several humanitarians and researchers refuted this purported phenomenon. A 1985 Refugee Policy Group document sardonically entitled 'The refugee dependency syndrome: physician, heal thyself!' interrogates the underlying issues of this so-called syndrome, writing, '[W]hile there is consensus that a problem concerning self-reliance exists, there is much less clarity about what the origin of the problem is.'[51] The article goes on to provide various explanations for refugees' lack of participation including the fact that:

> The refugee assistance system is directly involved in a wide range of areas of refugees' lives, including decisions about what kinds of food people will eat and how much, the kinds of housing they will have, the protection they will receive, their health care and education, their employment opportunities, and many others. Refugees who enter the official refugee assistance structure are confronted with a powerful, wide-ranging system which has primarily been created and designed by non-refugees. Further, the main policies and program[me]s of such systems typically take shape during the emergency relief phase, which bodes ill for refugee self-reliance.[52]

Nancy Hatch-Dupree, a prominent researcher of Afghan refugees, echoed the report in blunter terms: 'Thousands of rupee notes and other commodities are distributed indiscriminately [in certain RTVs], and only fools would fail to take advantage of such handouts and seek more from the next visitor. Outsiders must, therefore, share in the blame for these manifestations of dependency.'[53]

Interestingly, to a certain extent, this perception of 'refugee dependency' was empirically grounded. A survey undertaken by the United Nations Research Institute for Social Development (UNRISD) in 1987 found that,

---

[50] IRC (1988) 'Special report: integrating programs: education and self-reliance'. Quarterly Report April–June 1988. International Rescue Committee Pakistan Programme. A/FP 59.3 IRC in Box FA/FAP 59.3 A-Z.

[51] Clark, L. (1985) 'The refugee dependency syndrome: physician, heal thyself!' Refugee Policy Group. RSP Documentation Centre, A 59.1 CLA. The report opens ironically in the format of a doctor's report: 'Symptoms: Lethargy. Lack of Initiative. Acceptance of handouts with little attempts at self-sufficiency. Frequent complaints, especially about the lack of generous outside help. Diagnosis: Refugee Dependency Syndrome. Where Found: Reported by refugee assistance workers in countries around the world' (p 1).

[52] Clark, 'The refugee dependency syndrome'.

[53] Dupree, 'Demographic reporting on Afghan refugees', p 857.

regardless of their previous occupation, nearly two-thirds of Afghan men and one-ninth of women were gainfully employed in Pakistan.[54] However, this work was generally low-paid, part-time, and irregular, prompting assertions from multiple sources that Afghan refugees were dependent on both work and aid in order to survive, neither alone being significant enough to cover basic necessities.[55] The UNRISD survey showed that due to refugees' low income levels the majority would be in 'dire stress without aid',[56] demonstrating the limited extent to which self-reliance was occurring. Another side of the story was that, according to one report, many households had only one male family member working in Pakistan at a time, as many men took turns participating in the *jihad* in Afghanistan for several months. This meant that households earned much less than they might otherwise have and were using assistance to supplement lost wages.[57] Through this we see the explicit connection between foreign-provided military funding, refugee assistance, and the concept of dependency, as military support drew Afghans back into their country while humanitarian assistance provided support to those family members left behind.

From wage-based employment to psychosocial protection

By the late 1980s, the discourse of refugee dependency fomented an increased focus on self-reliance assistance not as a wage-based employment approach but as a psychosocial protection scheme. Self-reliance assistance was meant to address their war trauma and to rouse refugees out of their supposed apathy through 'self-help', viewed as a means of income generation. In contrast to the 'proud, independent refugee' of the early 1980s, Afghan refugees – and indeed, other refugees around the globe in protracted situations – now became people in need of treatment.

As part of this strategy, a 'Social Welfare Cell' funded by UNHCR was established to identify vulnerable refugees and promote 'community self-help activities'.[58] Organizations such as Rädda Barnen (the Swedish branch of Save the Children) opened training units in Peshawar 'to promote community-based social work in the refugee settlements' by training Pakistani social workers from the Social Welfare Cell who worked alongside UNHCR.[59] As Millwood describes:

54 Christensen and Scott, 'Survey of the social and economic conditions', pp v–vi.

55 Millwood, 'The Rädda Barnen Training Unit'; Morton, 'The socio-economic status of Afghan refugees in Pakistan'.

56 Christensen and Scott, 'Survey of the social and economic conditions', pp 11–12.

57 Millwood, 'The Rädda Barnen Training Unit'.

58 Rädda Barnen (1992) 'Workshop on assistance to disabled refugees'. 4–8 October. Peshawar, Pakistan. Available at: www.tinyurl.com/yaeeaj75 (accessed 1 July 2016).

59 Millwood, 'The Rädda Barnen Training Unit'.

> The plan that developed was concerned primarily with the psychosocial welfare of the refugees rather than their material needs and was based on ideas of self-help and community participation. It envisaged a network of social workers and self-help groups in the camps, with a team of Pakistani government officials to identify needy people – widows, children lacking one or both parents, the elderly, the sick, the disabled – and promote self-help efforts, including income-earning projects.[60]

Through this description we see psychosocial welfare at least ostensibly placed above material well-being, yet achieved through income-generating and other self-help efforts. Significantly, not just trained (foreign) social workers and Pakistani officials but refugees themselves were recruited for this undertaking. Through this we see refugees enacting both 'self-help' as well as becoming a part of the architecture of assistance, designated to carry out programmes that were not their own.

In addition to purportedly fostering refugee agency, this concept of self-help was also a means to shift the responsibility of both assistance and self-reliance onto refugees themselves, facilitated by the twinned concepts of vulnerability and dependency. Indeed, the focus on vulnerable groups aligned with the main aim of UNHCR's 1987 humanitarian assistance programme in Pakistan, which, agreed upon with the GoP, was the 'promotion of self-help activities, income generation and … vocational skill training'.[61] The intended objective of these projects was 'to lessen the refugees' dependency on external assistance'.[62]

1989–1995: self-reliance as a protection tool

Refugee self-reliance assistance was profoundly affected by the 1988 Geneva Accords, the peace treaty which signified the beginning of the Soviet withdrawal from Afghanistan and a marked increase in NGO cross-border activity into Afghanistan. Despite assertions of refugees' ongoing need for assistance, it was reduced by UNHCR and other INGOs, with the UNHCR budget for Afghan refugee programmes declining from $43 million USD in 1988 to $33 million USD in 1990 – almost a 25 per cent cut.[63] As one Rädda Barnen report stated, 'The phase-out policy of UNHCR assistance

---

[60] Millwood, 'The Rädda Barnen Training Unit'.

[61] UNHCR, 'UNHCR assistance programme for refugees in Pakistan'.

[62] UNHCR, 'UNHCR assistance programme for refugees in Pakistan'.

[63] ACBAR (1990) 'Overview of NGO assistance to the people of Afghanistan'. Agency Coordinating Body for Afghan Relief (ACBAR), Peshawar, Pakistan 1990. FA/FP 59.3 ACB in FA/FP 59.3 A-Z.

to the Afghan refugees has led to an emphasis on support for increased self-reliance and targeted assistance to the most vulnerable groups'.[64] In this way, the economic correlation between budget cuts and the promotion of self-reliance programmes was made explicit even as this assistance continued under the guise of 'social welfare' and 'social animation'.

Self-reliance assistance shifted from a psychosocial strategy to a protection tool for the most vulnerable beginning around 1989 and continuing into the mid-1990s. The 'neediest' were increasingly protected through ongoing material assistance as well as targeted for self-reliance programmes such as vocational training. This continued to take the form of organizing self-help groups among refugees, now to 'protect the rights of the vulnerable groups'.[65]

Self-reliance and cuts to food rations

NGO reports paint different pictures of the state of refugee self-reliance at the end of the 1980s and early 1990s. Some explain that many families were, by this point, self-reliant and that it was largely the 'extreme cases' that still required aid, while others discuss the challenges of supporting refugees on an increasingly minimalist budget. Regardless, the impact of these reductions in assistance was profound enough to alter the discourse of refugee self-reliance itself. Rather than being defined mainly as income generation, self-reliance was described by agencies in direct relation to reduced rations. One 1992 report stated, for example, '"Self-sufficiency" [is] defined as the ability of refugees to *maintain a minimum standard of living in the event of withdrawal of food aid* ... a function of income, household size, expenditure and definitions of poverty lines'[66] [emphasis added].

An NGO report written in the aftermath of a series of cuts to food aid discusses the challenges that agencies faced due to the sudden changes in modes of assistance, stating:

> It is a heavy task to motivate the refugees for self-reliance in this final stage of assistance especially with a population, where these concepts are not well clarified, and 15 years of free hand-out relief policies have created passivity and a growing 'dependency syndrome'. The skills and resources within the refugee communities themselves have not been

---

[64] Blomqvist, U. (1995) 'Follow-up study on the impact of the 1993 evaluations of the Rädda Barnen Training Unit [RBTU] in Peshawar, Pakistan'. The Emergency Standby Team (Swedish Save the Children), December. RSC Cardbox: FA/FP 625.25 BLO in FA/FP 62–62.25.

[65] Rädda Barnen, 'Workshop on assistance to disabled refugees'.

[66] Morton, 'The socio-economic status of Afghan refugees in Pakistan', p 21.

> properly used or developed. A lack in linking the refugee assistance to more long-term development programmes including the surrounding local communities is also a serious obstacle to achieving sustainability in the provision of basic community services once the outside support is withdrawn.[67]

The first food aid cuts to refugees, as previously discussed, occurred in the mid-1980s and continued into the early 1990s.[68] These reductions primarily happened due to the end of the Cold War and the West's decreased interest in financially supporting the proxy war, as well as due to a shifting focus to the rebuilding of Afghanistan and the repatriation of Afghan refugees. Those 'vulnerable refugees' who received more support were mainly defined as widows, the elderly, and the disabled; this rhetoric essentially targeted marginalized members of refugee populations who were not able to be economically productive. Therefore, by the early 1990s, self-reliance assistance had become a tool to aid the most vulnerable because they were the least 'marketized' population, primarily due to their lack of access to resources as minorities within the refugee population, and therefore the most reliant on aid.

The gendered nature of self-reliance

One so-called 'vulnerable group' was Afghan women. Although their targeted assistance increased in the late 1980s and early 1990s, a particular focus on the cultural complexity of assisting Afghan women is discussed throughout the 1980s. Countless reports from assistance agencies discuss the struggle of implementing programmes targeting women, demonstrating an under-explored aspect of refugee self-reliance assistance – its often heavily gendered nature.

Similar to the assistance provided in previous eras, Afghan men in Pakistan were provided with training in areas such as construction or driving while women were trained to sew or undertake other home-based activities. However, reports from the 1980s document extreme reactions to women seeking to become self-reliant in nearly any capacity. This was largely a result of the practice of *purdah*, the almost total seclusion of women. For many religious leaders and other refugees, *purdah* was an important means to uphold traditional values and 'ensure that "the honour of the fighting man" would not be avowed'.[69] Women were not expected to become self-reliant as

67 Blomqvist, 'Follow-up study', p 5.

68 Millwood, 'The Rädda Barnen Training Unit'.

69 Ullrich, 'Long-term aid'.

it was considered men's duty to provide for women.[70] Support by assistance agencies to foster the former was often viewed as an unacceptable violation of values. As one IRC report states, 'The cultural factors that make the Handicraft Project difficult also make it the most necessary'.[71] Despite the vastly altered lives of Afghan refugees in Pakistan, many agencies perceived that Afghans' traditional values were reinforced instead of loosened – regardless of the difficulties of thousands of women who no longer had the economic support of male relatives and therefore lacked a social structure that helped meet their needs.[72]

The result of these cultural restrictions was a limited ability for assistance agencies to offer livelihoods trainings, childcare, and literacy courses for women and schooling for girls. Two of the IRC handicraft centres were forced to close due to unrest owing to the opening of a Mother Child Center which then expanded to anger over the health clinic and handicrafts centre. As one report stated,

> In order to quell the rebellion, the Commissionerate for Afghan Refugees and IRC representatives met with the camp elders and agreed to discontinue the Handicrafts Program in these camps and close the Mother Child Center to women in return for being allowed to keep the health clinic open to women. The closure is for an indefinite period.[73]

Earlier reports on the handicrafts project cite it as being 'the most difficult' of the five self-reliance projects that IRC ran due to the conservatism of some refugees regarding the direct aid of women.[74] To accommodate these views, male personnel were strictly forbidden from entering the centre and the project was clearly marketed as a means for women to gain income within their own homes.[75] Yet the finished goods could still be controversial, as in the case of a single woman whose extended male relatives refused to sell her goods at the local bazaar as local Pakistani men and Afghans from other tribes were buying the items: 'To see crafts their women had made going out of the home into the possession of other men was unacceptable. Though this woman had no other way to support her family, it is still not acceptable.'[76]

---

70 ARC (Austrian Relief Committee for Afghan Refugees) (1988) 'Annual report 1987'. FA/FP 61 ARC in Box FA/FP Afghans in Pakistan, 59.3–64, pp 6–7.

71 IRC (International Rescue Committee) (1987) 'International Rescue Committee Pakistan program', August. FA/FP 59.3 IRC in FA/FP 59.3 A-Z, p 56.

72 ARC, 'Annual report 1987', pp 6–7.

73 IRC, 'Special report'.

74 IRC, 'International Rescue Committee Pakistan program'.

75 IRC, 'International Rescue Committee Pakistan program'.

76 ARC, 'Annual report 1987', p 9.

The situation of many Afghan women demonstrates the problems inherent to the view that self-reliance should be attainable for all refugees regardless of societal status, cultural norms, and other factors. We further see the provision of self-reliance assistance being mediated or denied based on the belief-systems of those refugees with the most authority, demonstrating its heavily contextualized nature as well as the power relations that dictate it – relations between not only agencies, governments, and refugees, but between refugees themselves. The larger cultural beliefs of international agencies are also revealed, reflecting a tension between assisting a refugee group and imposing particular values. This focus on rights and equality continued in the 1990s under the broader discussion of 'gender', reflecting a larger trend in international development.[77]

The early 1990s: repatriation and the 'Afghanisation' of NGOs

At the end of 1991 the US and USSR signed an Afghan arms halt, which quickly and drastically reduced the aid provided to the *mujahideen* as well as to Afghan refugees.[78] The decrease in funding was also blamed in part on 'donor fatigue', yet many humanitarians were under no illusions on the decreased geopolitical interest in the region as a factor of shifting post-Cold War utility and dynamics.[79] As one aid worker discussing increased violence by Afghans passionately wrote,

> I don't blame the Afghans for feeling angry. Nor do I fault their dependence on Western aid: More than 60 private charities, a bevy

---

[77] A Rädda Barnen report from 1995 states,

> Gender is now introduced as a development concern to be used as a tool to identify the different needs of women, men, boys and girls. In this way a process has been started, which aims at integrating the gender aspects in the implementation of all training activities. At field level new training packages have been introduced focusing on raising the awareness of the basic rights of women and girls. … Much more advocacy for and support to female field workers is called for to back up a development of activities organised and run by women themselves.

Source: Blomqvist, 'Follow-up study', p 2.

[78] Rubin, B. (1996) 'Afghanistan: the forgotten crisis'. 1 December 1996. Available at: www.refworld.org/docid/3ae6a6c0c.html (accessed 17 September 2019).

[79] Rose, C. (1991) 'Biting the hand …'. ICWA Fellow, Institute of Current World Affairs. Peshawar, Pakistan, 15 September 1991. RSC Cardbox: FA/FP 60 ROSE in Box FA/FP Afghans in Pakistan, 59.3–64, pp 2–3.

of United Nations agencies and the US Agency for International Development operate hundreds of projects for Afghans, both inside Afghanistan and in the Pakistan-based refugee camps. The total humanitarian aid budget for the Afghans is more than $200 million a year. Annual covert military aid to the mujahideen has been at least that amount. Time and again, I wonder if all this aid has hurt more than helped the Afghans.[80]

The withdrawal of assistance had myriad effects on the ground, including the loss of Afghan jobs attached to aid and development agencies, and the cutting of UN rations in refugee camps. ACBAR condemned the reduced rations, stating that Afghan refugees in 1990 still constituted the largest refugee group in the world and that '[r]educing assistance to refugees as an incentive for them to return to Afghanistan is in contradiction to the internationally accepted principle of voluntary repatriation'.[81] The coordinating body criticized the aim to, effectively, starve Afghan refugees back into their country. Despite such criticisms, the interest of international donors increasingly shifted from refugee assistance in Pakistan to repatriation, reintegration, and rehabilitation programmes in Afghanistan.[82]

Self-reliance for most Afghan refugees at this time was now defined in accordance with their (perceived) need for food aid, yet the early 1990s also saw a notable shift in the broader conception of Afghani independence through a process known as the 'Afghanization' of NGOs. After the Soviet withdrawal, and as development work inside Afghanistan became more feasible, there was a notable reconfiguration in refugee assistance emblematic of wider humanitarian trends promoting local participation. Afghan NGOs were formed and ultimately filled a void caused by decreasing international funding for assistance to Afghan refugees and repatriates, receiving international acclaim for their 'successful' participation in implementing assistance.[83] However, this process was also useful for donor countries such as the United States, which was eager to rebuild Afghanistan, reduce funding, and be free of obligations in the region. Supporting Afghan NGOs was a means to this end, and through

[80] Rose, 'Biting the hand …', pp 2–3.

[81] ACBAR, 'Overview of NGO assistance to the people of Afghanistan'.

[82] Blomqvist, 'Follow-up study', pp 5–6.

[83] Novak, P. (2013) 'The success of Afghan NGOs'. *Development in Practice* 23(7): 872–888 (p 873). Novak (2011) states, 'Afghan NGOs function as a key site of negotiation, contestation, and adaptation of the various, often contradictory, discourses and interests permeating humanitarian assistance'. Source: Novak, 'The institutional incompleteness of empire'.

the Afghanization of NGOs we see a larger expression of a reliance on community initiatives that the 'self-help groups' and 'social animation' of the previous years promoted.

Afghan-led assistance within Afghanistan also provided tangible benefits for development, such as wider access to populations, a clearer understanding of the context and needs, and a stronger ability to navigate varying political tensions than Western NGOs.[84] According to a 1991 feasibility study report on rural reconstruction in Afghanistan, only 1.5 per cent (266) NGO employees listed with ACBAR were expatriates; 92.9 per cent were Afghans and 5.6 per cent were Pakistanis.[85] However, it was noted that the 'expatriates are often in key managerial positions and that few expatriate NGOs are under Afghan management', reflecting an ongoing disparity in power relations between international agencies and those they were mandated to serve.[86] The Afghanization of NGOs sought to rectify this disparity, yet power relations did not disappear. Many Afghan NGOs were headed by Soviet-educated men, and an estimated 75 per cent were engineers who had been trained in the Soviet Union in infrastructure and agriculture. Thus, the majority of development projects in Afghanistan were initially in these areas.[87] However, the UNDP sought governance organizations that could contribute to the building of a stable democracy, and became attracted to the Afghan diaspora residing in Western countries such as the United States. Many Afghan expats thus moved to Peshawar and trained Afghans there; in so doing they promoted Western values of statebuilding as well as financial and organizational management and thus served ideological as well as practical agendas.

Self-reliance, dependency – and welfare?

The examination of refugee self-reliance assistance to Afghan refugees in Pakistan between 1979 and 1995 demonstrates a striking shift from the intention of assistance agencies to foster refugee self-reliance through wage-based employment in the early 1980s to the conceptualization of refugee self-reliance a decade later as support to vulnerable refugees struggling with

84 Holtzman, S., Herbison, O., and Qayum, A. (1990) 'A discussion on Afghan involvement in reconstruction and relief activities'. Peshawar: GTZ (Deutsche Gesellschaft fuer Technische Zusammenarbeit)/ACBAR (Agency Coordinating Body for Afghan Relief).

85 Weiner, M., Banuazizi, A., Barfield, T., Choucri, N., Gakenheimer, R., Moavenzadeh, F., and Rothenberg, J. (1991) 'A feasibility study prepared by the Reconstruction Group of the Center for International Studies of the Massachusetts Institute of Technology'. PN-ABS-658-90358, p 63.

86 Weiner et al, 'A feasibility study', p 63.

87 Interview, Jon Bennett, 24 November 2017.

food ration cuts and then to support Afghan organizations 'rehabiliating' their country. Far from isolated changes in programming, these phenomena link to larger economic and social events. The pivotal economic shift in the Western (non-Soviet) world from a Keynesian to a neoliberal model accounts for some of this, profoundly impacting diverse sectors of society around the world, including US and UK social welfare systems, international development – and refugee self-reliance assistance.

This section examines how global economic restructuring affected Afghan refugees – those in employment, those self-employed, and those out of work – in Pakistan throughout the 1980s and early 1990s. Using the case study of Afghan refugees in Pakistan, it argues that domestic welfare and economic discourse trickled down to refugee self-reliance assistance through international development, including through structural adjustment programmes. Thus, refugee self-reliance assistance came to echo dominant practices of American and British domestic welfare and neoliberal discourse.

The 'internationalization' of welfare and economic discourse

Values of individualism, an anti-dependency mindset, and an increasing focus on so-called 'vulnerable populations' became especially apparent in refugee self-reliance assistance in Pakistan throughout the 1980s, all of which strongly echo contemporaneous neoliberal doctrine governing welfare in the US and UK. This doctrine can be linked to the profound effect that changes in the international economy had on domestic welfare in the US and UK.[88] When viewed together, strong parallels are evident between Western stances on domestic welfare under neoliberalism and changes in the aims and practices of refugee self-reliance assistance.

Beginning in the early 1980s, doubt was cast on the sustainability of the international financial system's economic growth, in part after two oil crises led to widespread indebtedness throughout the world in the 1970s.[89] The world economy was considered by many to have permanently changed, which was seen as a catalyst for the acceleration of neoliberal policies and doctrine.[90] This period saw a Western shift from Keynesianism as the leading economic theory to neoliberalism, which demoted public goods

[88] Somers, M. R. and Block, F. (2005) 'From poverty to perversity: ideas, markets, and institutions over 200 years of welfare debate'. *American Sociological Review* 70(2): 260–287.

[89] Barsky, R. B. and Kilian, L. (2004) 'Oil and the macroeconomy since the 1970s'. *Journal of Economic Perspectives* 18(4): 115–134.

[90] Berger, M. T. and Beeson, M. (1998) 'Lineages of liberalism and miracles of modernisation: the World Bank, the East Asian trajectory and the international development debate'. *Third World Quarterly* 19(3): 487–504 (p 490).

and community in favour of individual responsibility and the privatization of previously state-owned industries. Neoliberalism was furthermore characterized by policies promoting government deregulation and free trade while limiting government spending, and an emphatic doctrine of self-reliance, self-determination, and freedom.[91]

A self-reliance discourse became evident in domestic welfare assistance in the US and UK, which in essence focused on ways to help the domestic poor survive without state benefits. Western conceptualizations of welfare in the 1980s increasingly took the form of individual employment through training and education to prepare welfare recipients to enter the workforce (known as 'workfare' programmes). Although these programmes began in earlier decades, it was in the 1970s and 1980s that US workfare programmes became compulsory for welfare recipients who were no longer to be 'rehabilitated' but rather forced to act 'responsibly' through work.[92] During the 1980s, for example, 40 US states created welfare-to-work programmes providing education and training to the poor. This trend coincided with an increased emphasis on 'do-it-yourself' rhetoric and practice, such as the UK's rise of 'big society' discourse. Peters writes of the impact of neoliberalism on education in the UK, noting a shift 'from an emphasis on a relationship based on professional authority [between welfare officers and recipients] to an emphasis on self-empowerment and self-help based on training, education, and the development of "personal skills"'.[93]

The US and UK were major humanitarian donors, opponents of Communism, and wielded considerable influence over entities such as the World Bank[94] and the International Monetary Fund (IMF); thus, their rhetoric and policies influenced development thought and practice around the world. The closely linked nature of the US government and the development work

[91] Reagan, R. (1981) 'Inaugural speech'. 20 January 1981. *Speaking My Mind: Selected Speeches*. Available at: https://www.reaganfoundation.org/media/128614/inaguration.pdf.

[92] Mittelstadt, J. (2005) *From Welfare to Workfare: The unintended consequences of liberal reform, 1945–1965*. Chapel Hill: University of North Carolina Press, pp 169–170.

[93] Peters, M. (2001) 'Education, enterprise culture and the entrepreneurial self'. *Journal of Educational Enquiry* 2(2): 58–71 (p 62).

[94] This became especially true with the nomination of Tom Clausen, former president of Bank of America, to lead the World Bank in 1981, replacing Robert McNamara. For example, a 1982 report by the US Department of the Treasury stated about the Bank: 'The international nature of the World Bank, its corporate structure, the solidity of its administrative team, and its strong voting structure have assured a strong consistency between its policies and practices and the long term economic and political objectives of the United States.' Source: USA (1982) *United States Participation in Multilateral Development Banks*. Washington, DC: Department of the Treasury, p 59.

of the World Bank and other multilateral financial institutions at the time is illustrated in a 1982 US Department of the Treasury report:

> By promoting economic and social development in the Third World, accelerating market orientated economic policies, and preserving a reputation of impartiality and competence, MDBs [multilateral development banks] encouraged developing countries to participate more fully in an international system based on liberalized flows of trade and capital. … This signifies the expansion of opportunities for American exportations, investments and finance.[95]

This rising influence of neoliberal thought on development can be seen through the changing application of the concept and practice of self-reliance to citizens and refugees alike. Against the backdrop of a discourse of emancipation, the Cold War, and the financial austerity of the global recession, it was market engagement and entrepreneurship – rather than strong state-sponsored welfare programmes – which were presented as means to combat the poverty of populations around the globe. A speech excerpt from then US President Ronald Reagan illustrates this well:

> The societies which have achieved the greatest and most spectacular economic progress in the faster time have not been the biggest, nor the richest in terms of resources; nor certainly have they been the ones controlled most strongly. *What these societies have had in common is the trust in the magic of the market. Millions of individuals making their own decisions in the market will always allocate resources in a better manner than any planning process of centrally planned government.*[96] [emphasis added]

As the participation of governments was rolled back, the subjects of self-reliance shifted accordingly to individuals in developing countries, with assistance increasingly aiming to help beneficiaries survive without government or international support.

Yet how did economic policies and welfare doctrine that originated in Western countries such as the US make their way to countries such as Pakistan, and ultimately to refugees? The answer became apparent in 1979. For Afghans and their Pakistani hosts, the invasion by the Soviet Union was the pivotal event of the year. Yet the end of the 1970s also

[95] USA, *United States Participation in Multilateral Development Banks*, p 48.

[96] *New York Times* (1981) 'Reagan talk to World Bank and I.M.F.' 30 September. Available at: www.nytimes.com/1981/09/30/business/reagan-talk-to-world-bank-and-imf.html (accessed 24 February 2017).

marked the beginning of another pivotal upheaval, though one meant to aid the economy: the structural adjustment loan.[97] These loans epitomize neoliberal policies in development and were offered to developing countries by international financial institutions such as the World Bank and the IMF. Premised on policy conditionality, including financial regulations, trade liberalization, and the privatization of state enterprises, these loans also significantly reduced the reach of the state into the welfare of citizens, including in social services. This gap led to increased service provision by civil society, including international organizations. In the 1980s, both the IMF and the World Bank were committed to restructuring developing country economies through these Structural Adjustment Programmes (SAPs). Pakistan was not exempt from this economic intervention.

Despite a recent history of socialism,[98] on 24 November 1980, the GoP signed an Extended Fund Facility through the IMF that continued until 1983. Five years later, in 1988, Pakistan established two new programmes, a Structural Adjustment Facility and a Standby Arrangement, ending respectively in 1990 and 1992.[99] These 'reforms' began with the reduction of measures limiting the private sector, but quickly became more pronounced: the public sector share of total industrial investment decreased from 74 per cent in 1977 to a mere 18 per cent by 1988. Reforms of Pakistan's financial markets and banking sector began in the late 1980s,[100] and in 1990

---

[97] Easterly, W. (2005) 'What did structural adjustment adjust? The association of policies and growth with repeated IMF and World Bank adjustment loans'. *Journal of Development Economics* 76(1): 1–22.

[98] For most of the 1970s (1971–1977), Pakistan had been ruled by Zulfikar Ali Bhutto and the Pakistan's People's Party (PPP). The PPP charter emphasized the importance of development through a socialism that integrated Islamic values, with some reforms initially restricting the power of the elites. Bhutto attempted widespread nationalization measures, which saw the share of the public sector in total investment rise from 5 per cent in 1971 to 74 per cent in 1977. After nationalization, the efficiency of industry, large-scale manufacturing, and agricultural production declined. Source: Anwar, T. (2002) 'Impact of globalization and liberalization on growth, employment and poverty: a case study of Pakistan'. WIDER Discussion Papers-World Institute for Development Economics (UNU-WIDER), No. 17, p 1. See also: Qureshi, S. (1980) 'Islam and development: the Zia regime in Pakistan'. *World Development* 8(7–8): 563–575.

[99] *The Express Tribune* (2016) 'Pakistan-IMF ties: a chequered history'. 5 August. Available at: https://tribune.com.pk/story/1156145/pakistan-imf-ties-chequered-history (accessed 30 November 2016).

[100] The goals of Pakistan's financial reforms were:

> (i) to liberalize interest rates by switching from an administered interest rate setting to a market-based interest rate determination; (ii) to reduce controls on credit by gradually eliminating directed and subsidized credit schemes; (iii) to create and encourage the development of a secondary market for

liberalized exchange controls, allowing foreign currency deposits by both residents and foreigners,[101] as well as other reforms meant to attract foreign investment and integrate Pakistan into the world economy.[102] As discussed in this chapter, refugees were embedded in World Bank development projects that sought to increase the possible economic exploitation of regions of Pakistan that had previously lacked infrastructure and faced environmental degradation. These projects ultimately were part of a 'Westernization' of Pakistan's economy, upheld in part by refugees.

The late 1970s and early 1980s saw the onset of the 'Second Cold War', the end of the period of détente, and the deterioration of US–Soviet relations. Whereas Western policy had previously focused on a strategy of Soviet containment, the 1980s introduced the so-called 'Reagan Doctrine', in which the US reaffirmed an allegiance to those countries resisting the Soviet Union.[103] This policy shift led to the support of freedom fighters such as the *mujahideen* and to formerly unfavourably viewed states such as Pakistan.

The US sought to support Afghan refugees through aid channelled through assistance agencies to strengthen the *mujahideen*'s opposition to the Soviets. In addition to other forms of support, providing humanitarian as well as self-reliance assistance to refugees in camps in Pakistan helped Afghans earn livelihoods and ostensibly lead self-reliant lives in exile – particularly those refugees left behind by fighters within Afghanistan. It also supported the *mujahideen* agenda of a free and independent Afghanistan. However, the US strongly benefited in this proxy Cold War as the fight for free-market capitalism over a government-controlled economy played out on foreign soil. American instrumentalism of Afghan refugees was enacted in large

---

> government securities; (iv) to enhance competition and efficiency in the financial system by recapitalizing and restructuring the nationalized commercial banks and allowing private banks to enter the market; and (v) to improve prudential regulations.

Source: Khan, A. H. and Hasan, L. (1998) 'Financial liberalization, savings and economic development in Pakistan'. *Economic Development and Cultural Change* 46: 581–598 (p 582). For more, see Khan, S. R. and Aftab, S. (1994) 'Assessing the impact of financial reforms on Pakistan's economy'. *Pakistan Journal of Applied Economics* 10 (1–2): 99–116.

[101] Bonaccorsi di Patti, E. and Hardy, D. C. (2005) 'Financial sector liberalization, bank privatization, and efficiency: evidence from Pakistan'. *Journal of Banking & Finance* 29: 2381–2406 (p 2385).

[102] Anwar, 'Impact of globalization and liberalization', pp 2, 3.

[103] The Reagan Doctrine is epitomized by Reagan's statement that, 'We must stand by all our democratic allies. And we must not break faith with those who are risking their lives – on every continent, from Afghanistan to Nicaragua – to defy Soviet-supported aggression and secure rights which have been ours from birth.' Source: Reagan, R. (1985) 'Address before a joint session of the Congress on the State of the Union', 6 February.

part through refugee assistance agencies themselves, which were used by but also benefited from American funding in exchange for adherence to foreign policy goals. These included CARE, Catholic Relief Services, the Church World Services, and the IRC.[104]

The economic reforms Pakistan undertook are also important to highlight due to the influential relationship with the US and other Western support that they evince: in each of the downturns of US aid, particularly in the early 1970s (due to Pakistan's uranium enrichment facility) and the late 1980s (with the Soviet withdrawal of troops in Afghanistan), Pakistan gained recourse to IMF funding with US support.[105] This suggests that the US 'stop-go' assistance was supplemented with IMF 'safety nets' in times of low US assistance levels. In this way, we see the instrumentalization of Pakistan by Western actors according to geopolitical interests, and can better understand the incentivizing role that funding to the Pakistani government for refugee and development assistance may have played.

Domestic to international policy shifts

Self-reliance assistance to refugees changed in part as an outcome of these structural adjustments in Pakistan and other refugee-hosting countries of the Global South. Humanitarian assistance became increasingly channelled through INGOs rather than host states, and reductions in service provision necessitated a narrower focus on those 'vulnerable' refugees incapable of living independently from humanitarian aid. Assistance agencies were entwined with the implementation and results of economic policies, as the types of assistance they offered refugees and other populations shifted according to the demands of donors, host countries, and, ultimately, the needs of the global economy. Thus, refugee assistance echoed domestic welfare practices through its alignment to larger economic interests.

As donor governments reduced funding for protracted refugee populations, higher importance was placed on the ability of these populations to live without aid and become self-reliant. Refugee self-reliance assistance shifted from a Keynesian public works model targeting collective self-reliance and socioeconomic equilibrium to individual vocational trainings and an emphasis on entrepreneurship. For example, refugee self-reliance assistance in Pakistan was first enacted through public works projects targeting regional development through building roads and other infrastructure funded by

[104] Baitenmann, 'NGOs and the Afghan War', p 69.

[105] Ehtisham, A. and Mohammed, A. (2012) 'Pakistan, the United States and the IMF: great game or a curious case of Dutch Disease without the oil?' Asia Research Centre Working Paper No. 57. London School of Economics.

international donors before it shifted to an individualized, urban approach. In theory, this latter approach would stimulate local economies and enable refugees to partake in income generation without the support of international agencies, which faced dwindling funds from disinterested donors as the Cold War ended. Hence refugee policy was revealed as more a facet of vested donors and less an outcome of addressing refugees' actual needs.

However, similar to Western 'workfare' programmes, by the mid-1980s, refugees in Pakistan were encouraged to gain the skills needed to find or create jobs themselves, rather than have them offered directly. Particularly after the end of the Cold War, when funds for Afghans declined and national and international labour demands shifted, education and training programmes were reconstructed to deliver the skills and productivity needed in a changing and increasingly competitive international economy.[106]

An emphasis on self-empowerment was applied in Pakistan through the creation of so-called refugee self-help groups, the members of which were encouraged by international organizations to work together for income generation. They demonstrate a departure from the top-down rhetoric of self-reliance assistance in authoritarian East African refugee settlements in the 1960s and 1970s, yet also demonstrate – despite an enlightened discourse of empowerment – a continuation of 'trainings' and 'education' for refugees. Through these self-empowerment programmes, reduced support by assistance agencies was legitimized as a means to respect refugee agency and avoid refugee dependency syndrome.

Correspondingly, Afghan refugees in Pakistan saw an increase in support for small-scale economic participation as 'refugee entrepreneurship' became a prevailing theme.[107] Funding increased for vocational training in areas such as business and cottage industries such as weaving and animal husbandry.[108] Refugees were also provided with increased opportunities for small loans to start or expand businesses. These practices supported refugees as individual workers rather than as a collective workforce, and upheld the neoliberalism doctrine of individualism, with the subsequent presumed responsibility for refugees to become self-reliant on their own.

After the Peace Accords were signed in 1988, the concept of self-reliance further morphed into the 'Afghanization' of NGOs as aid and development agencies in Pakistan and Afghanistan were part of a much broader shift of engaging in not only assistance but reconstruction and nation-building. Building on a shift in dominant development discourse toward participation

106 Peters, 'Education, enterprise culture and the entrepreneurial self', p 65.

107 Rolfe, C. and Harper, M. (1987) *Refugee Enterprise: It can be done*. London: Intermediate Technology Publications.

108 ILO, 'Tradition and dynamism'.

and civil society in the 1980s, refugee self-reliance assistance in the early 1990s was explicitly linked to liberal impulses to create or restore democracies in countries torn apart by war. Civil society became a main focus of development and was perceived as the key to both development and the protection of human rights.[109] As UNHCR High Commissioner Sadako Ogata ushered in the 'decade of voluntary repatriation', not only repatriated refugees but the agencies that moved in to assist them became embedded in these larger liberal projects. The incorporation of NGOs into broader aims was also linked to the professionalization of NGOs in Pakistan, which ultimately led to a loss of local knowledge and a freedom to implement programmes as aid and development workers saw fit.[110]

Notions of dependency and welfare

Writing of neoliberal 'market-like arrangements' of welfare and education in the UK, Peters writes:

> These new arrangements provide an increasingly accepted social recipe for individualizing the social by substituting notions of civil society, social capital or community for state. *At the same time, however, they carry the combined dangers, on the one hand, of pathologizing and stigmatizing those who are structurally excluded from the labour market*, and on the other, of weighing down with debt ... the next generation.[111] [emphasis added]

The stigmatization of those unable to economically contribute to society reflects a further key tenet of neoliberal discourse apparent in refugee assistance: a condemnation of dependency as the original sin of free-market thinking. This reflects a long-running debate in Western social policy on 'welfare dependency', with right-wing groups arguing that the provision of long-term welfare creates dependency, and left-wing groups challenging this implied view of the poor, instead arguing for the maintenance and extension of welfare policies.[112]

This conservative discourse is evinced in refugee self-reliance assistance through discussions of so-called 'refugee dependency syndrome', which were paramount in the second half of the 1980s. Dependency syndrome

[109] Edwards, M. and Gaventa, J. (2001) 'Global Citizen Action: Lessons and Challenges', in *Global Citizen Action*. London: Routledge, pp 275–287.

[110] Bennett, J. (nd) 'Afghanistan: Cross-border NGO coordination'. ICVA. RSC Cardbox: FA/FP 59.4 BEN in Box FA/FP Afghans in Pakistan, 59.3–64, pp 15–16.

[111] Peters, 'Education, enterprise culture and the entrepreneurial self', p 62.

[112] Harvey, P. and Lind, J. (2005) *Dependency and Humanitarian Relief: A critical analysis*. London: Humanitarian Policy Group, Overseas Development Institute.

reflected a pathologization of refugees who were not working and those who remained (at least partially) reliant on humanitarian assistance. This became evident in Pakistan as shifts from the employment of refugees in public works programmes in the early 1980s to the individual entrepreneurship trainings of the late 1980s and early 1990s were reinforced by a changing discourse of proud, independent Afghans to dependent refugees. In this way, the construction of Afghans shifted from workers in need of jobs to refugees requiring outside support such as 'social animation' to reach their own exogenously defined potential. Outside intervention such as trainings to encourage market engagement were legitimated, as was a larger process of accumulation through urban, market-based activities.

Notably, the condemnation of dependency was not confined to unemployed Afghans in Pakistan, but instead became cosmopolitan in protracted refugee situations across the globe. Discussing refugees in Africa in the 1980s, Stein stridently highlights the detrimental consequences of refugee dependency and how this phenomenon cripples refugees' independence:

> Failure to become at least self-supporting would mean lives of dependency and a loss of self-respect. … The longer the time that they are in camps … dependent and depressed, the harder it is to eventually make the refugees into independent integrated participants in society. Dependency is socially and psychologically damaging to refugees.[113]

As this quotation illustrates, dependency and indignity were perceived as intertwined, purportedly constituting an inability for refugees to become 'independent integrated participants in society'. In this way, dependency syndrome acted as contrived legitimation: of refugees as failed workers within capitalism who needed to be both emotionally and practically rehabilitated.

Vulnerable populations of refugees

In Western countries such as the UK, the costs of national social protection can be temporarily deferred onto future citizens through national debt; however, in refugee assistance, the more common method is for assistance to simply be reduced. As previously discussed, one result of movements toward reducing aid, partially as an outcome of refugees' purported dependency on assistance,[114] was

[113] Stein, 'Refugees and Economic Activities in Africa'. Report prepared for the Office of Policy Development and Program Review, Bureau for Program and Policy Coordination. Agency for International Development, p 5.

[114] A growing body of contemporary scholarship challenges notions of dependency in both refugee and broader humanitarian assistance, arguing instead the positive reality of social dependence. See for example: Ferguson, J. (2013) 'Declarations of dependence: labour,

that refugee self-reliance assistance in the late 1980s and early 1990s targeted so-called 'vulnerable populations'. This emphasis on vulnerability can be seen as the third key tenet of neoliberal doctrine: an outcome of an assistance model which assumed refugees' ability to become self-reliant through employment or entrepreneurship regardless of individual circumstances, and one which correspondingly sought to reduce levels of funding for humanitarian assistance such as food aid. The shift of self-reliance assistance from placing able-bodied men into employment to fostering the creation of small cottage industries for the most vulnerable demonstrates both a recognition of and a means to address the phenomena of those refugees who struggled to live independently in a competitive, market-based system.

The simultaneous reduction of assistance and targeting of the most vulnerable echoes welfare cuts in the US and Western Europe in the 1980s, as the 'decline' of the welfare state necessitated the directing of resources ostensibly to the most marginalized and economically depressed.[115] Notably, this conceptualization of refugee vulnerability arose as humanitarian aid began to be withdrawn, suggesting a larger dynamic of refugee self-reliance as a means to reduce aid to the majority of refugees.[116] In this way, and as will be discussed in the following chapter, self-reliance began to be framed as an exit strategy for assistance agencies and donors whose funds and gaze had turned elsewhere.[117]

Conclusion

The self-reliance assistance provided to Afghan refugees in Pakistan from 1979 to the early 1990s demonstrates the influence of Western economic and social welfare trends on development aid to refugees. During this period, refugees were deployed as labourers useful to the rising neoliberal global economy while other Western-armed and funded refugees fought the Communist economic model as part of the *mujahideen*. Engaged first in large-scale development projects funded by the West, and then supported to become individual entrepreneurs capable of navigating the market alone and without humanitarian assistance, Afghan refugees were economically

personhood, and welfare in southern Africa'. *Journal of the Royal Anthropological Institute* 19(2): 223–242; Easton-Calabria, E. and Herson, M. (2020) 'In praise of dependencies: dispersed dependencies and displacement'. *Disasters* 44(1): 44–62.

115 Esping-Anderson, G. (1990) *The Three Worlds of Welfare Capitalism*. Cambridge: Polity Press.

116 For a deeper historical discussion on the politics of aid provision in relation to categories of beneficiaries, see Feldman, I. (2018) *Life Lived in Relief*. Oakland: University of California Press.

117 Easton-Calabria, E. and Omata, N. (2018) 'Panacea for the refugee crisis? Rethinking the promotion of self-reliance for refugees'. *Third World Quarterly* 39(8): 1458–1474.

and conceptually instrumentalized through their own and assistance agencies' efforts to foster self-reliance. With parallels to the decline of the Western welfare state, self-reliance assistance sought to create productive subjects able to survive without government or other assistance. The purported fostering of Afghan refugees' self-reliance during this time aided the fight against Communism and the global expansion of a neoliberal economic model that condemned dependency and lauded self-reliance, regardless of the individual and collective needs and capabilities of the populations it targeted.

5

Dignity in Informality? Urban Refugee Self-Reliance Assistance in Kampala, Uganda

> [D]evelopment aid has a great … potential in terms of assisting the empowerment of refugees and enhancement of productive capacities and self-reliance … allowing them to be instrumental in … contributing positively to the development process.[1]

Introduction

On the side of a dusty road in Kampala, the capital of Uganda, Justin talks about his ongoing struggles to practise medicine. Nursing, his profession in the Democratic Republic of Congo, from which he fled years ago, is now barred to him because he cannot afford to have his certifications translated into English. He also has not been able to find any organization to support him in doing so. He lives and volunteers as an adviser at the Bondeko Refugee Livelihoods Centre, a community centre founded and led by refugees. While he offers support to the centre's members, he is too afraid of being penalized to offer medical advice or care. He shares, however, that InterAid, UNHCR's implementing partner in Kampala, knows that he is a nurse and has even requested his help:

> InterAid gathered all the refugee nurses for a meeting but trained us only to sensitise refugees in malaria … refugees must go all the way to InterAid just to get paracetamol. Or they go and wait two days to go to Mulago [Uganda's national referral hospital] for malaria. But there

[1] UNHCR (2003) 'Framework for durable solutions for refugees and persons of concern'. Geneva: UNHCR.

are many nurses here. We can diagnose and treat from right here at the Center![2]

The experience Justin relayed is echoed in the stories of many refugees in Kampala. Particularly for those who enter urban areas, informal work is their only option, despite many being professionally trained in their country of origin. Once doctors, nurses, lawyers, and teachers, many refugees are forced to become entrepreneurs in manual vocations in which they have only limited skills. Research shows that at least 52 per cent of refugees in Kampala are self-employed, while 41 per cent are employed by others, often fellow refugees, and 7 per cent are not employed.[3] Many refugees who had gained professional qualifications in their country of origin struggle to pay the fee to have their documents translated and notarized, or lost their documents in flight. These challenges, combined with Kampala's limited formal market, mean that often even desperately needed professions in the country are excluded from refugees.

However, although urban refugees in Kampala are considered self-reliant by the international community, this and other research has found that their lives and livelihoods remain precarious, and that even after becoming skilled through training they struggle to earn enough to cover basic necessities. This reality both aligns and significantly diverges from global discourse on self-reliance in the new millennium, including on protection and dignity for refugees.

This chapter juxtaposes 'global' narratives on refugee self-reliance with the local implementation of assistance through a case study of urban refugee self-reliance assistance in Kampala in 2015. It focuses more broadly on the self-reliance assistance – more commonly discussed at the time as 'livelihoods assistance' – offered to urban refugees since 2009, when the *UNHCR policy on refugee protection and solutions in urban areas* (the so-called Urban Refugee Policy) granted refugees the right to reside in urban areas and advocated for their protection in these spaces. As a result of this policy, many organizations began livelihoods operations in urban settings.

Rather than significantly investing in helping refugees to regain their former occupations, the international community has chosen to invest in livelihoods trainings as a main self-reliance assistance practice in cities and towns. In contrast to refugees in camps, refugees in urban areas do not receive material assistance such as shelter and food, but are instead expected to become self-reliant through entrepreneurship. Livelihoods trainings, such as in arts and crafts, business, IT, and tailoring, are the main source of support

2 Interview, Bondeko Center, Kampala, 20 June 2015.

3 Betts, A., Bloom, L., Kaplan, J. D., and Omata, N. (2014) *Refugee Economies: Rethinking popular assumptions*. University of Oxford, Refugee Studies Centre, pp 1–44.

they receive to do so. The lack of other means for refugees to utilize their existing skillsets, such as in the public sector, means that these trainings are in high demand. These trainings thus take on a heightened importance as they are essentially what urban self-reliance assistance constitutes. As examined here, livelihoods trainings place refugees under the 'protection' of the market, as livelihoods purportedly offer a path to self-reliance through sustainable work and thus a lack of need for international assistance.

Uganda, a small country in East Africa, is widely considered to be one of the world's most progressive host countries, allowing refugees the right to work and freedom of movement and promoting self-reliance through national strategies since the 1990s.[4] As of 2015, when this research was conducted, it hosted 500,000 refugees and asylum seekers, making it the third largest refugee-hosting country in Africa.[5] The majority of its refugees come from the Great Lakes region, with the most coming from the Democratic Republic of Congo (42 per cent), and South Sudan (39 per cent), followed by Somalia (7 per cent) and Burundi (6 per cent).[6] In recent years, Uganda has received increasing attention internationally for the livelihoods and self-reliance opportunities it affords refugees. Uganda was one of UNHCR's priority countries for livelihoods initiatives, for example, driven by the 2014–2018 Global Strategy for Livelihoods. Uganda's global standing as a model country for refugee self-reliance means that significantly more resources have been poured into self-reliance assistance there than in many other countries; thus the assistance provided there can be considered 'state of the art' for the time.

While previous historical chapters focus largely on refugee self-reliance from the perspective of international institutions, this chapter delves into how these macro institutional practices and discourses permeate the micro, local level of refugee self-reliance assistance as enacted by international, national, and local NGOs and community-based organizations (CBOs), including organizations led by refugees themselves (hereafter *refugee-led organizations*). This scope of research presents an opportunity to understand the extent to which the discourse present in policy and other guiding documents reflects

4 The 2006 Refugee Act and 2010 Refugee Regulations provide the legal and regulatory framework enabling refugees with the Right to Work and Freedom of Movement, while the Refugee Settlement Model enables refugees to live in settlements, not camps, and provides refugees with access to agricultural land for food production. Additionally, Uganda is party to the 1951 Refugee Convention, 1967 Protocol, 1969 Organisation of African Unity (OAU) Convention, and the 2015 Refugee Policy.

5 UNHCR (2015) 'Uganda hosts record 500,000 refugees and asylum-seekers'. 18 December. Geneva: UNHCR.

6 Uganda Government, Office of the Prime Minister (OPM), Refugee Information Management System (RIMS) (2015) 'Uganda – Monthly Refugee Statistics Update'. December 2015. Kampala: Government of Uganda.

and is suitable for the 'on-the-ground' reality of assistance meant to foster refugee self-reliance.

The following sections present a historical overview of refugee self-reliance assistance from the 1990s, where the previous chapter ended, up to early 2015, just when the so-called 'European refugee crisis' was beginning. In particular, international trends and initiatives that influenced global self-reliance discourse and practice are examined, followed by refugee livelihood programming and policies, and the state and results of livelihoods trainings in Kampala. The content and main details of these trainings are presented, as well as their contradictions: the results they offer as opposed to what they promise to provide. Challenges surrounding these trainings are discussed, which stem both from the local context as well as the institutional structure of livelihoods assistance. The discussion section presents the wider economic and social context that this assistance is embedded within, examining refugees as part of the informal labour force that has emerged as a key facet of globalization.

Repatriation, Targeted Development Assistance, and refugee livelihoods

In the 1990s, many refugee populations such as the Afghans began to return home, yet conflicts in other parts of the world began. The repatriation of refugees in the first half of the 1990s was largely due to the resolution of the Cold War,[7] yet the decade also saw the start of the so-called 'New Wars'[8] of the post-Cold War era, characterized by ethnic fighting and conflict in the name of identity politics as well as violence between state and non-state actors. The 1994 Rwandan genocide and the ensuing Congo Wars exemplify this trend, and resulted in the sudden influx of hundreds of thousands of refugees into Uganda as well as other countries in sub-Saharan Africa.

Despite UN High Commissioner for Refugees Ogata's call for the 1990s to be the 'decade of voluntary repatriation', by the end of the decade UNHCR had 22.3 million people of concern, with 1999 deemed 'one of the most challenging years in UNHCR's history'.[9] Crisp discusses UNHCR's focus on livelihoods and self-reliance at this time, writing:

---

[7] Based on UNHCR figures, more than 9 million refugees repatriated between 1991 and the beginning of 1996. Loescher, G. (2001) *The UNHCR and World Politics: A perilous path*. New York: Oxford University Press, p 280.

[8] Kaldor, M. (2005) 'Old Wars, Cold Wars, New Wars, and the War on Terror'. Lecture given to the Cold War Studies Centre, London School of Economics, 2 February; Duffield, M. (2014) *Global Governance and the New Wars: The merging of development and security*. London: Zed Books.

[9] UNHCR (2000) 'The global report 1999'. Geneva: UNHCR.

> To the extent that UNHCR was concerned with livelihoods issues during the 1990s, then the organization's interest and involvement was very much focused on the reintegration of returnees in countries of origin – rather than self-reliance amongst refugees in countries of asylum. Working on the assumption that repatriation now represented the only feasible solution to large-scale refugee situations, during this period UNHCR began to emphasize notions such 'sustainable reintegration,' 'returnee aid and development', and the 'relief to development gap.'[10]

As refugees were returning to their countries of origin, they had the right to work which was denied to them in many host countries, thus enabling livelihoods programming to emerge in the form of repatriation, reconstruction, and peacebuilding projects. The founding principles of returnee aid and development included that reintegration assistance was most effective when an entire community, and not just refugees or internally displaced person (IDPs), received support; that local development should be encouraged and dependency discouraged; and that the gap between humanitarian and development assistance should quickly be bridged.[11] In this way, many elements of the strategy emulated past principles in addition to providing a basis for future refugee self-reliance and livelihoods strategies. Short-term projects known as Quick Impact Projects often centred on income generation and provided important livelihoods and coordination experience for UNHCR and UNDP.[12]

In the second half of the 1990s, returnee aid and development was superseded by a larger focus on post-conflict reintegration, which in turn led to efforts to address the gap between humanitarian assistance and long-term development. The so-called Brookings Process beginning in 1999 was

[10] Crisp, J. (2003) 'UNHCR, refugee livelihoods and self-reliance: a brief history'. 22 October. Geneva: UNHCR. Available at: www.unhcr.org/cgibin/texis/vtx/search?page=search&docid=3f978a894&query=jeff%20crisp (accessed 1 July 2018). Crisp also posits that UNHCR gained valuable experience in self-reliance through reintegration programmes, a topic which is explored further in Skran, C. (2020) 'Refugee entrepreneurship and self-reliance: the UNHCR and sustainability in post-conflict Sierra Leone'. *Journal of Refugee Studies, 33*(1): 268–298.

[11] For more on returnee aid and development, see Crisp, J. (2001) 'Mind the gap! UNHCR, humanitarian assistance and the development process'. *The International Migration Review*, 35(1): 168–191 (p 179).

[12] Quick Impact Projects were part of a larger peace process known as CIREFCA from 1989–1994, which served to link the self-reliance and livelihoods of refugees and displaced populations with peace and democracy. For more information, see: Betts, A. (2006) 'Comprehensive plans of action: Insights from CIREFCA and the Indochinese CPA'. UNHCR New Issues in Refugee Research Working Paper No. 120. Geneva: UNHCR, Evaluation and Policy Analysis Unit.

led by UNHCR and the World Bank and arose out of a recognition of the ongoing relief-development divide in strategies and programming and the need for greater and more effective coordination between humanitarian and development actors.[13] The efforts of the Brookings Process demonstrated a renewed partnership between UNHCR and the World Bank, as well as a broader focus on engaging refugees and IDPs in development. As many projects were income-generating in nature, the process also paved the way for the broader focus on livelihoods that emerged in the 2000s.

The new millennium brought an emphasis on refugee self-reliance in the form of 'refugee livelihoods', defined by UNHCR as the means through which refugees 'secure the basic necessities of life, such as food, water, shelter and clothing'.[14] Self-reliance was presented as a way to achieve livelihoods – synonymous with labour market integration – which in turn was often presented as achieving local integration. This came in part through an international effort led by UNHCR to facilitate multilateral special agreements on refugee solutions, known as the Convention Plus Initiative, which took place between 2002 and 2005. Taking place on a larger scale than similar past conferences such as ICARA I and II, the Convention Plus Initiative was premised on both Northern states' desire to reduce Southern asylum seekers and the increased burden-sharing Southern states solicited.[15]

One of the three main strands of Convention Plus was 'Targeted Development Assistance' (TDA), essentially a repackaging of the previous era's 'Refugee Aid and Development' and characterized by constructions of refugees as displaced people and humans holding human rights – as well as potential security threats. In this way, Convention Plus reflected the broader UN discourse of the time, itself connected to attempts to increase global stability and security in the wake of the 2001 terrorist attacks in New York.[16]

---

13 Focusing on post-conflict regions, projects included the Georgian Self Reliance Fund managed by the World Bank and implemented by OCHA, UNDP, UNHCR, and the Swiss Government, created to support Georgian IDPs in reintegration and local integration. Others included the 'Imagine Co-Existence' community-based income-generating activities in Bosnia and Herzegovina and Rwanda. Source: Executive Committee of the High Commissioner's Programme (2001) 'Reintegration: a progress report'. Standing Committee 20th Meeting, 15 February. UN Doc. N. EC/51/SC/CRP.5, pp 200–201.

14 UNHCR (2014) '2014–2018 global strategy for livelihoods'. Geneva: UNHCR, p 7.

15 Betts, A. (2009) *Protection by Persuasion: International cooperation in the refugee regime*. Ithaca, NY: Cornell University Press. For more information on Convention Plus, see also: Betts, A. and Durieux, J. (2007) 'Convention Plus as a norm-setting exercise'. *Journal of Refugee Studies* 20(3): 509–535.

16 The 2005 UN Secretary General report cited, for example, the UN's aims to: 'strengthen development, security and human rights issues. ... On the development front ... reinvigorate the Millennium Development Goals ... On security, the goal is to adopt

One effect of the increased securitization of migration was restricted asylum options, as Northern industrialized countries became less and less inclined to resettle refugees.[17] Convention Plus sought to address this restrictive climate by focusing on supporting refugees in their region of origin. Ruud Lubbers, the UN High Commissioner for Refugees at the time, discussed this as well as the financial incentive of TDA:

> UNHCR is proposing a more coherent, wide-ranging effort by donor states to support refugees in their original host countries, and to find solutions by helping them return home, by resettling them to other countries or by helping them to start new lives locally in their region of origin. *But all this requires development assistance that would increase the self-reliance of refugees and benefit the countries that host them*, thereby reducing the pressures to seek asylum further afield. Indeed, each dollar or euro spent on solutions for refugees in regions of origin would have double value. That this is not happening is shameful and makes no financial sense.[18] [emphasis added]

The TDA strand of Convention Plus resulted in several projects in sub-Saharan Africa, including in Uganda, Zambia, and Ethiopia.[19] Although these projects were presented as 'examples of targeting development assistance in practice', no framework of understanding between states was achieved despite agreement that more needed to be done to involve refugees in development. Outcomes remained agreements in principle rather than formalized next steps in action. In 2005, the work of the Convention Plus Unit was mainstreamed into other UNHCR divisions and units, and it is largely remembered as a coordination exercise rather than a successful initiative connecting refugees to development.[20]

---

new ways of dealing with threats to international peace and security.' Source: UNHCR (2005) 2005 UN Secretary General report. Geneva: UN.

[17] Koser, K. (2007) 'Refugees, transnationalism and the state'. *Journal of Ethnic and Migration Studies* 33(2): 233–254; Van Hear, N. (2012) 'Forcing the issue: migration crises and the uneasy dialogue between refugee research and policy'. *Journal of Refugee Studies* 25(1): 2–24.

[18] Lubbers, R. (2003) 'Op-ed by Ruud Lubbers, UN High Commissioner for Refugees'. 20 June. Geneva: UNHCR. Available at: www.unhcr.org/uk/news/editorial/2003/6/3ef2e9094/op-ed-ruud-lubbers-un-high-commissioner-refugees.html (accessed 15 November 2017).

[19] UNHCR (2005) 'Progress report: Convention Plus'. High Commissioner's Forum, 8 November. FORUM/2005/6, p 2. Available at: www.unhcr.org/uk/protection/convention/4371c24c2/progress-report-convention-plus-forum20056.html (accessed 15 November 2017).

[20] UNHCR (2005) 'Progress report: Convention Plus', p 4.

Despite the lack of large-scale TDA outcomes from Convention Plus, a focus on refugees in development through livelihoods and self-reliance continued throughout the decade. Indeed, between 2000 and 2009, approximately 12,000 pieces of literature by academics and practitioners discussed refugee livelihoods – over double the number published the decade prior.[21] This number steadily rose, with close to 1,000 new publications on refugee livelihoods in 2015 alone;[22] there was an even more striking rise in publications on refugee self-reliance between 1990 and 1999 (209 records), 2000–2009 (1,134 records), and 2010–2019 (2,124 records).[23] Refugee livelihoods emerged as a main topic within debates surrounding rights-based approaches,[24] urban support programmes,[25] and micro-finance for refugees.[26] The UNHCR's Livelihoods Unit was established in 2008 and from 2010 to 2012 UNHCR's budget for livelihood programming increased by 66 per cent.[27] As UNHCR writes:

> [T]here has been a surge in the scale of livelihoods efforts across UNHCR operations in recent years. The global budget planned for livelihoods activities grew by more than 25% between 2011 and 2012 and by another 15% in 2013. In 2012, 18 operations had budgets ranging from USD 4 million to USD 24 million for livelihoods activities. In 2013, 87 operations conducted livelihood interventions, up from 79 in 2012. These programmes primarily benefit refugees (62%), followed by IDPs (22%) and returnees (13%). The greatest share of funds is invested in vocational and skills training, promoting

21 ProQuest (2014) 'Graph of search results: refugee livelihoods'. Available at: http://tinyurl.com/RefugeeLivelihoodsGraph (accessed 12 June 2014).

22 ProQuest (2015) 'Graph of search results: refugee livelihoods'. Available at: www.proquest.com/socialsciencepremium/results/AB2B3D6AE93D454APQ/1?accountid=13042 (accessed 27 June 2021).

23 ProQuest (2019) 'Graph of search results: refugee self-reliance'. Available at: www.proquest.com/socialsciencepremium/results/99A6F27A0E6740C9PQ/1?accountid=13042 (accessed 27 June 2021).

24 Crisp J. (2003) 'No solution in sight: the problem of protracted refugee situations in Africa'. Center for Comparative Immigration Studies (CCIS) Working Paper No. 68. CCIS: San Diego.

25 FIC (Feinstein International Center) (2012) 'Refugee livelihoods in urban areas: identifying program opportunities: case study Egypt'. Boston, MA: Feinstein International Center, Tufts University.

26 Bartsch, D. (2004) 'Microfinance and refugees'. *Forced Migration Review* 20: 20; Foy, D. (2006) 'The appropriateness and effectiveness of micro-finance as a livelihoods intervention for refugees'. London: Refugee Livelihoods Network.

27 UNHCR (2012) 'Livelihood programming in UNHCR: operational guidelines'. Geneva: UNHCR, p 14.

> entrepreneurship, supporting agriculture, livestock and fisheries, and strengthening access to financial services or microfinance.[28]

The practices of the UNHCR Livelihoods Unit have been labelled 'innovative' in development literature,[29] yet previous chapters reveal that these assistance practices have occurred since the first international institutional responses to refugees by the League of Nations in the 1920s. As discussed here, these practices have remained largely consistent from the 1920s up to today, as have international institutions' and host governments' aims for refugee assistance to lead to both refugee self-reliance and host country economic development. At the same time, after the new millennium vocational training and micro-finance were more heavily promoted in UNHCR and other INGO guiding frameworks and policies. These were seen as a means to promote entrepreneurship, which became a more popular form of livelihoods support in contrast to efforts to foster self-reliance mainly through subsistence agriculture, as had been more common in the interwar and post-Second World War period. The following sections explore tensions between the rhetoric and implementation of this new phase of refugee self-reliance assistance.

Refugee self-reliance assistance in Uganda

The evolution of refugee self-reliance assistance in Uganda since the late 1990s sheds light on the application of global self-reliance agendas in a national context. In 1999, the Government of Uganda (GoU) and UNHCR jointly launched the country's self-reliance strategy (SRS), and in 2003 Development Assistance for Refugees (DAR), part of the 'way forward' for the SRS. The SRS aimed to 'empower' refugees as well as nationals in refugee-hosting regions to support themselves, and 'establish mechanisms … [to] ensure integration of services for the refugees with those of the nationals'.[30] DAR, in turn, aimed to actualize the SRS and 'address some of the problems of poverty and under-development in refugee hosting districts which could promote further peace, security and stability in the region'.[31] It

[28] UNHCR, '2014–2018 global strategy for livelihoods', p 14.

[29] IFAD (2003) 'Five microfinance projects meet the rural pro-poor innovation challenge'. Available at: www.ifad.org/ruralfinance/poverty/rppic.htm (accessed 11 August 2014); Foy, 'The appropriateness and effectiveness of micro-finance'; IRC (2012) 'Urban refugees'. International Rescue Committee pamphlet. Available at: www.rescue-uk.org/sites/default/files/20.11.12%20Urban%20refs%20for%20ECHO%20advocacy%20event%20_0.pdf. (accessed 11 August 2014).

[30] GoU and UNHCR (2004) 'Self-reliance strategy for refugee hosting areas of Moyo, Adjumani and Arua Districts of Northern Uganda (SRS)'. Geneva: UNHCR.

[31] GoU and UNHCR, 'Self-reliance strategy for refugee hosting areas', p 6.

was created in line with the High Commissioner's Framework for Durable Solutions for Refugees and Persons of Concern, which developed protection tools such as DAR as part of Convention Plus. The framework described the broader DAR agenda as improving burden-sharing, increasing self-reliance for refugees, and enabling a better quality of life for both refugee and host communities. The incorporation of refugees into development was a central tenet of DAR and the ongoing search for durable solutions:

> [T]he needs of refugees and returnees have not systematically been incorporated in transition and recovery plans by governments concerned, the donor community and the UN system. Refugees and returnees are often not part of the national development planning. Ignoring the needs of displaced populations in development planning and most importantly, their positive contribution to society may result in returnees becoming a possible source of instability to the country's rebuilding efforts.[32]

Such quotes illustrate the purportedly limited extent of refugees' engagement with development, despite the wide-ranging efforts documented in previous chapters. The potential for refugees to be not just agents of development but of conflict and instability is also reflected here, illuminating how a focus on reducing violence was linked to development.

The development efforts in Uganda are described positively in many policy documents of the time; as one UNHCR report describes, 'SRS, over time has also helped in "attitude change" amongst refugees and host communities alike – from free handouts to self-help and capacity building'.[33] However, critiques of these approaches demonstrate that while UNHCR promoted 'empowerment' and 'self-reliance' through livelihoods and economic activities, they were impossible to attain without the right to work and right to freedom of movement, which were not then granted to refugees. Research also found that policies to promote self-reliance, such as reductions in food rations, were detrimental to refugee beneficiaries.[34] As Kaiser writes,

> The SRS evidently seeks to integrate refugee services into district service provision and from the point of view of the elimination of

[32] UNHCR, 'Framework for durable solutions', p 4.

[33] UNHCR (2003) 'Development Assistance for Refugees (DAR) for Uganda Self Reliance Strategy – way forward'. Report on Mission to Uganda 14–20 September 2003, RLSS/DOS Mission Report 03/11, p 3.

[34] Meyer, S. (2006) 'The "refugee aid and development" approach in Uganda: empowerment and self-reliance of refugees in practice'. UNHCR Evaluation and Policy Analysis Unit, UNHCR New Issues in Refugee Research Working Paper Series No. 131.

> wasteful parallel structures of refugee assistance, this makes good sense. However, the expectation that refugees will achieve and sustain 'self-reliance', in the absence of any substantial interventions designed to address the main obstacles to this goal, is less obviously well founded. The policy dialogue around the SRS in settlements usually fails to discuss such obstacles. How can refugees produce a surplus when their plot is too small, the soil exhausted, or when the rains fail to come, as in 2005?[35]

Uganda's legal context changed with the 2006 Refugee Act, which recognized human rights conventions and broadened refugees' rights, providing the ability to work and move freely between camps and urban areas. This theoretically addressed many of the critiques of the SRS but also meant that an important gap arose in the service provision to refugees in urban areas, as NGOs had up to that point mainly worked in settlements in Uganda. It was largely after the 2009 introduction of the UNHCR Urban Refugee Policy that most of UNHCR's urban implementing and operational partners in Uganda began offering livelihoods trainings. However these were largely restricted to Kampala, the only urban area where refugees were legally allowed to register. At the time of this research, most organizations had engaged in this work for five years. Uganda was also in the midst of finalizing a new national self-reliance strategy for refugees, which includes the promotion of urban livelihoods trainings.[36] This self-reliance strategy is known as the 2016–2020 Refugee and Host Population Empowerment (ReHoPE) Strategic Framework, formulated by UNHCR on behalf of the United Nations Country Team and World Bank.[37] However, at the time of this research it had not yet been implemented in Uganda.

[35] Kaiser, T. (2006) 'Between a camp and a hard place: rights, livelihood and experiences of the local settlement system for long-term refugees in Uganda'. *The Journal of Modern African Studies* 44(4): 597–621.

[36] UNHCR (2015) UNHCR Country Operations Profile – Uganda. Webpage. Geneva: UNHCR.

[37] It was considered one of the most progressive strategies in recent years involving refugees, host communities, and development. However, its aims were remarkably similar to that of the SRS. It too focused on developmental 'solutions' for refugees and aims to integrate refugees into existing institutional structures, as well as capitalize on their inclusion in the 2015/2016–2019/2020 National Development Plan II. Refugees' integration into national services was seen as having the potential to improve refugees' lives in a variety of areas, from providing access to loan services, more comprehensive healthcare, and government-sponsored livelihoods trainings. It epitomized the development approach that UNHCR has increasingly taken in recent years, and was considered an important pilot for the durable solution of local integration in host countries where refugees are provided with basic rights.

In 2015, Uganda had recently been selected as one of 13 priority countries for livelihoods in the UNHCR 2014–2018 Global Strategy for Livelihoods, the main guiding document on livelihoods and self-reliance at the time. As such, it was to be provided with additional funding and guidance on fostering refugee livelihoods and self-reliance. Notably, the term used repeatedly in the strategy document is 'economic self-reliance'. This is nowhere explicitly defined but is described as attainable through generating employment, job information and placement, skills and vocational training, entrepreneurship, and financial services.[38]

One of four five-year global strategies targeting different areas of UNHCR's work, the global strategy aims to define UNHCR's livelihoods programming, provide a global overview of its implementation, and guide national and local livelihoods strategies.[39] The guidelines consolidate many of the principles from the 2012 *UNHCR Livelihood Programming Operational Guidelines*, such as advocating for refugee rights and assisting refugees in accessing the services and tools needed for self-reliance. Building self-reliance at all stages of displacement is cited as key for helping people live with dignity; fostering livelihoods is presented as a central strategy in achieving this.

A main focus of the 2014 Global Strategy is on linking refugees to markets as well as 'scal[ing] up livelihoods programming'.[40] One important strategy for generating employment is by 'Identify[ing] new markets, value chains and potential employers for skilled refugees, including artisans, education or health care workers, technicians and other professionals'.[41] This includes job information platforms and job counselling services. It is notable in the attention it gives to refugees *after* skills training, as well as those seeking to utilize skills from previous livelihoods.

The following sections of this chapter are based on fieldwork in Kampala examining urban livelihoods trainings for refugees.[42] Livelihoods trainings

38 UNHCR, '2014–2018 Global Strategy for Livelihoods', p 32.

39 UNHCR, '2014–2018 Global Strategy for Livelihoods', p 8.

40 UNHCR, '2014–2018 Global Strategy for Livelihoods', p 8.

41 UNHCR, '2014–2018 Global Strategy for Livelihoods', p 28.

42 Note: The research was undertaken over three months between April and June 2015. The study is mainly qualitative and includes interviews with 119 refugees and 12 staff members from eight different organizations serving refugees in Kampala. The research employed a mixed-methods approach consisting of semi-structured in-depth interviews, focus group discussions (FGDs), basic demographics interviews, and non-participant observation. The majority of refugees interviewed (84 per cent) for this study were Congolese, which means a main limitation of this research is that of representativeness. The highest population of refugees in Uganda by nationality is Congolese (approximately 42 per cent), yet the data are not representative within the Congolese refugee community. Due to the lack of records on participants kept by institutions, it was often not possible to gain accurate numbers of trainees or break them down by demographic. Limitations therefore occurred due to the sampling method employed and the focus on livelihoods

at different organizations were observed, and individual refugees were also 'followed' in the process of their livelihoods creation, from participating in trainings to opening their own businesses. The main livelihoods trainings focused on are business, tailoring, arts and crafts, and hairdressing, as these were the most common trainings at the time. Micro-savings groups were also observed, and members interviewed. Information on other trainings offered by organizations was obtained through interviews with trainers and participants.

Providers of livelihoods assistance in Kampala

Livelihoods trainings in Kampala are led by some of UNHCR's most prominent operational partners in the city, including the Jesuit Refugee Service (JRS) and Finnish Refugee Council (FRC), and UNHCR's only implementing partner in Kampala, InterAid Uganda (henceforth, InterAid). As operational and implementing partners, these organizations represent the local instantiation of UNHCR's self-reliance and livelihoods discourse, although only InterAid is directly funded by UNHCR. JRS is an international Catholic organization that supports refugees and other forcibly displaced people through emergency aid, livelihoods and language training, and advocacy. It began offering livelihoods trainings in Kampala in 2010 with the aim of helping shift assistance from 'care and maintenance' to self-sufficiency.[43] In contrast, FRC is a religiously and politically independent organization that has operated in Uganda since 1997 and in Kampala since 2009. Its initial urban programmes were English lessons followed by business trainings. InterAid has implemented Kampala's Urban Refugee Programme under a tripartite agreement between UNHCR and the GoU since 1995; despite its esteemed role as UNHCR's implementing partner, it has a very negative reputation across Kampala's refugee communities, with allegations

arising after trainings undertaken at specific institutions. Corresponding to this, refugees interviewed were not evenly spread out across Kampala's neighbourhoods but instead mainly situated in the areas of Najjanankumbi, Nsambya, and Ndejje. Last, the qualitative nature of this study precludes the opportunity for detailed quantitative findings that a longer period of data collection and a primarily quantitative focus might have led to. Ethical review was undertaken by the National Geographic Society as part of the grant review process and approval for the grant was given based on meeting all criteria, including ethical considerations. Ethical permission was granted by the University of Oxford on 5 April 2019 after submission of a CUREC 2 form to the International Development Research Ethics Committee and Social Sciences and Humanities Research Ethics Committee.

43 JRS (2010) 'Uganda: JRS offers new training opportunities for refugees'. 16 April. Available at: http://en.jrs.net/news_detail?TN=news-20100421061545 (accessed 15 December 2017).

of corruption and frustration over long wait times for documents, trainings, and meetings.

Despite being vastly under-represented in literature, refugee-led organizations are widespread in Kampala and offer a variety of services to refugees, including livelihoods trainings.[44] Refugee-led organizations in Kampala include the Bondeko Refugee Livelihoods Centre, Young African Refugees for Integral Development (YARID), and Hope of Children and Women Victims of Violence (HOCW). Each of these organizations is led by Congolese refugees but has programmes led by refugees of various nationalities, including South Sudanese and Burundians. Generally, these organizations focus their work on livelihoods acquisition for refugees in the respective areas of Kampala in which they operate. Among Congolese organizations such as those researched here, livelihoods trainings comprise their main activities. While YARID and HOCW are more formalized than the Bondeko Centre, all three organizations offer similar trainings (see Table 5.1) and face ongoing challenges with organizational sustainability due to a lack of resources for teachers and students alike.[45]

Self-reliance assistance practices in Kampala

One popular livelihoods training takes place at JRS, which rests in a strikingly quiet street in the city, just up and off a big hill filled with crowded trucks and *boda-bodas*. The main buildings rest around a grassy courtyard that never seems to be used; the bulk of the activity occurs behind doors or buildings. Behind one of these buildings, just above a sloping dirt field that stretches down to a chain link fence, is the hairdressing livelihoods training. Dembe,[46] the Ugandan trainer, weaves in between students sitting alternately on small stools in patches of shade or standing above their seated counterparts wielding scissors, yarn, and hair extensions. The students – 30 women in total varying from teenagers to women in their thirties – generally spend most of their morning practising new styles

[44] For more information on refugee-led organizations, see Pincock, K., Betts, A., and Easton-Calabria, E. (2020) *The Global Governed? Refugees as providers of protection and assistance*. Cambridge: Cambridge University Press; and the *Forced Migration Review* (2018) 'Special Supplement on Refugee-led Social Protection'. Oxford: Refugee Studies Centre, University of Oxford.

[45] Each of their leaders, for example, discussed needing more training resources, such as further skills development for teachers and basic materials (such as cloth or notebooks) for trainings. Source: Interviews, Bondeko Centre leader (15 May 2015), HOCW leader (16 May 2015), YARID leader (20 May 2015).

[46] Not her real name.

Table 5.1: Livelihoods training for refugees in Kampala

Training types	Organizations offering trainings
Arts and Crafts	4 (HOCW, JRS, InterAid, YARID)
Baking	1 (Bondeko Center – initiated through FRC)
Business	4 (Bondeko Center, FRC, HOCW – initiated through FRC, YARID)
Carpentry	1 (JRS)
Catering	1 (JRS)
Cobbling	2 (Bondeko Center, InterAid)
Computer Skills	4 (FRC, HOCW InterAid, YARID)
Hairdressing	4 (FRC, HOCW, InterAid, JRS)
Mushroom Growing	2 (FRC, HOCW – initiated through International Rescue Committee)
Pedicure/Manicure	1 (InterAid)
Tailoring/Fashion and Design	4 (Bondeko Center, HOCW, JRS, YARID)
+ Micro-savings/loans group	4 (Bondeko Center, HOCW, InterAid, JRS)

on each other, with Dembe occasionally bringing the group together to instruct on a particular topic. Sometimes she demonstrates the proper angle with which to hold scissors; another time students gather around her as she weaves a student's hair into an intricate plait, pointing out the particular pattern she follows.

Dembe's students are mainly Congolese and South Sudanese with varying levels of English. Dembe's English is loud and slow, but many of the lessons take place through demonstration and practice. The training itself lasts a year and is held five days a week full-time. Each of the students applied to take part and was interviewed by JRS staff, who emphasize they seek to match candidates' personal interests and visions for the future with a specific training. Two specific aspects of the hairdressing training stand in contrast with JRS' and other organizations' livelihoods trainings: first, students are provided with an internship in a hair salon in Kampala after graduation and, second, most of these students secure a job once they finish their training. This was attributed to hairdressing being a competitive skill in Kampala, which has small hair salons scattered across the city, as well as to the fact that internships provide a means to access and build on an established network of both employers and clients. The relatively small amount of material needed to work as a hairdresser also helps; as the JRS training coordinator explained of hairdressing, 'After training you don't need capital, because the capital is your hands'.

However, many refugees trained in other skills or at other organizations are not so lucky.

On the outskirts of Kampala, after the giant shopping centre ('Freedom City') on Entebbe Road and past goats and cows ambling on dirt side streets, is the refugee-led organization HOCW. Bolingo, the founder, is a Congolese refugee who started HOCW out of a recognition of the particular vulnerabilities faced by women and children. Interestingly, in contrast to the majority of refugee-led organizations interviewed in Kampala, HOCW serves both refugees and Ugandans. The organization offers a variety of support, including children's activities, English lessons, and livelihoods trainings. These trainings are known as the 'Community Collective' and began with a tailoring training in 2013.[47]

The tailoring training was initiated by an international volunteer who bought a sewing machine with which 20 people began training. Due to the high level of interest, HOCW requested more sewing machines from an international women's organization and received two more machines.[48] In September of 2013, a South Korean volunteer came to help with livelihoods trainings. Recognizing the need for resources, he started a crowdsourcing campaign through Gofundme and was able to raise $5,000 USD. Twelve new sewing machines and three design machines were bought with this money, as well as cloth and stools for trainees to sit at.[49] Therefore, although this and other trainings were initiated out of refugees' interests, they were partially enabled through volunteer donations and initiatives as well, thereby illustrating the importance of both resources and social networks for refugee-led organizations undertaking livelihoods trainings. Yet despite the significant effort put in by organizations to create trainings and students to learn new skills, viable livelihoods are not assured.

The structure of livelihoods trainings

Most livelihoods training participants have no prior experience in the skills they are acquiring. On one hand, this is due to refugees' personal challenges to make a living in Kampala through their former livelihoods, which range from farming to pastoralism to highly skilled public sector jobs, which leads them to look elsewhere for skills. On the other hand, organizations prefer to train refugees without past experience in the

---

47 Interview, Bolingo, HOCW Founder, 12 June 2015.

48 Interview, Bolingo, 12 June 2015.

49 Interview, Bolingo, 12 June 2015.

particular livelihoods skill they aim to acquire. JRS and InterAid actively screen potential participants for past livelihoods experience in training areas, seeking to support people in learning entirely new skills. They explained this as an effort to support vulnerable people, such as those without any experience in viable livelihoods, as well as a way to keep their trainings cohesive and streamlined. The refugee-led organizations YARID and Bondeko Centre lead trainings similarly, although they are less stringent in picking participants. HOCW adjusts training durations based on a participant's existing skillsets. Table 5.1 details the main livelihoods trainings offered to refugees in Kampala in 2015.

The number of refugees trained every year per organization varies. At any given time, JRS trains 120 refugees in its five livelihoods areas, while FRC trains 600 refugees per year in two cycles of business classes, and smaller numbers of refugees in other sectors. Refugee-led organizations train between 30 and 300 refugees per year. InterAid was the only organization interviewed that does not directly implement livelihoods trainings but instead offers them through existing service providers. Refugees apply at InterAid for a particular training, and successful applicants are then matched with an organization offering trainings near the refugee's location.

The number of participants per training ranges from six to 30, depending on the amount of space and available materials. For example, the tailoring training at the Bondeko Centre is held by three volunteer teachers who are fellow refugees. During the time observed, 12 refugees (nine women, three men) were taking part in a six-month training. Due to the limited number of sewing machines, the trainees were split into three groups and four participants undertook training for three hours twice per week.

The nationality of participants is most diverse in trainings led by INGOs. JRS trainings have a mixture of Congolese, Rwandan, Burundian, and South Sudanese refugees. FRC also supports these nationalities but generally holds trainings that are de facto separated by nationality, as trainings take place in areas of Kampala with high concentrations of particular refugee populations. The same is true of the refugee-led organizations interviewed, which mainly serve Congolese refugees. An exception, however, is HOCW, which aims its activities toward the community the organization is based in, and estimates that 30 per cent of training participants are local Ugandans.

It was not possible to accurately break down participants by gender, as organizations had varying levels of documentation on participants. However, 80 per cent of the participants in the trainings observed were women. The exception was business trainings, where participants' genders were more evenly divided. The high number of female participants in livelihoods trainings was considered problematic by several organizations, which discussed male refugees' complaints about the minimal training available in 'male' professions. To address this, JRS began a carpentry programme in

June 2015, and InterAid planned to offer trainings in mechanics, electric installation, and plumbing beginning in 2016.

Notably, both institutional and refugee-led organizations cited the genesis of trainings as driven by refugees' desire to work; as one InterAid protection officer stated, "Livelihoods are the most important issue among refugees".[50] JRS, InterAid, and FRC had conducted needs assessments and identified livelihood skills as a major need of refugees, while refugee-led organizations created trainings based on anecdotal evidence. JRS offers three months of emergency assistance for food and rent to eligible refugees, but recognized that refugees needed more sustainable assistance after this time. As the JRS livelihoods coordinator stated, "Refugees asked to fish for themselves, instead of being handed the fish". Several initiatives led by refugee-led organizations began with support and training from the IRC and FRC and thus were influenced by these organizations to offer trainings in particular sectors. Mushroom growing and business trainings were initiated by IRC at HOCW, while FRC helped start mushroom growing, business trainings, and baking at the Bondeko Centre. The organization African Centre for Treatment and Rehabilitation of Torture Victims (ACTV) also provided four sewing machines to the tailoring group at the Bondeko Centre, although this was to strengthen and not start the existing training.

The challenges of creating livelihoods

The ability to participate in livelihoods trainings does not guarantee that refugees are able to find or create jobs *after* their training. Each organization interviewed had conducted needs assessments of refugees that reflected refugees' desire for skills training and micro-finance loans. However, despite being a priority country for livelihoods programming, neither the GoU, UNHCR, nor any of the organizations interviewed had, at the time of research, conducted a market assessment of Kampala.[51] This precluded knowledge of viable sectors for refugees to become skilled in, and ultimately calls the impact of trainings into question. This lack of knowledge is reflected in refugee informants' livelihoods struggles, which often centre around finding markets in which to sell their goods and services. This problem stems

---

50 Interview, InterAid Protection Officer, 16 June 2015.

51 The most recent UNHCR document related to livelihoods is the 'UNHCR operational guidelines on the minimum criteria for livelihoods programming', published in 2015. The guidelines demonstrate UNHCR's emphasis on refining livelihoods programming, and seek to establish criteria when planning, implementing, and monitoring livelihoods programmes. This includes the establishment of baseline and market assessments, and a 3–5-year context-specific livelihoods strategic plan. However, at the time of research these guidelines were not being implemented in Kampala.

from a variety of factors, including an oversaturated informal sector with few opportunities in the formal sector and, more recently at the time, barriers that the specific legal context of Kampala poses (expanded on below). The high unemployment rate and high level of poverty are crucial compounding factors. As one participant in the tailoring training explained:

> We are trying to become self-reliant but not that many of us are. We are facing many challenges. Some of us women have husbands that drink alcohol and eat the money. When we have skills like sewing, our problem is getting capital. With the savings group this is solved a little. We produce good items, good quality! We can compete with Ugandans but another problem is the markets … we cannot find the markets.[52]

Refugees' struggle to foster livelihoods was also acknowledged by livelihoods trainers and employees of JRS and other organizations, who saw their roles as helping 'enhance livelihoods' but often were not certain of training outcomes. While the JRS livelihoods coordinator stated, "Emergency help is the short-term and this is the long-term to give skills so that refugees can work",[53] when asked about the monitoring of training participants after training, the coordinator admitted that JRS had only recently begun keeping track of how many people found or created viable jobs for themselves. This was openly discussed as an important and currently missing component of demonstrating training 'impact'. This lack of data was common across all organizations interviewed, with the exception of FRC, which had undertaken a monitoring study on post-training livelihoods success. The study provided fairly positive figures, showing that 69 per cent of livelihoods groups formed through FRC are viable, 20 per cent break even, and 11 per cent collapse. It was therefore estimated that 70 per cent of refugees use the skills gained to start businesses after finishing trainings.[54] While this could be considered a significant success, it was not clear how long these businesses lasted. The majority of refugee informants interviewed who create their own informal business struggle to make regular profits, as a result of lack of capital to expand,[55] and struggle to access markets, often due in part to enforcements from the local city authorities. Therefore, while they may

52 Interview, training participant, 20 May 2015.

53 Interview, JRS Livelihoods Coordinator, 15 June 2015.

54 Interview, FRC Project Officer [2], Kampala Urban Project, 11 June 2015.

55 This is consistent with broader struggles for Africans to access capital for entrepreneurship at the time. See: Global Entrepreneurship Monitor (2015) '2014 Global Report'. GEM. Available at: https://www.gemconsortium.org/report/gem-2014-global-report (accessed 22 February 2022).

have businesses in some form, they do not necessarily have successful or sustainable businesses that generate enough income to meet basic needs or anything beyond them.

Access to markets and capital

The barriers to creating livelihoods after trainings that many refugees cited demonstrates the importance of national and local contexts in the fostering of self-reliance. The struggle for refugees to access markets across sectors in Kampala is exemplified by refugees engaged in arts and crafts, as many organizations and refugee informants cited this business area as 'non-essential' and dominated by Ugandans. Craft skills' lack of practical applicability was explained by one Sudanese refugee, who stated, "These goods are the extras, but here people do not have money for extras, for beautiful things". A UNHCR Livelihoods Officer echoed this, writing, 'I would also be critical of organisations and projects that pursue handicrafts. Unless the project is a major tourism destination, which Uganda is not, we are merely "trinketif[ying]" an entire workforce and providing occupational therapy to people.'

Despite this, arts and crafts trainings were offered by all organizations interviewed, and are very popular for female refugees in particular. Arts and crafts trainings occur three to five times a week for three to six months, depending on the programme. They often focus on learning how to make paper bead jewellery, purses, shoes, sisal earrings, and cloth bangles. The knowledge that refugees gain in these trainings is vast, yet many refugees post-training – even three years later – are unable to make a livelihood from this. Many are discouraged and frustrated. Barriers are faced at different stages, depending on the amount of capital they start with. Some struggle to buy enough material to make even one handbag, and have formed groups to combat this lack of capital. However, once made, profits must be shared among group members, which also proves challenging.

Other refugees interviewed are able to buy material and make products, but struggle to sell them. This is due to various factors, such as lack of English skills, an exclusion from trade shows and exhibitions due to xenophobia, and not having a registered business with a storefront.[56] Registering businesses in permanent locations is a multifaceted and important factor in job success and livelihoods creations in Kampala. Refugees from all sectors believe that they could sell more products and market themselves better if they were able to rent a small stall or container, simply because their business would then have a 'face'. Despite their desires, this is impossible for most, as they

[56] Interviews, Refugee Informants 19–30, 1 May 2015–30 June 2015.

lack the capital to pay three months of rent upfront and organizations rarely offer this form of tangible support post-training.

Eugenie, a charismatic Rwandan woman and JRS arts and crafts trainer, was trained in making jewellery and handbags after she arrived in Kampala in 2008. She explains the informal way that she was able to gain a formal job as a livelihoods trainer:

> I made a friend who helped me learn these skills, and then another friend who charged me only 300 Ugandan shillings to teach me. After the training, this friend gave me beads, pliers, and metal clips so that I could make these on my own. I made 20 necklaces at a time and started selling them to door-to-door at people's houses and their offices. The money I made, I saved some, bought food, and left the rest to buy more jewellery [material] … I started my own jewellery making group for lady refugees, and then in September 2010 was asked by JRS to become a trainer for crafts.[57]

A rare success story herself, Eugenie now teaches arts and crafts at JRS every weekday morning from 8.30 to 12.30 pm to 30 students, who undertake eight-week training courses. Her current class is comprised of 22 students, 12 women and 10 men. She feels frustrated by how hard it is for her students to find work and sell wares after their training: "Since 2011 I have trained over 150 students and in my heart I feel it is useless. We need to help raise our voices where we are not: How can we make money through art, get capacity-building skills, and a permanent exhibition?"[58]

This quote illustrates the breadth of support refugees need in order to create viable businesses, ranging from networks ("We need to help raise our voices where we are not") to skills training to sustainable forms of marketing. However, Eugenie also attributes some of the failure of her students' livelihoods to the structure of assistance, which she perceives as largely corrupt and exclusive of refugees:

> Right now aid goes from the 50th floor to the 1st. We don't want that … It's time for people from abroad to come and work with us directly. Because we're not working with InterAid, OPM [Office of the Prime Minister] … we're not. They'll make budgets and budgets but no money will reach refugees.[59]

57 Interview, Eugenie, JRS Livelihoods trainer, 12 June 2015.
58 Interview, Eugenie, 12 June 2015.
59 Interview, Eugenie, 12 June 2015.

Rather than truly build on refugees' capacities, such as supporting them in translating certificates of existing skills, or ensuring that entrepreneurs are equipped with capital and market access after trainings, she feels that organizations are offering livelihoods trainings that often leave refugees in equally vulnerable situations to those they were in before. In this way, those actors tasked with helping refugees foster self-reliance are instead perceived as utilizing the concept to gain funding for themselves.

Local authorities and livelihoods

In addition to teaching at JRS, Eugenie has a registered arts business that she would like to become a permanent workshop. She takes skilled former students and pays for their labour, and then seeks to sell their goods. Every other Saturday, the group gathers on Eugenie's living room floor, beading necklaces and stitching handbags while they discuss business challenges and next steps. Discussions with this group revealed a lack of access to capital and to markets as their main challenge. Members described an additional, new barrier to accessing markets in the form of crackdowns on informal work in Kampala. In contrast to when Eugenie first began selling goods door-to-door, refugees and other petty traders are now restricted from selling wares informally around the city. For people striving to make their income through selling small pieces of jewellery or handbags, this is especially challenging as they do not earn enough to formally register businesses and thus to become 'legal' sellers.

In 2011, the Kampala City Council Authority (KCCA) created a law that prohibits the selling of goods in public spaces without a business licence or petty trading (hawker) permit. The KCCA law is applied equally to refugees and nationals. More stringently enforced in 2014, KCCA officials move through Kampala in plain clothes, stopping street sellers and at best confiscating their goods or fining them, or at worst imprisoning them. This formerly took place only in the city centre, but at the time of research increasingly occurred in all areas of Kampala.

This has heavily impacted both refugees and nationals. The majority of refugees survive through the informal sector and still attempt to sell their products on the street, because they feel they have no other option. Many echoed the sentiment of one informant, who stated, "I still go to sell, but I am fearing. KCCA comes … they take all from you, they beat you … sometimes you go to prison."[60] Indeed, the behaviour of KCCA has become violent enough that a local organization, African Centre for Treatment and Rehabilitation of Torture Victims (ACTV), held a one-day awareness

[60] Interview, KCCA refugee informant, 10 May 2015.

training in 2015 with 30 KCCA law-enforcement officials on the concept of torture and the anti-torture law.

The challenge that KCCA poses also extends to organizations helping refugees. As one FRC employee stated, "KCCA is one of our biggest problems we face in our livelihoods section". To exemplify this, she explained that half of the businesses run by women belonging to a FRC-sponsored savings group were demolished in December 2014:

> In Kisenyi [a neighbourhood in Kampala] KCCA demolished the roadside businesses of these women. They were selling vegetables and fruit, jewellery, dried fish. They do not make enough to rent a small shack so they just sit on the ground and sell like many others. But KCCA came and destroyed. … It was very demoralizing and traumatic for these ladies, and some were even beaten and chased away. Now they struggle to repay their loans to the savings group, which means the whole group suffers. They do not know what to do, and they come to us for help but we are also constrained … we talk with other NGOs and are trying to make a new strategy but it is hard when this is the law.[61]

Organizational responses to the KCCA law vary. The issue has grown pressing enough that the Refugee Law Project (RLP) has held a series of stakeholder meetings with KCCA, in an attempt to negotiate and highlight the challenges this law posed to refugee informal business owners. KCCA had not previously known that refugees were among the business owners in Kampala. However, while sympathetic, KCCA insisted that any exceptions were impossible. Instead, certain days where it is 'legal' to sell on the streets have been declared, but these average only a few days a month at most and therefore offer very few the chance to make a livelihood solely in this way. These meetings also discussed creating gazetted areas where people, including refugees, could legally sell goods, such as the large Usafi market in town. However, the promised construction of six modern markets to provide legal selling space to vendors across Kampala has yet to materialize. Although refugees had different reactions to the idea of selling in markets, many worried that it still would not be viable, due either to competition or a lack of customers.

InterAid also reported that 25 refugees who had been assisted by them in starting livelihoods were arrested and detained in 2015 for hawking in the city centre. It planned to address the barrier posed by KCCA through renting out several stalls for refugees in local markets and paying the first

[61] Interview, FRC Project Officer, Kampala Urban Project, 10 June 2015.

three months of rent. FRC has dealt with the challenge by paying for the licences of three livelihoods groups for one year. Although helpful for some refugees, neither of these options is sustainable for these organizations on a wider scale, particularly given their limited funding for livelihoods programming. Discussions with KCCA have included negotiating a reduced licence fee for refugees; this seems helpful on a wider basis yet it is unclear if it will materialize.

Overall, for the refugees of Kampala, KCCA represents one of the biggest barriers to creating sustainable small businesses – and, thus, to becoming self-reliant. The members of Eugenie's business discussed the near impossibility of sustainable livelihoods through arts and crafts given the risks of hawking jewellery. As one participant explained, "We can make good money with just a few nice necklaces if we can move freely ... I used to go to big businesses and sell to ladies at lunchtime but now I get chased."[62]

The result of KCCA enforcement is the constraint of selling space for refugees and vulnerable nationals in Kampala. InterAid estimates that 95 per cent of refugee businesses are unregistered, partially due to the burdensome and expensive process of business registration. In order to become a registered business, refugees must undergo an often lengthy process of paperwork, which averages around 225,000 Ugandan shillings (about $75 USD). This registration fee is in addition to the costs of renting a selling space, for which paying three months of rent upfront is standard. The cost of rent generally ranges from 250,000 ($70 USD) to 750,000 ($200 USD) Ugandan shillings. However, it is impossible for many urban refugees to obtain their own space to sell from, as many struggle to earn even the public school fee of 10,000 Ugandan shillings per term (approximately $3 USD).

Fostering livelihoods, promoting protection?

Ultimately, KCCA's law infringes on the protection space available to refugees in Kampala. This is especially relevant for female refugees, as hawking jewellery, fruit, and clothes are common livelihoods for women. Rukiko, a Congolese woman from Goma, seeks to circumvent KCCA's law by selling most of her goods while walking through neighbourhoods at night. She has been in Kampala with her husband and four daughters for five years. Her husband was a businessman who owned a general store in Goma and travelled regionally for trade; Rukiko was the store manager. However, the government kidnapped her husband for four years and, although he was released, he remains in hiding in Kampala. This means that Rukiko is the family's sole breadwinner. She strives to do this by selling jewellery and other

62 Interview, Arts and crafts business member, 10 May 2015.

small goods around Kampala, but stopped doing so during the day after her wares were taken twice by KCCA. While selling at night, she was recently raped by two Ugandans. Despite this, she continues to sell jewellery and hairnets in the evening, as this is the only way she can support her family.

Local and international discourses on self-reliance

Despite immensely challenging situations such as that experienced by Rukiko and her family, the discourse used by both refugee participants and organizations regarding refugee livelihoods in Kampala largely echo guiding policy documents on the topic, such as trainings constituting a key step to self-reliance. Participants perceived trainings as a way to learn new skills to help them survive in Kampala; as one refugee explained, "The livelihoods training is to give us knowledge on how to becom[e] self-reliant. Knowledge on how to create an income generating activity". An FRC employee explained the role of trainings similarly:

> We are trying to reduce poverty here through self-reliance. Trainings are one way to do this because refugees can strengthen their business skills and manage the competition of Kampala. We want to give new skills to people, who were maybe farmers before but fear being in settlements and can't grow crops in the city. They need to learn something new to survive here.[63]

Interview responses overall demonstrate that livelihoods trainings are perceived by participants, trainers, and other members of organizations as useful for the fostering of refugee self-reliance. Some organizational staff qualified positive statements, such as the UNHCR officer who expressed doubt about the value of arts and crafts trainings, yet none suggested trainings be replaced with other forms of livelihoods support.

However, due to the local context of constrained informal work in Kampala, the value of these livelihoods trainings – which largely teach skills for the informal labour market – as well as the level of responsibility of organizations promoting 'illegal' work are called into question. Indeed, one significant point of departure from the contemporaneous global discourse on refugee self-reliance at the local level in Kampala is the lack of discussion by training participants on these trainings as contributing to their 'dignity' and 'protection'. Instead, participants from all areas seek training to gain or improve their livelihoods, and cite paying for food, rent, and school fees as predominant reasons for needing to earn money. In this way, many refugees'

[63] Interview, FRC Project Officer, Kampala Urban Project, 10 June 2015.

aim of joining a livelihoods training is humble: survival to makes ends meet in the city. Interestingly, the main necessities refugees cited as aiming to buy through income generated from training skills are those covered by the international community in camps and settlements: food, shelter, and education. This suggests that livelihoods trainings merely – and in the best case – help refugees secure basic necessities rather than increase protection or significantly advance their income or career.

Non-economic benefits of livelihoods trainings

Although organizational employees were generally evasive about the outcome of livelihoods trainings for refugees, they were quick to cite benefits aside from the direct applicability of trainings. One repeated example was the importance of the certificates awarded upon completion of a livelihoods training. These certificates are useful documents for demonstrating skills and are often one of the only forms of documentation that refugees have in displacement. An FRC employee mentioned, for example, several refugees who had returned to the organization to personally thank her, stating that attaching copies of training certificates to CVs had helped them secure jobs.[64] This demonstrates the value of helping refugees gain 'institutional' recognition of any kind, which can be an important means to help them enter the formal sector.

Even when refugees are unable to develop viable livelihoods directly after trainings, all participants cited the positive effects of trainings on their lives. Trainings provided refugees with a structure for their day, a chance to make friends and form networks, and a way to feel supported in starting a new life in a foreign place. Theories on integration and social interactions emphasize the importance of creating social connection within and between groups,[65] which livelihoods trainings provide through creating spaces for refugees to meet each other. Their social and psychosocial effects, therefore, may well be significant – although it is due to other often unmaterialized promises that refugees join livelihoods trainings at all.

The disappointing gap between refugee livelihoods' rhetoric and reality

Efforts to assist refugees in entering Kampala's market are fraught with myriad challenges and contradictions, and ultimately represent a disappointing gap

64 Interview, FRC Training Officer, 7 June 2015.

65 Ager, A. and Strang, A. (2008) 'Understanding integration: a conceptual framework', *Journal of Refugee Studies* 21(2): 166–191; see also: Putnam (2002) *Democracies in Flux: The evolution of social capital in contemporary society.* Oxford: Oxford University Press, p 5.

between the rhetoric of refugee self-reliance and its on-the-ground reality. A lack of understanding of this reality, under-resourced programmes, and limited attempts to investigate the impact of trainings (likely due in part to limited programme funding) mean that livelihoods trainings appear to rarely achieve their purported intention of refugees' successful livelihoods creation. This was apparent in statements by informants, who commonly lamented their inability to create jobs that could cover the cost of food, rent, and educational supplies for their children, as well as by many livelihoods trainers within organizations, who are at best unsure or at worst disillusioned with their students' livelihoods prospects. Yet without a means to access substantial material support from the international humanitarian community, urban refugees are reliant on the help they can receive – even when it does not go far enough to be helpful, or reflects larger trends of dubious outcomes, as further discussed here.

The gap between the rhetoric and reality of fostering livelihoods is further evident when refugees' livelihoods in Kampala are compared with a suite of UNHCR guiding documents on refugee self-reliance, which frame self-reliance and livelihoods as both a right and a tool to prevent the derogation of other rights.[66] This discourse presents refugee self-reliance as a natural state offering security and well-being to refugees. As UNHCR writes, '[Livelihoods activities] provid[e] goods and services to a market economy based on cash exchange or barter. Work provides the basis for their food security and self-reliance, *adding stability, prosperity and peace to the community at large*'[67] [emphasis added]. In this view, work leads not only to self-reliance but regional security and community cohesion, thereby benefiting host countries as well as refugees. However, while the potential benefits of self-reliance appear to be expansive, at a declaratory policy level, the concept of self-reliance has become progressively narrower in the 21st century than earlier definitions, more focused on individual economic rather than on communal, social (or political) dimensions.

Indeed, although UNHCR documents discuss the challenges, barriers, and limits to supporting refugee self-reliance, nowhere is the merit of introducing refugees to markets questioned. Instead, refugees are touted as a

---

[66] Documents include: UNHCR (2005) *Handbook for Self-Reliance*. Geneva: UNHCR; UNHCR (2011) 'Livelihood programming in UNHCR: operational guidelines'. Geneva: UNHCR; UNHCR (2011) 'Encouraging self-reliance'. Geneva: UNHCR; UNHCR (2011) 'Promoting livelihoods and self-reliance: operational guidance on refugee protection and solutions in urban areas'. Geneva: UNHCR; UNHCR (2014) 'Global strategy implementation report'. Geneva: UNHCR; UNHCR (2014) '2014–2018 global strategy for livelihoods'. Geneva: UNHCR; UNHCR (2015) 'Operational guidelines on the minimum criteria for livelihoods programming'. Geneva: UNHCR.

[67] UNHCR, '2014–2018 global strategy for livelihoods', p 7.

means to 'enhance local markets' while livelihoods programmes themselves 'will strive to strengthen the local market by providing an injection of labour, consumers, and traders'.[68] A main aim of the UNHCR's 2014–2018 Global Strategy for Livelihoods, for example, is to '[i]dentify new markets and value chains for agricultural products, assist producers in production and marketing'.[69] Thus, a focus on linking refugees to markets is consistent regardless of the nature of their work. For several years the drop-down menu of UNHCR's Livelihoods webpage offered readers the opportunity to learn about 'safe value chains', 'wage employment', 'micro, small and medium enterprises', the 'graduation approach', and 'private sector engagement', thereby similarly presenting livelihoods assistance as a means to introduce individual refugees to markets, finance, and business.[70] Refugees participate in urban market engagement in an era premised on the modern urbanization of capital in part through urban entrepreneurialism,[71] thus illustrating the wider trends that refugee self-reliance exists within. While some scholarship has critically examined this premise, such as discussing those refugees who, due to disability, discrimination, or other circumstances, will likely never be able to be financially independent,[72] this is rarely broached in documents at the time.

The concept of refugee self-reliance has also remained explicitly linked to aid reduction, as we saw in the case of Afghan refugees toward the end of the Cold War. In the 2011 UNHCR operational guidelines, for instance, staff were reminded that any cash or food assistance should 'be short-term and conditional and gradually lead to self-reliance activities'.[73] Ensconced in this rhetoric is an enduring condemnation of dependency on humanitarian assistance. In 2015, for example, former UNHCR Deputy High Commissioner Alexander Aleinikoff published a policy brief entitled 'From dependence to self-reliance', which focused on 'changing the paradigm in protracted refugee situations'. This illustrates a simplistic and problematic binary of self-reliance and dependency which assumes that

---

68 UNHCR, '2014–2018 global strategy for livelihoods', p 11.

69 UNHCR, 'Global strategy for livelihoods', p 28.

70 UNHCR (2018) Livelihoods. Webpage. Available at: www.unhcr.org/uk/livelihoods.html (accessed 14 September 2018).

71 Harvey, D. (1985) *The Urbanization of Capital: Studies in the history and theory of capitalist urbanization*. Baltimore, MD: Johns Hopkins University Press; Moreno, L. and Bang Shin, H. (2018) 'Introduction: the urban process under planetary accumulation by dispossession'. *City* 22(1): 78–87.

72 Easton-Calabria, E. and Omata, N. (2018) 'Panacea for the refugee crisis? Rethinking the promotion of self-reliance for refugees'. *Third World Quarterly* 39(8): 1458–1474.

73 UNHCR (2011) 'Promoting livelihoods and self-reliance: operational guidance on refugee protection and solutions in urban areas'. Geneva: UNHCR.

dependency should naturally progress to self-reliance, as also explored in the previous chapter.

Refugees as urban market subjects

Rather than achieving self-reliance with 'dignity' after participating in livelihoods trainings, refugees in Kampala often end up in informal work, which may be exploitative or dangerous and usually is not lucrative enough to bring them out of poverty. Despite working, refugees struggle to pay rent, feed their families, and send their children to school – in short, to meet the basic necessities that comprise UNHCR's definition of 'livelihoods': the means through which refugees 'secure the basic necessities of life, such as food, water, shelter and clothing'.[74] Indeed, through the practice of offering livelihoods trainings to refugees in urban areas instead of material items, humanitarian assistance becomes linked to work rather than to 'hand-outs'. In this way, refugees are supported to rely not on the international community for assistance but instead on the market itself.

This echoes ongoing practices of self-reliance assistance from the previous century but also holds specific parallels to contemporaneous trends in broader welfare assistance in the US and UK, which seek to relieve national welfare programmes of beneficiaries through similarly supporting citizens to work, sometimes to the point of making benefits contingent on this. This includes the American 1998 Workforce Investment Act, which aimed to implement programmes to prepare youth and unskilled adults to enter the workforce,[75] and the UK's 2012 Welfare Reform, which sought to reduce welfare spending, in part through increasing employment training and opportunities.[76] These agendas were bolstered by a rhetoric of dignity through work. UK Prime Minister David Cameron stated, for example, "Compassion isn't measured out in benefit cheques – it's in the chances you

[74] UNHCR, 'Global strategy for livelihoods', p 7.

[75] US Government (1998) Workforce Investment Act of 1998. Public Law 105-220-Aug 7. Available at: www.congress.gov/105/plaws/publ220/PLAW-105publ220.pdf (accessed 1 August 2018).

[76] Critiquing the contemporary concept of 'workfare' in UK politics, which originally meant reforms forcing welfare claimants to work in exchange for benefits, Grover (2003) writes, for example:

> 'workfarism' [now] represents a reorientation of social policy to make it more 'in tune' with neoliberal growth, for example, the facilitation of flexible labour markets through social policy in the pursuit of a competitive edge in global markets. In this sense social policy has become central to economic restructuring aimed at supporting 'free' markets, rather than being concerned with protecting universal rights that were associated with Keynesianism. p 18.

give people. The chance to get a job."[77] Such statements – also present in US discourse at the time[78] – encapsulate the role of education and training in what has been termed 'enterprise culture'. As Peters writes,

> At one and the same time enterprise culture provides the means for analysis and the prescription for change: education and training are key sectors in promoting national economic competitive advantage and future national prosperity. They are seen increasingly as *the passport for welfare recipients to make the transition from dependent, passive welfare consumer to an entrepreneurial self.*[79] [emphasis added]

Self-reliance assistance for refugees through livelihoods trainings operates in a similar way, promoting the training of individual refugees as entrepreneurs, rather than, for example, facilitating their entry into formal markets through recertification or expanded professional employment options. This reflects the neoliberal tenets of individualism and entrepreneurialism, as well as emphasizes the responsibility of refugees to support themselves through their own job creation. Similar to the discussion of Afghans in Pakistan in the previous chapter, refugees are encouraged to become independent market subjects integrated into local economies.

Lack of practical steps to support individual refugee self-reliance

Self-reliance assistance for refugees in Kampala frames refugees as small-scale market subjects in the informal sector who become self-reliant through entrepreneurship and pose no threat to Kampala's limited formal market. Yet the irony of this stance is the lack of practical steps offered to refugees in Kampala to enter and compete successfully in the local market. Notably, there is a lack of market assessments by organizations to determine which livelihoods trainings might most effectively offer viable livelihoods. The paucity of follow-up support in the form of micro-finance to refugee entrepreneurs post-training is also striking given research on non-displaced

77 *The Telegraph* (2012) 'David Cameron's welfare speech in full'. 25 June. Available at: www.telegraph.co.uk/news/politics/david-cameron/9354163/David-Camerons-welfare-speech-in-full.html (accessed 15 September 2018).

78 As Speaker of the US House of Representatives Paul Ryan stated, "Our goal must be to help people move from welfare into work and self-sufficiency". See Tirado, L. (2015) 'America's "welfare state" is shameful: the UK shouldn't follow our lead'. *The Guardian*, 18 November. Available at: www.theguardian.com/politics/2015/nov/18/us-welfare-shameful-uk-public-services-private-profit (accessed 1 September 2018).

79 Peters, M. (2001) 'Education, enterprise culture and the entrepreneurial self'. *Journal of Educational Enquiry* 2(2): 58–71 (p 60).

populations indicating that the level of start-up capital is a strong predictor of business success.[80] As non-nationals, refugees face more barriers than nationals in accessing formal finance, meaning that access to capital through entities such as aid and development agencies becomes more necessary. Yet despite awareness of refugees' need for loans and grants in order to start or grow businesses, such capital access by refugee-serving organizations remains inadequate in Kampala.[81] This lack of practical support to better enable successful refugee entrepreneurship is compounded by a lack of widespread programming to help refugees access markets or address significant barriers such as efforts to formalize the local economy through restrictions enforced by KCCA.

The structural factors of self-reliance

The result is limited efforts to truly help refugees competitively enter the local market. Problematically, the emphasis on refugees as individuals and entrepreneurs ultimately places the onus of self-reliance and economic mobility solely on themselves, minimizing the structural factors of poverty that refugees encounter in host countries the world over. Indeed, much of the growing criticism or at least scepticism of self-reliance as a policy arises out of a recognition that refugee self-reliance (broadly understood in this context as some level of economic independence) is not 'achieved' in a vacuum. Research undertaken by Zetter and Ruaudel indicates that many of the world's refugees are unable to fully exercise their right to work due to restrictive host governments which are reluctant to allow refugees to enter labour markets due to a fear that refugees will take away jobs available to citizens.[82]

These considerable legal and political constraints are often not adequately reflected in the implementation of self-reliance and livelihoods assistance for refugees. Instead UNHCR and other relief agencies tend to approach the

---

80 See Bates, T. (1997) *Race, Self-employment, and Upward Mobility*. Baltimore, MD: Johns Hopkins University Press; Fairlie, R. W. and Robb, A. (2008) *Race and Entrepreneurial Success: Black-, Asian-, and White-owned businesses in the United States*. Cambridge, MA: MIT Press.

81 For more on the provision of micro-finance loans in refugee contexts, see: Easton-Calabria, E. and Omata, N. (2016) 'Micro-finance in refugee contexts: current scholarship and research gaps'. Refugee Studies Centre (RSC) Working Paper Series No. 116. Oxford: University of Oxford. For more on micro-finance groups in Kampala run and led by refugees themselves, see: Easton-Calabria, E. and Hakiza, R. (2020) 'In the interest of saving: refugee-led micro-finance in Kampala, Uganda'. *Development Policy Review.*

82 Zetter, R. and Ruaudel, H. (2016) 'Refugees' right to work and access to labor markets – an assessment. Part I: Synthesis (Preliminary)'. KNOMAD Working Paper and Study Series. Washington, DC: World Bank.

issue of livelihoods and self-reliance from a technical perspective without taking appropriate steps to account for the constraints on refugees' rights and entitlements.[83] Patricia Ward writes that the problem of self-reliance is primarily one of application because 'achieving self-reliance is case-dependent on the political and social context of the country [of] asylum' and refugees' ability to access' those rights.[84] While the international discourse on refugee self-reliance discusses fostering livelihoods as a means to increase refugee protection, and thus for UNHCR to fulfil its mandate, stories detailing the destruction of refugees' livelihoods by KCCA echo Ward's findings, demonstrating the significant extent to which local contexts influence the attainment of refugee livelihoods and self-reliance, and ultimately their protection.

While practical implementation is undoubtedly important – such as providing livelihood trainings – the provision of self reliance assistance makes sense only when refugees have enabling environments to pursue economic autonomy. Indeed, the environment in which trainings in Kampala take place does not necessarily support refugees' 'entrepreneurial selves'[85] to emerge. Despite the generous laws that Uganda affords refugees, livelihoods opportunities for refugees in Kampala are so constrained that InterAid projects that refugees will begin leaving the city within one to two years. It was explained that, "[L]ife in Kampala is growing more expensive. The cost of living is growing, and these new by-laws of KCCA are also pushing people away. We [InterAid] expect that soon many refugees may not be able to manage life in Kampala."[86] This is particularly significant given that Uganda is considered one of the best places for refugees to live in the world.[87]

The structural constraints faced by refugees in creating livelihoods in Kampala are reminiscent of the legal environment that impeded refugee 'empowerment' and 'self-reliance' before the 2006 Refugee Act was passed. These restrictions serve as a reminder that refugee livelihoods and self-reliance depend on access to resources and networks, which institutions, laws, and policies inhibit or engender. Indeed, these challenges evoke Meyer's 2006

---

83 Omata, N. (2013) 'Repatriation and integration of Liberian refugees from Ghana: the importance of personal networks in the country of origin'. *Journal of Refugee Studies* 26(2): 265–282.

84 Ward, P. (2014) 'Refugee cities: reflections on the development and impact of UNHCR urban refugee policy in the Middle East'. *Refugee Survey Quarterly* 33(1): 77–93 (p 79). Available at: https://academic.oup.com/rsq/article-abstract/33/1/77/1570430. (accessed 29 June 2018).

85 Peters, 'Education, enterprise culture and the entrepreneurial self'.

86 Interview, InterAid Protection Officer, 20 May 2015.

87 Hattem, J. (2017) 'Uganda may be best place in the world to be a refugee. But that could change without more money'. *The Washington Post*, 20 June. Available at: https://tinyurl.com/ycfryldz (accessed 15 September 2018).

critique of the SRS, which centred on an approach that 'proposes refugee empowerment without taking into account the social, political and economic context'.[88] This is particularly problematic as members of national and international organizations – and even refugees themselves – stressed the importance of livelihoods creation as a means to access basic necessities, including food, shelter, and education. In this way, engagement in Kampala's local market becomes a substitute for a functioning social welfare system – or for the provision of assistance and protection by international organizations such as UNHCR.

Self-reliance and quality of life

This reflects one of the problematic paradoxes of current refugee livelihoods and self-reliance programmes: the lack of discussion on the quality of life afforded to those who become 'self-reliant'. Duffield critiques broader development interventions in supporting populations to achieve only a limited level of improvement in life circumstances, writing:

> [O]ne of the problems is that for the non-insured humanity, international intervention in support of the underdeveloped state promises little. What are being reconstructed are *human* security rather than forms of *social* security states. Compared to the welfare safety-nets and social insurance of consumer society, the future being scripted for the larger part of humanity is a more basic non-material stasis of self-reliance.[89]

The perpetuation of this 'basic … statis of self-reliance' is further evident in Kampala through what organizations are *not* doing to foster refugee self-reliance: rather than providing refugees with both material and livelihoods support, helping refugees gain access to the formal market through offering trainings in areas necessitating highly skilled workers, or significantly addressing structural barriers to entrepreneurship, organizations provide trainings in low-skilled sectors offering generally small financial returns and fail to help refugees in a widespread manner beyond these trainings. The level of interest in the welfare of these refugees is debatable given the fact that the impact of trainings is only rarely tracked by these organizations. This calls into question the ultimate aim of livelihoods support to refugees in Kampala and the interests they actually serve.

---

88 Meyer, 'The "refugee aid and development" approach in Uganda', p 22.

89 Duffield, M. (2008) 'Global civil war: the non-insured, international containment and post-interventionary society'. *Journal of Refugee Studies* 21(2): 145–165 (p 161).

The instrumentalization of refugee self-reliance assistance

Refugees become instrumentalized by the international donor community through livelihoods training themselves when the outcome they are intended to create remains at odds with the reality of refugees' lives in their aftermath. The global discourse on refugee self-reliance and the local discourse surrounding livelihoods trainings in Kampala largely align in that both put forth intentions for refugees to become self-reliant through market engagement. However, to assume that simply providing livelihoods trainings is enough to foster self-reliance is to ignore the significant – and increasing – barriers to employment that many refugees in Kampala and elsewhere face. Framing these trainings as a reasonable step toward self-reliance runs the risk of providing aid organizations with a justification for reducing assistance to long-term refugees – without the economic structures, policies, or protection measures in place to truly foster self-reliance. UNHCR writes, 'Investing in livelihoods activities helps reduce the costs associated with the provision of aid and protection'.[90] While saving funds is not inherently problematic, the provision of trainings without corresponding support or evidence-based research becomes a cost-effective exit strategy which leaves refugees without follow-up support and programmes, and ultimately at the 'mercy' of the market.

If a main intended outcome of livelihoods trainings is to save international organizations money, then it may not be problematic for donors that trainings in Kampala rarely match market demand and lack the necessary follow-up of capital investment or market access. After receiving livelihoods training, refugees often remain in Kampala and struggle to become self-reliant, thus relieving the industrialized North of the 'burden' of these refugees crossing into their countries and either entering the economy or 'draining' social services.

The manifestation of refugee self-reliance assistance as (limited) support to individual refugee entrepreneurs in need of skills training to foster livelihoods also sidesteps critical conversations between donor countries of the Global North and the refugee-hosting countries of the Global South regarding refugees' rights in exile and quality of life – which in turn links to wider discussions on the international asymmetry of global refugee burden- and responsibility-sharing. Given donor countries' disinterest in widening channels to receive asylum seekers in their own countries, it is no wonder that the Government of Uganda is also lauded internationally through the enabling environment it provides refugees, and thus receives funding and positive acclaim it may otherwise not accrue. In this way, the very concept

[90] UNHCR (2015) 'Livelihoods'. Available at: http://www.regionaldss.org/wp-content/uploads/2017/09/TCM-Dev-Jacobsen-FINAL.pdf (accessed 29 April 2022).

of refugee self-reliance is also instrumentalized for the benefit of maintaining asymmetrical refugee-hosting arrangements that benefit donor governments and particular refugee-hosting countries (or at least government officials within them) rather than refugees themselves.

Conclusion

When we examine the global rhetoric of refugee self-reliance assistance and how it is implemented at the local level in Kampala, we see that livelihoods are presented as one important pathway to self-reliance but fall short of offering the security and economic stability that discourse commonly espouses. The livelihoods trainings offered to refugees provide them with skills but not with start-up capital or access to the markets they need to create viable businesses. Livelihoods trainings in Kampala are under-resourced and largely unsuitable for the local economy. The livelihoods programming of refugee-serving organizations also does not adequately address the local law enforced by KCCA of registering businesses and only selling goods with proper licences.

Refugee participants are assumed to be able to become entrepreneurs after trainings but generally lack the necessary follow-up support to create sustainable livelihoods. Many remain unemployed or with haphazard livelihoods, and thus face little to no improvement in welfare upon completion of a training. The 'mismatch' of skills that these trainings offer, combined with the lack of investment in necessary resources for entrepreneurship represent at best negligence by organizations and at worst the undertaking of programming without the expectation of impact – in other words, the use of livelihoods trainings as a cost-effective exit strategy that mainly benefits international humanitarian and development agencies seeking to reduce the financial burden of protracted refugee situations and avoid uncomfortable discussions with host country governments regarding refugee rights and wider responsibility-sharing. Yet in the current age of globalization, high unemployment, and growing informalization in the Global South, it is little wonder that livelihoods trainings cannot live up to their rhetoric. Instead, as the case of urban refugee livelihoods trainings in Kampala demonstrates, the 'fostering' of refugee self-reliance is ultimately the normalization of urban refugees living at the mercy of the market – largely unassisted, impoverished, and confined to informal work with few chances for upward economic mobility.

6

Livelihoods 2.0? Refugee Self-Reliance and the Digital Gig Economy

> Enabling refugees' resilience goes hand-in-hand with achieving durable solutions. … Better self-reliance means refugees and host communities are better able to meet their essential needs, enjoy their human rights and live with dignity.[1]

Introduction

Evident to those of us engaged in refugee humanitarian and development work, and to many Europeans and refugees overall, 2015 marked a turning point in the wider contemporary recognition of refugee issues. The so-called 'European refugee crisis', wherein a record 1.3 million forcibly displaced people sought asylum in Europe in 2015 alone, has received large-scale attention and significant amounts of funding. It also arguably led to the political watershed of the 2016 New York Declaration, the Comprehensive Refugee Response Framework (CRRF), and ultimately to the 2018 Global Compact on Refugees, the world's newest instantiation of responsibility-sharing and cohesive responses to refugee flows.

This chapter has little to do with this. Instead, it is concerned with a related but parallel, still nascent movement in refugee livelihoods and self-reliance. Indeed, in many ways its focus is on changes still to come rather than what is already fully fledged. This chapter's subject is the so-called new world of work and how refugees are – and are not – involved in it. The so-called European refugee crisis is important in terms of larger political agenda-setting, which has continued the restrictionist and anti-immigrant

[1] UNHCR (2020) 'Global report'. Geneva: UNHCR, p 110.

trend arguably more present since the 1980s. The primary character in this chapter, Alaa, is also a Syrian refugee originally displaced due to the war that led so many others to flee first throughout the Middle East and then onwards to Europe. And the COVID-19 pandemic, while only peripherally present here, assuredly plays a role in the ongoing reality of digital work today.

Indeed, the nature of work is vastly changing for people around the globe. In the age of COVID-19, remote work has changed from constituting a luxury for a few to a public health strategy for the masses. Yet changes in the world of work had already started long before the pandemic. As the many reports on the future of work[2] indicate, the rise of gig economies and innovations in technology, AI, and robotics are some drivers of this change. While these phrases may seem flashy, zero-hour contracts and jobs without rights and benefits attached to them are on the rise, while at the same time automation could displace up to 30 per cent of existing workers by 2030, affecting 800 million people.[3] The increasing conversion of work into digital form – a process known as *digitalization* – has myriad effects on society and presents both opportunities and challenges for us all.

A broad range of types of digital work exist, ranging from simple image categorization for AI learning to high-skill online consulting. Common types of work and ways to access digital skills and livelihoods include online work platforms; graphic design, web design, and coding schools; e-commerce platforms; and language and translation businesses. At the most basic level, NGOs offer refugees basic ICT training and digital literacy to undertake digital work, while at the most advanced, refugees are supported to enter highly competitive digital markets via online work or e-commerce platforms as freelancers and entrepreneurs, or else employed directly by corporations and social enterprises.

This chapter focuses on the intersection of this new world of work with efforts by humanitarian and development actors to foster refugee self-reliance, with a particular focus on the role and outcomes of these actors in mediating the relationship between refugees and digital economies. It draws on research spanning 2019–2020, including a scoping study identifying over 100 digital work initiatives for refugees around the world and 35 semi-structured qualitative interviews with members of humanitarian, development, and

[2] See, for example, reports from the ILO's Future of Work Centenary initiative on technology and jobs, the World Economic Forum's Future of Jobs Report, and the Oxford Internet Institute's iLabour project, particularly their online labour index.

[3] McKinsey & Company (2017) 'Jobs lost, jobs gained: what the future of work will mean for jobs, skills, and wages'. 28 November. Available at: www.mckinsey.com/featured-insights/future-of-work/jobs-lost-jobs-gained-what-the-future-of-work-will-mean-for-jobs-skills-and-wages.

private sector organizations leading these programmes.[4] The following sections review the context that these initiatives take place within, followed by a case study of one refugee's digital livelihood, and an overview of the landscape of digital work for refugees. The discussion raises key questions and concerns for the humanitarian and development community to address as efforts to foster refugee self-reliance through digital work continues.

'Enhancing' refugee self-reliance and digital access

> The Syria crisis has highlighted the need for new approaches to livelihoods and self-reliance and for possibilities for promoting the inclusion of refugees in the formal labour sector, particularly in countries where refugees are present in large numbers.

As this quote from a 2016 UNHCR Executive Committee (ExComm) document – aptly titled 'Livelihoods and self-reliance' – illustrates,[5] the large-scale displacement of Syrians in 2015–2016 played a significant role in the reconsideration of self-reliance by a variety of humanitarian, development, and government actors. However, as has been discussed in previous chapters, this focus was hardly new. Nor was the background of this discussion a novel situation: the increasingly protracted nature of displacement, heightened donor fatigue, and political restrictionism which has decreased rates of resettlement in the so-called Global North and eroded refugee rights in regions of origin. The document goes on to succinctly summarize the issues at hand:

> Most of the world's refugees are unable to earn sufficient income to meet their basic needs. With growing demands placed on the humanitarian response system and a widening gap between humanitarian needs and resources available to address them, enabling refugees to be productive and self-reliant has never been more crucial.[6]

The importance of self-reliance was recognized in the 2016 New York Declaration for Refugees and Migrants, and the resulting Global Compact on Refugees (GCR) in 2018. Hailed as landmark cooperation between countries to quickly address refugee situations with a focus on fair and equitable burden- and responsibility-sharing, the Global Compact on

---

[4] Some of this research was published in the report: Easton-Calabria, E. (2019) 'Future of work, digitalization, and livelihoods for displaced people and people on the move'. Migrant Nations Initiative, UNDP. Geneva: UNDP.

[5] UNHCR (2016) 'Livelihoods and self-reliance'. Geneva: UNHCR. Available at: www.refworld.org/pdfid/585163cf7.pdf.

[6] UNHCR, 'Livelihoods and self-reliance', para 3.

Refugees was signed by the UN General Assembly in 2018. One of the Compact's key pillars is to 'enhance refugee self-reliance', although the term itself is never defined in the document. A definition does appear in the 2019 GCR Indicator Framework, and follows a narrower version of the 2005 UNHCR Handbook as 'the social and economic ability of an individual, a household or a community to meet essential needs in a sustainable manner and with dignity.' However, the indicator itself only focuses on refugees' economic inclusion, thereby keeping with a broader trend of focusing primarily on the definition's economic dimensions.[7]

The aim of refugee self-reliance is also core to the CRRF, a series of initiatives in so-called CRRF pilot countries which are envisioned to act as roadmaps for the implementation for the GCR:

> When refugees gain access to education and labour markets, they can build their skills and become self-reliant, contributing to local economies and fuelling the development of the communities hosting them. Allowing refugees to benefit from national services and integrating them into national development plans is essential for both refugees and the communities hosting them, and is consistent with the pledge to 'leave no one behind' in the 2030 Agenda for Sustainable Development.[8]

Entrepreneurship as a pathway to self-reliance has remained a high priority for UNHCR since 2015,[9] continuing with the focus from the previous chapter. During this time there has also been growing recognition of the need for financial services for refugees, which has resulted in partnerships between UNHCR and financial service providers (FSPs) as well as the non-profit organization Social Performance Task Force to develop guidelines and generate evidence to garner support for refugee entrepreneurs. Yet entrepreneurship in 2015 and 2016 rarely extended beyond local markets, and indeed was partially epitomized in the livelihoods trainings in Kampala discussed previously. As the ExComm update on refugee self-reliance and livelihoods explains, 'Globally, UNHCR is focusing on the artisanal, agricultural and information technology sectors, which have high growth potential and offer prospects for absorbing refugee labour'.[10]

As alluded to in the reference to the IT sector, what began to change after 2010, and increasingly since 2015, is a heightened awareness of the importance

[7] UNHCR (2019) Global Compact on Refugees: Indicator Framework. Geneva: UNHCR. Available at: https://www.unhcr.org/5cf907854.pdf p. 22.

[8] UNHCR (2018) 'Comprehensive Refugee Response Framework'. Geneva: UNHCR. Available at: www.unhcr.org/comprehensive-refugee-response-framework-crrf.html.

[9] UNHCR, 'Comprehensive refugee response framework', para 13.

[10] Ibid. P. 6.

of digital connectivity for refugees and some nascent efforts to connect refugees to digital work. Some of this early work was piloted through the UNHCR Innovation Unit, established in 2012 to experiment and problem-solve within the agency. Focusing at the time on areas called Innovation Labs, the unit emphasized self-reliance in addition to ICT, access to energy, data and communication, and field delivery.[11] One of these projects was Community Technology Access (CTA) in Kenya's Dadaab refugee camp, a programme which was seen as a 'holistic and expansive approach to formal education, vocational training and community e-learning'. This project has since expanded to both camps and urban areas, and forms the practical basis for UNHCR's focus on helping refugees access digital work – what UNHCR originally termed teleworking activities – and wider digital skills. Another innovation project was 'Impact Sourcing', an early if not the earliest effort by UNHCR to connect refugees to digital work. Its aim was to identify 'opportunities for employment for persons of concern using cloud computing, mobile payment for performing micro tasks – those that can be performed online and linked to business process outsourcing centres',[12] and was a partnership between a range of organizations and enterprises, including Anudip (which promotes digital inclusion) and iMerit (which specializes in AI). While this project never got off the ground, its tenets are similar to other current efforts linking refugees to online micro-work through smartphones, discussed in more depth below.

Despite these mentions of digital work in documents, the 2014–2018 UNHCR Livelihoods Strategy does not mention it. The 2019–2023 Global Strategy Concept Note on Refugee Livelihoods and Economic Inclusion also does not discuss digital work; it does however discuss the importance of refugees in national education systems as important to help 'ensure that younger generations develop problem-solving and other cognitive, interpersonal, social, civic, academic and *computer/digital literacy skills needed for the labour market*'.[13] [emphasis added] Instead, UNHCR's main work in the digital sphere is comprised of two strands: increasing internet access to refugees through initiatives such as 'Digital Access, Inclusion and Participation', which replaced 'Connectivity for Refugees' in 2020,[14] and promoting digital identity to combat the lack of legally recognized identity

[11] UNHCR (2014) Update on Innovation. Executive Committee of the High Commissioner's Programme Standing Committee, 59th Meeting. EC/65/SC/CRP.4. Available at: https://www.unhcr.org/5319e6109.pdf.

[12] Ibid.

[13] UNHCR '2019–2023 Global Strategy Concept Note on Refugee Livelihoods and Economic Inclusion'. Geneva: UNHCR, p 7.

[14] UNHCR (2020) Space and Imagination: Rethinking Digital Access for Refugees. Geneva: UNHCR. Available at: https://www.unhcr.org/innovation/wp-content/uploads/2020/04/Space-and-imagination-rethinking-refugees%E2%80%99-digital-access_WEB042020.pdf.

documents (or any documents whatsoever) which many refugees face. One UNHCR document explains:

> In our modern world this [lack of documents] excludes from services and socio-economic participation, it limits access, for example, to work, housing, a mobile phone and a bank account. In fact, the lack of a documented identity constitutes for vulnerable and already marginalized people a constant risk of transgressing the lines between legal and illegal.[15]

As we will see, despite the fact that digital work does not occur 'in real life', many of these same barriers remain in the digital sphere.

The following section presents a case study of one refugee's pathway to remote work. Alaa, a Syrian refugee who lived in Cairo, Egypt, for many years, illustrates both the success that digital work can bring as well as the many barriers that refugees face in creating or obtaining it. A brief overview of the refugee context in Egypt is presented, followed by information about Alaa and his work.

Tomooh: a digital livelihood in Cairo, Egypt

Egypt has hosted many groups of refugees and migrants since the early 1900s, including Armenians, Palestinians, Iraqis, Sudanese and other African refugees. However, the arrival of significant numbers of Syrian refugees in Egypt beginning in 2012 significantly affected the country's refugee regime and the composition of its refugee population. As of 2021, Syrians make up the largest number of refugees in Egypt's population of over 250,000 formally registered refugees.[16] However, there are estimates that the actual number of Syrian refugees alone is closer to 250,000.[17] As Egypt does not have camps, most refugees live in Greater Cairo, which in 2020 had approximately 20.9 million inhabitants.[18]

Egypt is a signatory to the 1951 Refugee Convention and its 1967 Protocol as well as to the 1969 Organisation of African Unity (OAU) Convention. However, Egypt has placed restrictions on five articles of the 1951 Convention

15 UNHCR (n.d.) UNHCR Strategy on Digital Inclusion and Identity. Geneva: UNHCR. Available at: https://www.unhcr.org/blogs/wp-content/uploads/sites/48/2018/03/2018-02-Digital-Identity_02.pdf p 1.

16 UNHCR (2021) 'Global focus: Egypt'. Webpage. Available at: https://reporting.unhcr.org/egypt.

17 UNHCR (2016) '3RP Regional Refugee & Resilience Plan 2016–2017 in response to the Syria crisis – Egypt'. Available at: https://reliefweb.int/report/egypt/3rp-regional-refugee-resilience-plan-2016-2017-response-syria-crisis-egypt-enar.

18 *Egypt Independent* (2020) https://egyptindependent.com/population-of-greater-cairo-tripled-since-1980-national-population-council/.

relating to access to primary education (although as of 2017 all Sudanese and Syrian children can in principle access public education), access to public relief and assistance, labour legislation, personal status, rationing, and social security. No restriction has been placed on refugees' paid employment (Article 17) and the Egyptian Constitution states that political refugees may be eligible for work permits (Article 54), although in practice it is challenging for refugees to obtain a work permit. That said, the pre-pandemic informal economy constituted approximately 50 per cent of the country's GDP and provided 68 per cent of new jobs.[19] As one informant put it, 'The informal economy is the heart and soul of the poor and the marginalized in Egypt – it plays a huge role for the poor.'

Syrians in Egypt as well as those elsewhere in the Middle East receive the bulk of international assistance, as seen in the Syrian Regional Response Plan. Indeed, many international agencies in Cairo and elsewhere, such as UNHCR, IOM, Caritas, CARE, and Catholic Relief Services work with 'Syrians' and 'non-Syrians' (or 'Africans and Iraqis'), leading to an artificial division in refugee populations that manifests in unequal programming. UNHCR has direct responsibility for refugees in Egypt based on a 1954 Memorandum of Understanding, meaning that both legal documentation procedures such as refugee status determination as well as social services and livelihoods assistance are assumed by the agency.

Despite public statements by the Government of Egypt about welcoming refugees, local integration is not a preferred durable solution and there are limited policies to facilitate this, including no pathway to acquiring Egyptian citizenship, which is only granted on the basis of descent (*jus sanguinis*). In the absence of the possibility for legal integration, refugees must apply every six months for a residency permit. This stressful and lengthy bureaucratic procedure also serves as a regular psychological reminder of instability, as it is never guaranteed refugees will receive a permit.[20]

While refugees can largely work in the informal sector without repercussions, many still face challenges in having legal documentation recognized, which in turn makes formal banking difficult or even impossible. This presents challenges such as an inability to take out loans from micro-finance institutions or banks, meaning that taking out loans – an important livelihood strategy for many[21] – must take place informally or through expensive and exploitative lenders.

---

[19] Soliman, M. (2020) 'Egypt's informal economy: an ongoing cause of unrest'. 29 October. *Columbia Journal of International Affairs* 73(2). NYC: Columbia.

[20] For more information see the box on p 9 in: Miranda, P. (2018) 'Getting by on the margins: Sudanese and Somali refugees. A case report of refugees in towns, Cairo, Egypt'. Boston, MA: Tufts University.

[21] Jacobsen, K., Ayoub, M., and Johnson, A. (2014) 'Sudanese refugees in Cairo: remittances and livelihoods'. *Journal of Refugee Studies* 27(1): 145–159.

A 2014 study found that although 89 per cent of refugees were economically active in Cairo, their earnings hardly covered their food and rent, leaving them subsisting from day to day and month to month.[22] In recent years the devaluation of the Egyptian pound and inflation have contributed to raising rents and overall prices in Cairo, with the poorest disproportionately affected. Refugees have been even more heavily affected due to rent discrimination and inflated water and electricity bill prices.[23]

It is against this backdrop, which is similar in context to the poverty and informality that many refugees face elsewhere in the world, that the concept of digital livelihoods is emplaced.

Tomooh

Alaa, a Syrian social entrepreneur and NGO worker who lived as a refugee in Cairo, Egypt, from 2012 to 2019, illustrates both possible success and limits to scale that many refugees face in digital work. In 2016, with two other Syrians, Alaa started the website Tomooh (www.tomooh.org) offering information in Arabic for Syrian refugees on navigating Egyptian and other bureaucracy, including how to obtain marriage and birth certificates, and register with UNHCR. The website has expanded to offer support to Syrians in Turkey, Jordan, and Lebanon, as well, and also began providing information about university scholarships that Syrians could access. It currently has over 70,000 followers on social media. While Alaa and the other founders started the website as volunteers, they now earn income through ads based on web traffic. "It's good," Alaa explained, "because the refugees don't pay for the help – Google does. It's enough for three families to live in Egypt."

However, because of Egypt's strict laws, Alaa could not open a bank account with his refugee ID to get paid for Tomooh; although his refugee ID is valid, it is not recognized. His Syrian passport had expired. While the income he made from Google was sent via Western Union, he was prevented from expanding the business due to the lack of a bank account. He even had to turn down offers from organizations to provide funding to grow. In 2019 he explained, "We can't register as an organization because we are Syrians, which means we don't have an office or a bank account. The organization couldn't give us money without a bank account, so now we are working with them on a voluntary basis."

Alaa graduated as a computer science engineer from Damascus University and taught computing and maths before leaving Syria. He arrived in Cairo in 2012 but initially went back to the United Arab Emirates where he had

[22] Jacobsen et al, 'Sudanese refugees in Cairo'.

[23] Abdel Aziz, N. (2017) 'Surviving in Cairo as a closed-file refugee: socio-economic and protection challenges'. Center for Migration and Refugee Studies, The American University in Cairo. Paper No. 10.

been living, because work prospects seemed better there. However, he was ultimately refused residency there and in January 2013 arrived back in Egypt. Because he could not find work initially, he started to volunteer. As he explained,

> I started my real life in Egypt when I started volunteering in Greater Cairo, in Giza. I started noticing the work around me and what the refugee life looked like. I found myself very happy providing services to my community and the refugee community. I decided this is the work I will do. After six months of volunteering [at the Psycho-Social Services and Training Institute in Cairo (PSTIC)], I got my first paid job at Tadamon, the Egyptian Refugee Multicultural Council. I started as volunteer community outreach and then got paid starting in September 2013.

Alaa's idea for Tomooh came in 2015. He was working with Tadamon at a community centre in a poor area of Cairo called Faysal where many refugees, mainly Syrians, live. The centre was a project funded by UNHCR which offered advice, activities, and a social space for refugees. UNHCR was in negotiations with Tadamon about extending the project but then in May 2015 the funding stopped. Without the funds from UNHCR, the community centre was forced to close. "It was the only community centre in that area", Alaa shared,

> So many people relied on it. It was the only place to go for some refugees. It answered a huge need. We, a few other paid staff and volunteers, did our best trying to get it to stay open, we tried to mobilize the press and to pressure UNHCR. We failed. Then we started talking in my apartment, let's create our own community centre. But we had the challenge of not having enough money for a physical space. So we said, let's start with the virtual … we decided it was our responsibility as a community to fill that gap.

Tomooh was first created with the intention of sharing information online relevant only for refugees living in Faysal. Alaa and others started collecting resources and putting them online:

> We wanted to put those resources in front of refugees. We shared how to support themselves if they need psychosocial services, health, legal services: you have to go there, this is the phone number, address, and so on. We also started to contract Syrian clothing factories to get free clothing for refugees living there, and food donations. The idea started like this.

Over time Alaa and the website's other co-founders realized that through online tools they could provide services and information to more people in Greater Cairo and not only in Faysal. The idea then expanded to people in Egypt, and then to refugees across the Middle East: "We are now active in Turkey, Lebanon, and Jordan in addition to Syria", Alaa explains, "We provide immigration information to refugees, information about resettlement, and we have a small section on educational scholarships, but it's not that active because there aren't many."

The physical side of Tomooh also grew. Alaa and others expanded their team to almost 40 volunteers, who began teaching English courses and basic livelihoods training such as sewing, as well as continued to distribute clothing and food. At first activities were delivered under the auspices of other organizations. This arrangement started when one INGO implemented a new project in the same area for children and then wanted to expand their activities to target mothers. "But they had an issue with outreach – they weren't at all able to find people, to reach the community. We realized we could help." Alaa and several other members of Tomooh offered their time in conducting outreach for INGO projects like CARE International and Terre des Hommes in exchange for space on specific days to run their own courses and activities. As Alaa explained, "We promoted ourselves as an outreach team to big organizations because they don't have access to the community. It was win-win."

After that they began working with a local Egyptian charity which worked out of an apartment. "They gave us the space", Alaa said. "We helped them with finding Syrian students because they had a project to run a community centre. This relationship still exists with them until now. This is the other side of Tomooh which continued on after I left Egypt."

In 2019 Alaa was resettled with his wife and toddler to Vancouver, Washington, USA, a small city just across the river from Portland, Oregon. They have since had one more child. His work with Tomooh has continued and he has even started another website which is also generating income. But here in the US his digital work is his side work. He explained:

> I don't invest so much time in the website now because I have to focus on my work. You know the life in the US: no work, no life. I have to work, my wife has to work, I have to keep Tomooh active, and with two kids, it's really hard to put so much time in the website … Tomooh is enough to be extra income but it's not enough to be my only income in the US with a family of four.

To help him with the website he works alongside four people that he quickly stresses are not true employees:

> I don't know if I can call them that because we don't pay that much money for them – they are a kind of employee-volunteer. We pay them money but not enough money, around 100 dollars for each which for people living in Egypt is not enough for a family to live, but maybe enough for a student to go forward. We also have people working with us working from Syria. For them 100 dollars is enough for them to survive, it is now good money for them.

These contractors (for lack of a better word) mainly focus on creating content for the website, which is then put on social media, where Tomooh is advertised. Facebook is the main social media site, followed by Telegram, Foxpush, and WhatsApp. Alaa explained they do not use Instagram because they cannot share links to the website on it, or Twitter, as not enough Arabic speakers in their target audience use it.

Depending on how much the website is advertised and the resulting stream of visitors, Alaa and his team make more or less money each month. "The maximum amount I can keep after paying everyone else is $2,000 USD", he explained, "and the minimum amount if we haven't done much with the website is 600. I average about $1,000 USD per month with the website [of take-home pay]." Other friends of his who have created websites are able to earn more because of the amount of time they invest in them. "But my colleagues who are making more than me are not living in a country like the US, their life in their country is easier than me," Alaa explains. "They don't have to have another job so they can double or triple their income from websites because they can invest all their time in them."

Alaa considers himself self-reliant, which he explains as meaning, "I can pay all my expenses, starting from houses, transportation, clothing food and maybe entertainment from my own pocket, without receiving any extra money from the government. Yes, we are now self-sufficient here."

As a side job, Tomooh is helpful for Alaa and his family, but as he explained, it is not enough. Refugees in the US are notoriously under-supported, with most benefits cut off after just 90 days, at which point refugees are expected to be in employment. This model of refugee resettlement is underpinned by the 1980 Refugee Act, which aims for 'economic self-sufficiency' to be achieved for refugees 'as quickly as possible'.[24] At the same time, many refugees are under-employed in the US, with their skills and credentials

[24] US Government (1980) Public Law 96-212--Mar 17, 1980. 96th Congress. Available at: https://www.govinfo.gov/content/pkg/STATUTE-94/pdf/STATUTE-94-Pg102.pdf.

unutilized,[25] likely due in large part to the push to find work – any work – as soon as they can. In contrast to many, Alaa was able to work in the same field as he had in Cairo and now works for an NGO in Portland assisting newly resettled refugees. He shared,

> In general it's going well for me and my family. I came prepared. Many of my colleagues in Cairo are from the US and Europe, so I came to the US knowing that I have to work here. Because we are both working – I am working full-time, my wife is working part-time – we are moving forward. We have some savings, we have a good life. All the benefits from the government are done, we are self-sufficient 100 per cent. But I have a lot of friends from Syria and other places who are here in the United States and they have a different story. My story is different, you can't say my life is 'the refugee life' in the US. Some arrived five or six years ago and are still struggling to get by.

When Alaa reflects on the start of Tomooh he is clear that the idea started as a way to fill the gap that UNHCR left in the neighbourhood:

> We had a belief in ourselves at that time that we are better than UNHCR and that we can provide better services than them, we don't need their money, we can provide the services to their community. The relationship between UNHCR and refugees is really bad – maybe that was also our motivation. Up to now, people in Egypt, especially in greater Cairo, most of them know Tomooh, they know us. We opened our door, but our door is much smaller than the UNHCR door because they have the funds, the money. Creating Tomooh was an opportunity to serve the community but for the community it was a huge loss at the end of the day. That community centre changed the life of many people and then it closed.

And other impacts of Tomooh on Alaa? "It's a good work, it helped us to survive in Egypt when I came."

The digital livelihoods landscape for refugees

Alaa's work helps us understand one form of digital work – itself borne out of the loss of humanitarian and development support for a refugee community – but nothing of current efforts undertaken within the

25 MPI (2017) www.migrationpolicy.org/sites/default/files/publications/TCM-Asylum-USRefugeeIntegration-FINAL.pdf.

humanitarian architecture to support refugees to enter the digital economy. As will be discussed more here, much of the work on digital livelihoods for refugees is small-scale, undertaken by smaller NGOs or as pilot projects of INGOs. The ILO has only recently re-broached the topic of refugees and work, mainly as a result of Syrian refugees in the Middle East and in Europe, and only more recently still has included digital refugee livelihoods as a topic relevant to its decent work agenda. Much of the expertise, funding, and digital infrastructure needed to make digital work for refugees a reality, much less a successful one, lies beyond the realm of humanitarianism and development in the private sector. At the end of the day, it is the private sector offering and seeking jobs in the digital sphere. As one UNHCR think piece stated, 'The $25 billion humanitarian sector continues to grow, and yet its way of working has not kept pace with the digital revolution'.[26] The following section explores what is already taking place.

The geography of digital work initiatives for refugees

Initiatives and pathways to digital and digitally mediated work exist in many places around the world but are concentrated in several main areas.[27] Corresponding to other literature on digital projects for refugees,[28] in the Global North Germany is the most common site for initiatives, followed by the Netherlands and the UK. In sub-Saharan Africa, the most common region for initiatives is in East Africa, primarily Kenya and Uganda. In Asia, multiple initiatives exist in India, while Turkey, Israel, Palestine, and Jordan are common sites in the Middle East. Most of these initiatives have arisen since 2010 and largely since 2015 when mass arrival of asylum seekers in Europe put refugees more at the forefront of public thought and increased private sector interest in refugees, often as social corporate responsibility projects.

While the majority of identified initiatives in sub-Saharan Africa and the Middle East are based in camps, initiatives in urban areas are more common in Europe, Latin and South America, and South Asia. The individual

[26] UNHCR (2022) Connectivity for Everyone. Webpage, available at: https://www.unhcr.org/innovation/connectivity-for-everyone/.

[27] As the scoping study was not exhaustive and was based in part on snowballing research, these regions are not definitive areas where the most activity is occurring. One key limitation of the research was that the scoping study was conducted in English. While findings available in German and Spanish were captured due to the author's language skills, the actual search terms and scoping methods were conducted in English.

[28] betterplace/Nesta (2018) 'Mapping digital social innovation: migration and innovation'. European Commission. Available at: www.nesta.org.uk/feature/mapping-digital-social-innovation/mapping-dsi-migration-and-integration/.

refugees interviewed who had created or founded digital livelihoods were all based in urban areas. While this is likely not representative of the location of individual engagement in digital work, given that the lack of humanitarian assistance offered in urban areas compared to camps forces many refugees to become entrepreneurs in the informal economy, this phenomenon may translate into digital entrepreneurship, as well.

Types of digital work for refugees

At its most valuable, digital work can open up new opportunities, markets, and networks for refugees beyond their immediate physical location. Relatedly, people can match their skills and services with a market that may not exist where they physically are, even allowing them to work with or sell goods to diaspora markets around the world as well as international customers and employers. Due to the remote and mobile nature of digital work, it remains available to people on the move or those who settle in multiple host countries. In many instances, it circumvents local work restrictions, allowing people access to jobs they would be unable to legally receive in their host countries, though regulations on transnational work appear to vary by country. It may also help displaced people bypass informal barriers to work, such as xenophobia by national employers. Indeed, some researchers posit that the majority of displaced people pursue digital work only when all of their other options for in-person work in the informal and formal economy are denied.[29] Depending on their circumstances, displaced people may even start or continue remote work that is based in their home country, thus allowing them to utilize their existing social networks.

Most digital work occurs on an individual basis with refugees becoming members of the online gig economy. While there are risks attached to this, benefits include refugees managing their own time and tasks and thus making work fit into their life circumstances, even if they suddenly change. Relatedly, some work is accessible by smartphone rather than computers, with reimbursement almost immediate through mobile money. One example of digital work currently undertaken by refugees and local Ugandans is through the 'LevelApp' from the NGO RefUnite, which allows users to sign up, download datasets, and complete 'tasks' such as categorizing images on their phone to train AI. Users are paid for completed work through mobile money, meaning they are quickly reimbursed and do not need to have a formal bank account, thereby avoiding many of the challenges faced by other refugees engaged in digital work. The LevelApp was

[29] Key informant interview, Andreas Hackl, Senior Research Fellow, University of Edinburgh; Key informant interview, Julie Zollman, Researcher, The Fletcher School, Tufts University.

enabled through a 300,000 GBP grant from the Global System for Mobile Communications Association (GSMA) to pay users and create a body of evidence to prove displaced people's capacity to be competitive in the digital market. While refugees were LevelApp's target beneficiaries, about half of LevelApp's current users are Ugandans, likely reflective of the high rate of unemployment in Uganda among nationals. Uganda was selected as a pilot country because refugees have the right to work there – and because the cost of living is low. As the chief operating officer of LevelApp conceded,

> It would be hard to be competitive in Lebanon versus in Uganda if refugees have the same skill level because their low prices is what makes them competitive. But through this work we can push up the bottom [billion]. Young people will take up digital work very quickly, particularly because there are limited work opportunities in countries like Uganda. I don't see any better way getting thousands and thousands of people into employment.

The founders aim to use outcomes of the pilot to secure large-scale private sector contracts to create a sustainable service. Users may soon have the option to have a small fee deducted from their monthly earnings to provide life insurance – very important in high mortality settings such as Uganda. As of 2019, the project targeted 5,000 users and aimed to scale to 25,000 and then beyond. LevelApp illustrates how with just a phone and a phone number, refugees can both access and be paid for digital work. As the case of Alaa illustrated, this can be particularly helpful for those lacking official identification, unable to open a bank account in their host country, or on the move.

Types of assistance actors promoting digital livelihoods

A wide variety of actors are involved in fostering digital livelihoods for refugees. Particular actors are often active at certain 'levels' of the international system, as summarized in Figure 6.1. Transnational actors such as private sector companies and international organizations often provide the infrastructure to enable digital work, be it access to internet and computers, digital trainings, or undertaking market assessments to match supply and demand. International organizations, in particular, often see one of their main roles as offering humanitarian protection and upholding labour standards. The ILO's Decent Work Agenda, for example, cuts across country priorities, is relevant for refugees, and also transcends into digital work.[30]

[30] ILO (2019) 'Decent work'. Webpage. Geneva: ILO. Available at: www.ilo.org/global/topics/decent-work/lang--en/index.htm.

Figure 6.1: Overview of actors involved in digital livelihoods creation at different levels of the international system

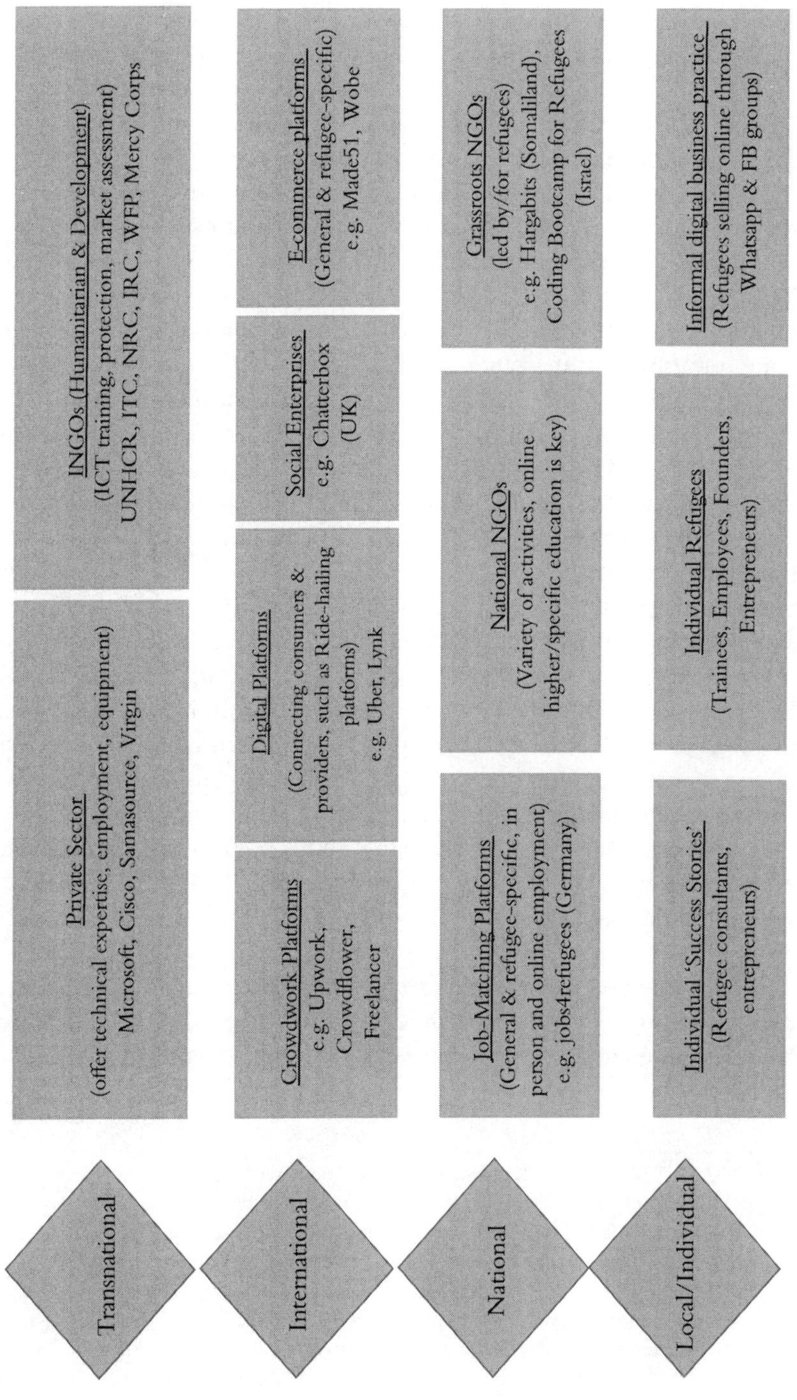

Transnational actors can mobilize resources, forge strategic partnerships, and make use of extensive social networks and social capital, and thus play a key role in large-scale programming. GSMA, for example, a corporation representing the interests of more than 400 companies in the 'mobile ecosystem', has created a Humanitarian Innovation Fund to test and scale the use of mobile technology to address humanitarian challenges, including displacement.[31] It is through this fund that LevelApp was created. For these telecom operators, refugee camps are not just sites of humanitarian intervention but also marketplaces where they can make significant profits. This growing interest is based on research showing that refugees are spending about a third of their disposable income on connectivity – thereby demonstrating its importance in their lives.[32] At the same time, both the private sector and international organizations engaged in humanitarian digital work training and infrastructure are often constrained by bureaucracy, and international organizations face the additional burden of short funding cycles, which often require demonstrating impact more quickly than they are able to within a given time period.[33] This limits their ability to scale their programmes.

At the international level, digital labour platforms such as Crowdwork and e-commerce platforms offer jobs that some refugees can directly access. Job-matching platforms, while sometimes international such as Talent Beyond Boundaries, are often national, targeting a domestic market, such as jobs4refugees in Germany or Refugee Talent in Australia. The majority of these job-matching platforms use digital databases to link potential employees and employers rather than offer digital jobs *per se*. National NGOs are among the most common actors to offer digital and ICT skills training to displaced people, and often target refugees. Grassroots NGOs also play a role in this, such as Hargabits in Somaliland, which trains IDPs in digital design and other skills demanded by the local market.[34]

Locally, refugees access work through digital platforms linking consumers and providers, such as ride-hailing platforms like Uber in East Africa.[35] They also often undertake informal trade through WhatsApp and Facebook

---

31 GSMA (2022) Mobile for Humanitarian Innovation. Webpage, available at: https://www.gsma.com/mobilefordevelopment/mobile-for-humanitarian-innovation/.

32 GSMA (2017) 'Mobile is a lifeline: research from Nyarugusu Refugee Camp, Tanzania'. Available at: www.gsma.com/mobilefordevelopment/wp-content/uploads/2017/07/TWP98_1-Refugee-Report_WebSpreads_R1.pdf.

33 Key informant interview, Norwegian Refugee Council country director, Kenya.

34 Key informant interview, Khadra Ali and Ahmed Ali, Team Leads, Hargabits Academy.

35 Key informant interview, Julie Zollmann, Researcher, The Fletcher School, Tufts University. Learn more about Julie Zollman's in-progress research at: www.juliezollmann.com.

groups. Grassroots and community-based organizations often provide computer and internet access as well as many displaced people's only access to ICT trainings.[36] While individual displaced people can and do obtain digital work internationally, this research found that many of the digital or digitally accessed job opportunities are actually *local*.[37] This suggests an interesting, though not necessarily widespread, potential for digitalization to foster job creation in a refugee's own environment (potentially by avoiding local labour barriers) as well as beyond borders.

Online work platforms and refugee self-reliance

Upwork and Figure 8 are two online work platforms that have partnered with organizations supporting displaced people to support access to digital work. One example of this is the Refugee Employment and Skills Initiative (RESI) led by the International Trade Center (ITC) and the Norwegian Refugee Council (NRC) in the Kakuma and Dadaab Refugee Camps in Kenya, as well as in Jordan, Gaza, and Somaliland. ITC provides the development, market, and trade experience to RESI while NRC offers protection and addresses local barriers through dialogue and advocacy. Technical experience and a direct pathway to the private sector are offered by, respectively, the technology company Samasource and Upwork. The programme was piloted in 2016 and began running in 2017. Refugees are trained in two main value chains, online freelancing and artisan crafts. The online freelancing component, as one employee involved in the programme explained, "is sexy and fundable". As refugee camps often lack large-scale markets and livelihoods trainings rarely meet existing demand, RESI trains refugees as digital consultants through providing intensive ICT and trainings in online skills and seeks to connect refugees to online international markets through Upwork. From the RESI training, the 'Dadaab Freelancing Collective' was created, an online refugee consulting business advertised on Upwork.

[36] The Bondeko Refugee Livelihoods Centre discussed in the previous chapter is one example of a refugee-led organization based in Kampala, Uganda, that has teamed up with the NGO Xavier Project to offer a 'tech hub' under its auspices. Refugee teachers train fellow refugees in ICT on computers donated by the Xavier Project, and internet is accessible for a small fee to the local community. See: www.bondekocenter.com. Source: Key Informant Interview, Paul Kithimba, Bondeko Centre Director.

[37] Key informant interviews: Julie Zollmann, Researcher, The Fletcher School, Tufts University; Khadra Ali and Ahmed Ali, Team Leads, Hargabits Academy; Katie Schlinder, Director, RESI Programme, International Trade Center.

RESI does not offer only a simple technical skills training but instead walks participants through a series of hard and soft skills development courses aimed to help them become competitive freelancers. This includes mentoring, networking connections, and coaching in CV writing, interview skills, and more. Jean-Marie Ndikumana, a RESI participant and winner of the online freelancing Kakuma competition, shared, for example:

> I have come across different opportunities, but the Kakuma (online freelancing) boot camp is the best and I believe it will change our lives and mindsets. Since we are talented in different areas and have many skills, but we didn't know how to sell them online. The boot camp we have undergone was a great opportunity for us to learn new things and work beyond the refugee status. First and foremost, being taught on how to work online made me feel rejuvenated despite my refugee status.[38]

The RESI programme also illustrates how digital work encompasses development, humanitarian, technical, and private sector realms – and competing aims. NRC initially sought to have the most vulnerable inhabitants of camps join RESI. As the NRC country director explained: "As a humanitarian organization we look at vulnerability and need first. If we don't, what happens to poor, female-heading households with no income or education? In humanitarian terms, they are more deserving of help." However, ITC was clear that a basic foundation of literacy and skills, as well as owning a smartphone, was needed in order to give participants the best shot at becoming competitive freelancers. The end result is, among other characteristics, a larger gender discrepancy, with a majority of male participants. Of the 32 active members of the Dadaab Collective Freelancing agency on Upwork, only two are women. As one NRC employee said:

> We lose on who to help, so we need to do digital work but we also need to assist more with other livelihoods … the role of humanitarian organizations is protection and advocacy in relation to displacement. There remains a lot of barriers to self-reliance in Kenya. Participants may be trained [through RESI] but what about a bank account? A business permit? Freedom of movement to get new stock or equipment? Even certification, because they can't sit school exams without a birth certificate.

[38] ITC (2018) 'The refugee employment and skills initiative'. Geneva: ITC, p 13.

While most of these barriers are ones refugees face both off- and online, some have been successfully addressed to better enable access to digital work. Initiatives such as the World Food Programme's Empact programme work in a similar way to RESI by linking trained participants to online work platforms. The programme helps refugees find remote digital micro-work mainly categorizing images to train AI, similar to LevelApp. In this way, the programme trains refugees to become more competitive in global gig work but does not employ them. Instead, they seek out work opportunities for refugees on open-access platforms such as Figure 8. As of 2019 they had trained 3,000 refugees, half of them women. Of those, 33 per cent had found jobs, 17 per cent of those worked in the local tech industry, and 22 per cent were engaged in remote online work. They operate in Lebanon and Iraq, have a pilot in Kenya and plans to open up programmes in Ghana, Libya, Tanzania, and Bangladesh. Their aim? To "help refugees make money as fast as possible to become financially sustainably so they don't need WFP [World Food Programme] to succeed".[39]

In addition to helping refugees find work, humanitarian and development agencies such as Empact in cases address specific barriers refugees face, such as a lack of legally recognized documentation. Empact has direct relationships with work platforms themselves to ensure refugees are able to register on them.[40] Similarly, after realizing that refugee IDs were not recognized as legal documentation on Upwork, RESI partnered with Upwork to 'support the verification of identification of refugee freelancers through locally emitted documents.'[41]

Informal digital trade

While digital work is being promoted by organizations, it is of course also happening independently from them. Digital entrepreneurship may take the form of Alaa's website but often occurs through using the internet to sell goods that are then provided in person. Informal digital trade is under-researched globally, yet work on how to measure this type of trade is being promoted by actors such as OECD and the World Trade Organization due to the growing recognition of its widespread use.[42] A small body of research

39 Key Informant interview, WFP Empact Programme.

40 ITC (2018) 'RESI: The Refugee Employment and Skills Initiative (Brochure)', Geneva: ITC.

41 Key Informant interview, Katie Schlinder, Director, RESI Programme, International Trade Center.

42 Fayyez, S. (2018) 'A review on measuring digital trade & e-commerce as new economic statistics products'. Paper prepared for the 16th Conference of IAOS, OECD Headquarters, Paris, France, 19–21 September. Available at: www.oecd.org/iaos2018/programme/IAOS-OECD2018_Item_3-D-1-Fayyaz.pdf.

demonstrates that refugees in East Africa, for example, sell goods and services informally through posting on social media groups, often reaching thousands of members – potential customers.[43] WhatsApp and Facebook groups, including those for churches, diaspora groups, and shared interest groups, as well as Instagram followers, offer a customer base for refugees to offer goods and services both locally and internationally. Facebook pages and Facebook marketplace are other common ways to sell online. These offer pre-made networks that are ideal for selling, particularly in situations where people have few local contacts.

In Nairobi, for example, South Sudanese refugees sell peanut butter to WhatsApp group members while Congolese and Burundian refugees commonly sell clothing over Facebook.[44] Goods and services are bought via digital money transfers and either sent by post, transferred from trusted person to trusted person, or picked up in person, such as a refugee in Uganda selling jewellery through a church WhatsApp group who agrees to give the already bought jewellery to buyers at church the following Sunday. Selling in these fora offers a means to circumvent local work restrictions, such as the barring of informal street hawking in cities such as Kampala.[45] At the same time, displaced people are often still vulnerable to other restrictions, such as refugee IDs not being considered valid ID with which to purchase SIM cards, and thus can face challenges in accessing informal social media markets. An unpublicized cancellation of phone numbers held by those using refugee ID in Kenya, for example, left many refugees without recourse to their digital livelihoods.[46]

Challenges and barriers to digital work for refugees

While a huge opportunity for some, the changing nature of work replicates some of the skillset and socioeconomic divides that refugees and refugee-serving organisations alike still struggle to address in the non-digital world. For refugees with low socioeconomic backgrounds, for example, specific disadvantages from displacement – such as a lack of national identification documents, language skills, or long-developed social networks in a host country – are compounded by other barriers that the changing world

[43] Key informant interview, Julie Zollmann, Researcher, The Fletcher School, Tufts.

[44] Key informant interview, Lisa Poggiali, Price Mellon Postdoctoral Fellow, University of Pennsylvania.

[45] Easton-Calabria, E. (2016) 'Refugees learned to fish for themselves'. UNHCR Working Paper Series.

[46] Key informant interview, Lisa Poggiali, Price Mellon Postdoctoral Fellow, University of Pennsylvania.

of work creates for the poorest.[47] This includes a loss of menial jobs to automation, lack of access to Smart devices to find or create digital work, and limited social networks with which to digitally trade. The challenges specific to refugees in accessing digital work and other more general barriers raise the question of whether digital work is a true option to foster large-scale refugee self-reliance (still broadly defined here as the ability to live independently from humanitarian assistance). This question arises because many of these barriers are broad and systemic, including work regulations in host countries, limited access to electricity and internet, and struggles with obtaining legal documentation.

The organization NaTakallam, a digital platform that employs refugees for language services including translation and language tutoring, is an example of how remote work can address limitations refugees face in accessing local labour markets. In countries like Lebanon, where many of NaTakallam's employees reside, restrictions on rights affect refugees' ability to work regardless of their capabilities. Several NaTakallam employees also moved from the Middle East to Europe without the necessary credentials or language skills to find employment in their new country. Despite changing countries, they are able to continue to work and earn their living through NaTakallam. However, finding ways to pay refugees living in countries where they cannot even legally open a bank account has proved challenging, and was a barrier cited by multiple other initiatives as well as experienced directly by Alaa in the case study above.

Some refugees also face the challenge of lacking the necessary capabilities to be competitive in the eyes of potential employers. While so-called 'hard skills' and 'abilities' (generally technical) are commonly offered in digital livelihoods trainings, other less tangible skills are also critical for successful digital and other employment. So-called soft skills are interpersonal 'people' skills as well as character traits, and include communication skills such as listening. Some organizations, such as the Gaza Sky Geeks expanded on below, have identified that these 'soft' elements of capability are often harder to teach but crucial to have, and have thus sought to integrate different skillsets into their training programmes. This includes interview techniques as well as cover letter and CV styles, which differ widely from country to country and even sector by sector. These findings echo broader research on the skills needed for future sectors of work, which discuss that the ability to communicate well within teams as well as having resilience and flexibility in the workforce will be increasingly important.[48]

[47] Hackl, A. and Gardiner, D. (2021) *Towards decent work for young refugees and host communities in the digital platform economy in Africa: Kenya, Uganda, Egypt*. Geneva: ILO.

[48] Accenture (2018) 'It's learning. Just not as we know it'. Dublin: Accenture Available at: https://www.accenture.com/_acnmedia/thought-leadership-assets/pdf/accenture-education-and-technology-skills-research.pdf.

It is also clear that many refugees have the requisite skills to work but lack the material or regulatory foundation to use them. Host country regulations strongly mediate displaced people's access to both digital and non-digital work. As mentioned earlier, Zetter and Ruaudel[49] found that approximately 50 per cent of states party to the Geneva Convention restrict, in part or in full, refugees' right to work, as do many states that are not party to the Convention at all. The 10 million stateless people in the world face similar restrictions on work, often related to a lack of recognized ID or not being afforded the same rights with the IDs they do hold, as do millions more so-called economic and other migrants around the world. While digital, remote work may offer a solution for some to bypass host country restrictions, refugees still have difficulty navigating restrictive laws and regulations. While a refugee in the Dadaab refugee camp in Kenya may, for example, have a thriving e-commerce business, this is dependent on being able to travel to access the goods they aim to sell.[50] Similarly, a tech entrepreneur such as Alaa in Egypt will struggle to create a sustainable digital business due to not being able to open a bank account with a refugee ID.

These issues represent critical obstacles that organizations seeking to place refugees in digital work must also find ways to overcome. One initiative, Gaza Sky Geeks, which trains Palestinian refugees in digital work including coding and web development, has used legal loopholes to establish much of the business infrastructure abroad. Thanks to a relaxed banking law in one US state, for example, graduates are able to open up an American bank account while in Gaza, thereby overcoming barriers to financial inclusion.

Identifying creative solutions like this requires knowledge and often particular connections in the first place. Yet a rupture in social networks is a common theme in displacement,[51] with myriad resulting challenges. Even people with high capabilities and high levels of access to resources may lack the networks to obtain digital and other work if they are in a new place. As discussed here, linkages to markets and jobs occur formally through humanitarian and development organizations as well as informally through digital networks. However, these connections are often dependent on participation in a formal NGO-led skills training or employment programme, or in informal cases dependent on access to internet and

[49] Zetter, R. and Ruaudel, H. (2016). 'Refugees' right to work and access to labor markets – an assessment'. World Bank Global Program on Forced Displacement (GPFD)/Global Knowledge Partnership on Migration and Development (KNOMAD) Thematic Working Group on Forced Migration. KNOMAD Working Paper. Washington, DC: World Bank Group.

[50] Key informant interview, Refugee (preferred to remain anonymous), Nairobi, Kenya.

[51] Horst, C. (2006) 'Introduction: refugee livelihoods: continuity and transformations'. *Refugee Survey Quarterly* 25(2): 6–22.

knowledge of relevant social media platforms and groups to join. While digital livelihoods may represent successful work for some, the barriers for many refugees remain high.

'Ideal' refugee self-reliance and the (worrying) future of work

As Alaa himself describes, his story is both the ideal – and the exception. He arrived in Egypt alone, a young able-bodied male, and a Syrian, one of the more 'privileged' categories of refugees in Egypt. He was educated and spoke English well, which provided him with additional skills to make himself an asset at the organizations he first volunteered for. This set him up to become one of the few refugees formally employed in the public sector in Cairo, at a refugee-serving organization. This in turn helped him secure a job in the US upon resettlement at the refugee agency where he now works. While in no way easy, and further enabled by his perseverance and capability, Alaa's trajectory demonstrates what refugees' livelihoods *could* be like – and often are not. As previous sections of this chapter have explored, channels to livelihoods are in no way assured through digital work, and many 'in real life' challenges and barriers are replicated or even exacerbated online.

When overviewing the landscape of current formal and informal initiatives and pathways to find or foster digital work for refugees, several interesting insights emerge. First, the trends in the type of assistance provided largely mirror key features of the changing nature of work, namely the need for upskilling, online work platforms and the online gig economy as the workplaces of the future, and even the types of digital work in which refugees are engaged, including coding, web design, and translation.[52] In this way, we see, yet again, how efforts to foster refugee self-reliance are embedded within wider global trends. In this case, digital work is linked to the global gig economy, itself inherently intertwined with job precarity, which is in turn just as reflective of social relationships and micro and macro (im)balances of power as it is of the rapid evolution of technology.[53]

[52] Lehdonvirta, V. (2017) 'How the world's largest companies use online freelancing platforms: New report'. Oxford Internet Institute, Oxford. Available at: www.oii.ox.ac.uk/blog/how-the-worlds-largest-companies-use-online-freelancing-platforms-new-report/.

[53] Stanford, J. (2017) 'The resurgence of gig work: historical and theoretical perspectives'. *The Economic and Labour Relations Review* 28(3): 382–401.

Linkages to the future of work

As discussed earlier in the chapter, one of the main mediums for refugees to access digital work is through online work platforms, where they can join as freelance consultants and offer skills such as translation and interpreting, data entry, and administrative support to companies.[54] Online labour platforms area a rising phenomenon, with an estimated growth of 30 per cent per year – highly significant compared to traditional labour markets.[55] They enable corporations to source freelance work from around the world, thus comprising a significant part of the so-called 'online gig economy'. This economy is highly transnational, with services on one large platform conducting 89 per cent of transactions across national borders.[56] Increasingly large firms including Fortune 500 companies are utilizing these platforms, demonstrating a shift in the world of work from global business influencers. As Corporaal and Lehdonvirta write, 'It's one thing when independent consultants and startups experiment with new ways of organizing work; it's something else when corporations employing hundreds of thousands of people adopt such models'.[57] One former Microsoft manager explained how the tech industry followed the model of Uber, 'providing services without employees. Instead services are provided through thousands of screens and web addresses. You get remote workers for cheap.'

These remote work platforms, and the casual contracts they promote, are one of the clearest manifestations of the so-called new economy and world of work. As the internet has more widely become both a necessity to work and for accessing work itself in the new millennium, there has been a rise of digital gig work in contrast to permanent jobs. Digital platform work typically involves performing work on an on-demand or as-needed basis, which is compensated by pieces of work or tasks rather than generally by workers' time. Gig workers must supply their own equipment, such as a car, a smartphone, or a computer (plus internet access). There is also often a triangular relationship between the gig worker (the 'producer'), the end-user,

54 World Economic Forum (2018) 'Future of jobs report'. Geneva: WEF. Available at: www3.weforum.org/docs/WEF_Future_of_Jobs_2018.pdf.

55 Corporaal, G. (2019) 'Intermediaries should be worried about the platform economy'. The iLabour Project, Oxford Internet Institute. Available at: https://ilabour.oii.ox.ac.uk/intermediaries-should-be-worried-about-the-platform-economy/.

56 Lehdonvirta, V., Barnard, H., Graham, M., and Hjorth, I. (2014) 'Online labour markets – levelling the playing field for international service markets?' Paper presented at the IPP2014: Crowdsourcing for Politics and Policy conference, University of Oxford, 25–26, September 2014.

57 Corporaal, G. F. and Lehdonvirta, V. (2017) 'Platform sourcing: how Fortune 500 firms are adopting online freelancing platforms'. Oxford Internet Institute, Oxford. Available at: www.oii.ox.ac.uk/blog/how-the-worlds-largest-companies-use-online-freelancing-platforms-new-report/.

and an intermediary.[58] This digital intermediation, such as an online work platform, is used to commission, supervise, and deliver work, as well as facilitate payment.

What role for humanitarian and development organisations?

In the case of current efforts to foster refugees' self-reliance, humanitarian and development organizations often take on the role of an additional intermediary, commonly in the form of connecting refugees to a primary intermediary (such as Upwork in the case of the RESI programme), through which they then go on to find work. NGOs also take a more removed role in this situation through providing digital training and ICT literacy to improve refugees' chances of competitively accessing work online.

But what sort of work are refugees ultimately able to access through these efforts to foster self-reliance?

Both online and off, precarious employment contracts are becoming the norm, defined by the ILO as work that is low-paid, insecure, with minimal worker control and unprotected,[59] as well as 'work relation[s] where employment security, which is considered one of the principal elements of the labour contract, is lacking'. As Zwick writes, 'Words such as "flexibility" and "competitiveness" become euphemisms for denying workers' rights and engaging in a race-to-the-bottom in terms of wages and benefits'.[60] An ILO report explains:

> The global financial, economic and social crisis we have been experiencing since 2007 has intensified these problems. Instead of drawing lessons from the crisis and changing a failed economic model, governments have allowed themselves to be governed by financial markets. Public sector employment is being slashed, workers' rights have been further eroded, wages have been cut, and millions of additional workers have been pushed into precarious, temporary, and insecure employment, with undeclared work on the rise in many countries.[61]

In addition to reducing benefits to workers, such contracts in fact transfer risk from businesses to workers.[62] The rise of gig work rather than standard work contracts also accounts for billions of dollars in lost tax revenues at local and federal levels as companies are able to avoid the payroll taxes

58 Stanford, 'The resurgence of gig work'.

59 ILO (2016) *Non-Standard Employment Around the World*. Geneva: ILO, p 18.

60 Zwick, A. (2018) 'Welcome to the gig economy: neoliberal industrial relations and the case of Uber'. *GeoJournal* 83(4): 679–691.

61 ILO (2012) 'From precarious work to decent work'. Geneva: ILO, p 3.

62 Beck, U. (2000) *The Brave New World of Work*. Oxford: Blackwell.

that ultimately pay for social protection programmes, including workers' insurance.[63] Thus the notion of precarious work extends in some form to even salaried, permanent workers.

The replacement of employees with independent contractors, alternately known as freelancers and contingent workers, drives down costs and allows quick shifts to new market conditions. It also means that it is often the most economically vulnerable who are employed, with resulting assertions that the 'the last remnants of a Keynesian middle-class economy are being torn down'.[64] Zwick discusses this as a purported aim of corporations, who use the 'neoliberal handbook … to empower themselves at the expense of workers', through a blend of (mis)classifying the legal category of workers, who are erroneously considered independent contractors when they should in fact be employees; 'regime shopping', wherein labour markets are sought on the basis of minimal costs and maximal flexibility, which often results in international outsourcing; and, last, relying on economically vulnerable labour – which often tends to be migrant labour.

These and other characteristics of contemporary gig labour arrangements of course pre-existed the internet and to some extent have been present throughout the history of paid work.[65] Major features of platform work existed in earlier periods of capitalism, but became less popular in the 20th century with the rise of the 'standard employment relationship' which connected workers to steady, contracted employment including benefits.[66] And even the current characterization of digital forms of labour – labour fragmentation, under-payment, and piece-work[67] – began not with the internet but with neoliberal economic restructuring. However, digital access to labour has changed the speed, scope, and scale of such change.[68]

While some initiatives target the vulnerable and lower classes, some of the platforms and initiatives identified here clearly cater to a 'middle class' of refugees such as Alaa who hold prior skills or the social and other capital to access education or undertake work. However, the vast majority of refugees are not part of this digital trend. A much riskier and exploitative informal

---

63 Zwick, 'Welcome to the gig economy'.

64 Zwick, 'Welcome to the gig economy', p 679.

65 Stanford, 'The resurgence of gig work'.

66 Stanford, 'The resurgence of gig work'.

67 Irani, L. (2015) 'Difference and dependence among digital workers: the case of Amazon Mechanical Turk'. *South Atlantic Quarterly* 114(1): 225–234; Lehdonvirta, V. (2016) 'Algorithms that Divide and Unite: Delocalization, Identity, and Collective Action In "Microwork", in J. Flecker (ed) *Space, Place, and Global Digital Work*. London: Palgrave-Macmillan, pp 53–80.

68 Zwick, 'Welcome to the gig economy'.

economy continues to be a daily reality for many.[69] The resulting lack of access stems from a variety of barriers, including lack of proper or recognized identification, host country regulations, and social networks to find or be selected for work. This means that while digital or digitally mediated work opportunities exist, they are ultimately not often accessible to refugees, due in part to the same barriers they are confronted with 'in real life'.

But even if digital work were more accessible to refugees, the risks, challenges, and vulnerabilities present in the global gig economy raise the question of whether decent work can be attained through online work – and what the role of humanitarians in helping refugees access it actually is.

As previously discussed, NGOs working to place refugees in remote digital work today find themselves in the peculiar position of acting as market intermediaries between refugees and corporations offering work in the digital gig economy. Their roles vary from 'linking' refugees to digital work through private sector companies and online work platforms, to acting as third parties seeking to ensure the safety and protection of refugees, to envisioning their role as ultimately leaving the scene once refugees are trained and have connections, if not a job, in the digital gig economy.

As previous chapters have illustrated, this intermediary role between refugees and work is longstanding, such as through providing particular trainings to help refugees fill host country labour gaps. The direct engagement of organizations with private corporations, such as RESI's role in advocating for the adjustment of documentation criteria on platforms like Upwork, is in fact similar to ILO's oversight role in employment-matching in the 1920s. The elephant in the room, however, is that the relationship being mediated is not ultimately between employer and future refugee employee, but rather between refugees and other intermediaries such as online work platforms which do not offer job security, protection, or stability … because they do not actually offer jobs. Instead, the 'gigs' that refugees are encouraged to apply for are often one-off, part-time, and not necessarily well-paid endeavours.

As an example, cumulatively, the Dadaab Collective Freelance Agency members have earned over $3,000 USD for their work, which based on the total number of hours calculated on Upwork averages to almost $20 USD per hour – significantly higher than the US minimum wage and certainly a good hourly rate for people based in Kenya. However, these hours are not necessarily reflective of the actual time undertaken, and a purview of members' hourly rates for significant skills such as Somali–English translating and interpreting shows a general range of $5–12 USD per hour. One freelance member of the group accounts for over $2,000 of

[69] ILO (2016) 'The access of refugees and other forcibly displaced persons to the labour market'. Geneva: ILO. Available at: www.refworld.org/pdfid/58bd53f14.pdf.

the dollars earned, thus significantly skewing the notion of the collective's success as a whole. Most members last worked over a year ago. While the collective is a positive example of what digital skills training and links to online platform can in theory achieve, these figures challenge the idea that – at the moment, at least – digital work is a feasible and large-scale pathway to refugee self-reliance.

It is also important to reflect on the wider trend that humanitarian and development agencies become part of through this type of work. Growing research focuses on the exploitative use of migrant labour to feed the 'flexible' work demanded of many private sector corporations today. Refugees commonly become part of the outsourcing agenda of firms seeking to reduce costs, as discussed earlier, in part through recruiting temporary work agencies and subcontractors to identify, recruit, transfer, and set up workers for employment in a host country.[70] These workers are generally paid far less than local workers (hence their desirability) and are even used to undermine collective bargaining efforts,[71] thus eroding other workers' rights.

It is also crucial to recognize that the demographic of people that humanitarian and development agencies are seeking to help make competitive in the digital gig economy – refugees in some of the world's poorest countries – are effectively competitive because they are cheap labour. As one head of a major digital livelihoods skills training programme for refugees put it, "The work is high volume, low skills … we're not prepping people to become software developers". This raises questions of whether humanitarian and development agencies working to foster refugee self-reliance through digital work become complicit in corporations' efforts to increase profits, slash wages, and outsource jobs to places where workers are cheap and their responsibility is limited – in essence, an arguable undermining of human rights and decent work.

Is this where we want humanitarianism to be going?

Evaluating these different roles – including the main one as an interlocutor between refugees and the digital economy in its many forms – is important for both the well-being of refugees as well as for how humanitarian ethics and organizational mandates may or may not be put to the test. As mentioned in the previous chapter as well as throughout this one, the 'market' is portrayed in current humanitarian practitioner rhetoric on refugees as a gateway for

---

70 Sporton, D. (2013) '"They control my life": the role of local recruitment agencies in East European migration to the UK'. *Population, Space and Place* 19(5): 443–458.

71 Lillie, N. and Greer, I. (2007) 'Industrial relations, migration, and neoliberal politics: the case of the European construction sector'. *Politics and Society* 35(4): 551–581. doi:10.1177/0032329207308179.

(re)-claiming rights and dignity. Yet a broader survey of the current state of work, and projections of the future of it, are not so clear. The casualization of work, the growth of the gig economy, and the largely unregulated digital economy all point toward present and future precarity in digital work in particular.

This suggests that the promotion of refugees' digital livelihoods may ultimately – whatever the intentions – act as yet another exit strategy for donors rather than a true pathway to refugee self-reliance. While there are still grey areas and conflicts over labour regulations, the digital gig economy is also considered by many host governments to be a more appealing 'place' for refugees to work than within these countries themselves, as local jobs are protected and national competition for work is reduced. Given this, humanitarian and development agencies promoting digital work instead of the actual right to work in host countries may be able to avoid tricky conversations about the need for local integration, or worse still, refugees' rights.

Yet, at this point in time at least, it is unclear how successful on a wide scale digital gig work or digital entrepreneurship can be for refugees. Most of the digital training programmes are fragmented and small-scale; significant challenges abound in identifying corporations interested in working with refugees for anything more than a social corporate responsibility stunt. Take Alaa, who is an individual success story but one that may not be widely replicable due to both the likelihood of market oversaturation and the specific skillsets and needs that led to Tomooh.

Following on from this, it is also clear that the story of Tomooh is not just of digital entrepreneurship or successful digital work; it is one of a shuttered community centre in an impoverished environment, of an unfunded project to assist refugees, and of lost access to resources, including mutual aid and information. One of the many broader issues presented is thus also that of what is lost in the digitalization of refugee assistance. While Tomooh as a website and a livelihood is a success story, it also signifies a failure. A website cannot reconstitute a place for children to play or a room to sit in and make friends. 'The digital' may be a space but there is much it cannot hold. As international agencies and organizations continue to examine 'innovative' ways to assist refugees, this should be remembered – particularly in the ongoing face of COVID-19, where the digitalization of many services may exclude many more than it can include.

Conclusion

Currently, literature on the future of work rarely addresses the needs of and possibilities for refugees. Even today, governments and international labour bodies generally focus on placing refugees in 'traditional' sectors of work, including an enduring focus on agriculture and artisanship, thereby bypassing chances for this population to become part of the so-called 'next economy'.

While the Sustainable Development Goals and the Global Compact on Refugees offer important frameworks for action, digital work for refugees has largely remained disconnected from these frameworks' objectives, including critical considerations of how this type of work can truly combat poverty, offer decent work and economic growth, and 'leave no one behind'.[72] The technology and enterprise community have also largely not engaged beyond small corporate social responsibility-esque efforts, leaving opportunities for engagement and a variety of risks to attend to in this still emerging global phenomenon. This is all the more glaring in the face of the COVID-19 pandemic, which illuminates both the value of digitalization for work and other areas of life, and the reality of how much of the world remains excluded from not just internet connectivity but the basic infrastructure to establish it. If these and other issues are left unaddressed, the likelihood is high that many refugees will remain both non-self-reliant and further left behind as huge shifts in work and the global economy continue without them.

[72] Learn more about the Global Compact on Refugees here: www.unhcr.org/uk/the-global-compact-on-refugees.html, and the Sustainable Development Goals here: https://sustainabledevelopment.un.org/?menu=1300.

7

Conclusion

After a century of humanitarian and development practice, the concept of refugee self-reliance endures. And the question remains: What do we mean when we speak of refugee self-reliance? And who is speaking – or should be – about it, anyway? Past chapters of this book explored specific practices intended to foster refugee self-reliance, its constructed 'beneficiaries' (such as vulnerable refugees or refugee entrepreneurs), and how refugee self-reliance assistance has evolved in parallel with broader trends in global economic and political history. This history reveals self-reliance assistance as not only an inherently contested but a *constricted* concept, as seen by outside actors such as the donors, humanitarians, and states imposing programmes on refugees as subjects, be they considered beneficiaries, entrepreneurs, or livelihoods training participants.

The implications of many findings from the history of refugee self-reliance assistance are moral, practical, and problematic: this assistance purports to offer refugees the ability to enact their own agency – a situation many would agree is inherently in conflict – and in doing so reveals relationships of power and instrumentalization. This history has demonstrated both continuity and change in the conceptualization and practices of refugee self-reliance by dominant actors – and a century of disappointing outcomes in the institutional fostering of refugee self-reliance by many of the very actors purporting today to uphold refugees' dignity and enhance their protection.

Theoretical contributions to the study of refugee self-reliance

This book's critical reading of history illuminates the role of capital in shaping refugee self-reliance policy, and treats refugee self-reliance assistance itself as a shifting set of practices intimately connected to the capitalist system. In so doing, several particularly valuable elements of critical theory for the study of refugee self-reliance emerge: first, an examination of structural causes of a given phenomenon using the logic of the capitalist system – with the intent then, as Schuurman states, 'to do something about it'.[1] This element helps us ask everything from why particular humanitarian and development programmes are structured the way they are, with a given set of objectives, to what structural economic forces are impacting the actual outcomes of such programmes.

Relatedly, the framework of instrumentalization used here expands on this focus through an explicit examination of how assistance can serve other interests besides those of its beneficiaries. In other words, *cui bono* (who benefits)? Notably, the concept of instrumentalization as used here is not limited to an analysis of refugee assistance but instead can be extended to other sectors that entail provider–beneficiary relationships in the international sphere. These include humanitarianism, development, and even the field of health.

Refugees provide an important case study for examining the power relations present in the provision of international assistance, and this conceptual framework offers Refugee Studies in particular an opportunity to engage with critical development theory through a structural examination of other types of refugee assistance, as well. Taking refugee self-reliance assistance as its central focus, this book demonstrates the utility of critical development theory not just for studies of refugee self-reliance but for Refugee Studies as a whole, and contributes to work linking humanitarianism and capitalism.[2] To the best of my knowledge, this perspective has not previously been brought to Refugee Studies.

Take-aways for policy and practice: what have we learned?

First, what has not changed? There is a striking similarity in self-reliance assistance across time and place as 'help' that primarily treats refugees as sources of labour. While the intended outcomes of engaging refugees in work have varied, ranging from boosting refugee-hosting economies, contributing to national and international development projects, and relieving the 'burden'

1 Schuurman, F. J. (2009) 'Critical Development Theory: moving out of the twilight zone'. *Third World Quarterly* 30(5): 831–848 (p 836).

2 Ashworth, J. (1987) 'The relationship between capitalism and humanitarianism'. *The American Historical Review* 92(4): 813–828; Haskell, T. L. (1985) 'Capitalism and the origins of the humanitarian sensibility, Part 1'. *The American Historical Review* 90(2): 339–361; Haskell, T. L. (1985) 'Capitalism and the origins of the humanitarian sensibility, Part 2'. *The American Historical Review* 90(3): 547–566.

of refugees from humanitarian donors, the main practices to foster refugee self-reliance have remained similar. Agricultural settlement, vocational training, micro-finance, public works, and employment-matching are all types of self-reliance programming that have endured over the past century despite significant changes of global power and economic, political, and social systems.

This continuity in practices also mirrors another persistent trend in self-reliance assistance: linking refugees to national development programmes and agendas. Different eras saw multi-pronged efforts to foster refugee self-reliance through various forms of labour while simultaneously boosting host countries' infrastructure and economic development. This ranged from agricultural production in interwar Greece and post-colonial Tanzania to World Bank-led public works projects in Cold War Pakistan to a shifting focus on refugee entrepreneurs and refugee employment in the informal sector in the new millennium and beyond. The previous chapters detailing 'model' refugee self-reliance assistance programmes found that they were often conceived of as new at the time of implementation. Through these case studies, 'reincarnations' of similar practices are clearly evident, such as zonal development, which became popular in the 1960s and 1970s in Africa. Sometimes, these repetitions have been obscured by discursive changes, such as from the 1920s' 'rehabilitation' and 'self-sufficiency' to the 1960s' 'animation' of refugees, yet strategies virtually identical to zonal development – offering assistance that benefits both refugees and locals in particular areas – appeared under other names in the 1980s and more recent decades. However, zonal development has been largely forgotten and these later programmes remain largely ascribed to the 1979 Arusha Conference, which sought to address Western restrictionism and the rise of protracted refugee situations in sub-Saharan Africa. The aims of linking refugee self-reliance and national development have therefore remained consistent throughout the history of the international refugee regime.

At the same time, important changes within self-reliance assistance practices are evident. For example, refugee self-reliance assistance has, since its inception, shifted from emphasizing the placement of refugees into formal work, such as the ILO's employment-matching scheme in the 1920s, to promoting refugees' informal work through livelihoods training and entrepreneurship today. There has also been a shift from focusing on refugees' agricultural livelihoods to urban (self-)employment, which is generally in the informal sector. The advent of internet technology and the growing digitalization of work constitutes perhaps the most striking shift in practices; however, the nascent outcomes of this focus suggest that they may be similar to other more recent efforts to bring refugees into the market: low-paid, part-time work on short-term or no contracts at all.

Throughout the history of refugee self-reliance assistance, focus has also shifted from supporting the collective self-reliance of populations, including those living in refugee settlements, to promoting individual forms of self-reliance, such as providing livelihoods trainings to foster individual entrepreneurship. Refugee self-reliance assistance from the interwar period up to the early 1980s demonstrates a focus by assistance agencies on collective self-reliance at the level of communities, such as the growing of cash and subsistence crops in rural Tanzanian settlements. However, the self-reliance assistance practices after the mid-1980s de-emphasized this approach, in part due to urbanization. For example, self-reliance assistance for Afghan refugees shifted in the 1980s to vocational training targeting individuals as entrepreneurs rather than addressing mass unemployment through public works projects. This individual focus has extended to the present day, illustrated by the primary emphasis on livelihoods trainings as self-reliance assistance for urban refugees in Kampala and individualized efforts to engage refugees in the digital economy through small-scale IT training.[3] These changes in self-reliance assistance's intended beneficiaries stem in part from a larger economic shift in development from collective efforts to address poverty and inequality to focusing on individuals' ability to navigate adversities alone.

Self-reliance, development, and welfare

Examining the *longue durée* of refugee self-reliance also reveals trends that rise and fall with broader social and economic phenomena elsewhere in the world. This includes parallels to broader shifts in development and welfare practice, such as strengthening the protection that states are capable of offering to fostering self-reliance in the *absence* of states. As explored in the chapter on Afghan refugees in Pakistan, Western welfare reforms have progressively stripped welfare programmes of their core linkages to central governments, and have instead increasingly advocated beneficiaries' reliance on the market through their own employment to attain basic necessities. The 1980s saw a shift in both domestic and international welfare to neoliberal modes of self-reliance assistance that promote market engagement through individualism and entrepreneurialism over Keynesian-esque collective employment initiatives. The trend has continued in recent decades. Under the 'Self-Reliance' component of UNHCR's programmatic response in

[3] For a further contemporary discussion on collective versus individual refugee self-reliance programming approaches see: Carpi, E., Field, J. A., Dicker, S. I., and Rigon, A. (2020) 'From livelihoods to leisure and back: refugee "self-reliance" as collective practices in Lebanon, India and Greece'. *Third World Quarterly* 42(2): 421–440.

the 2020 UNHCR Global Report, for example, the only activities listed were vocational training, entrepreneurship/business training, and advice on labour markets.[4]

Through these livelihoods and self-reliance initiatives undertaken by the international refugee regime, the main 'solution' for refugees is challenged: refugee assistance does not only aim to restore people into the nation-state system but into *economic* systems, as well – or perhaps even primarily. Indeed, this latter aim is arguably at the forefront of protection and assistance today given increasing restrictions on accessing asylum in the Global North and restrictions on refugees' rights in refugee-hosting countries of the Global South. Despite important ongoing rights advocacy by UNHCR and other humanitarian and development actors, labour market integration, rather than the local integration once conceived of as a full set of rights leading to citizenship per the 1951 Convention, appears to be considered the most feasible path forward.[5]

And yet – writing this now in 2021 – the COVID-19 pandemic should in many ways have shattered our illusions (if we still had them) about the 'safety' of the market for refugees. Many of the Congolese refugees interviewed in Uganda in 2015 have had their livelihoods destroyed by government responses to the COVID-19 pandemic. Although Uganda had one of the harshest lockdowns in the world, it is notable that it did not take the weeks and months of the first lockdown, and then the second, to destroy these livelihoods. Instead, in under a week many people started to go hungry. This has not gone unnoticed. Promisingly, even prior to the pandemic, there have been more discussions and work on the need for refugees' inclusion into national social protection systems. As discussed in more depth, if ever there was a time to seriously consider expanding the right for refugees *not* to work, it is now.

From bottom-up to top-down

Another change in practice is the level of agency and engagement refugees have had in the practice of humanitarian assistance and self-reliance programming. While some level of refugee agency was in instances welcomed in the interwar years, the more predominant story throughout this history is a lack of true agency in refugees' ability to foster their self-reliance as they see fit. We see this through the larger trends of self-reliance assistance itself, which changes focus and scope alongside national and international economic and social trends rather than sitting primarily with the interests and skills of refugees themselves.

[4] UNHCR (2020) '2020 global report'. Geneva: UNHCR.

[5] DRC (2021) Which Refugee Self-Reliance? Whose Durable Solution? Copenhagen: Danish Refugee Council. Available at: https://prod.drc.ngo/media/od0i2zb4/drc-refugee-self-reliance-report-final.pdf.

And, likely, when gazing from the vantage point of national and international institutions and programmes, we just don't see refugee agency at all. Think of Alaa, self-reliant in Cairo but under the radar, online, and out of sight.

As the first chapter on Greek refugees in Greece and elsewhere in Europe found, refugee self-reliance assistance was bottom-up and largely ad hoc during the interwar years yet became part of top-down, technocratic development efforts after the Second World War. In the 1920s and 1930s, refugee self-reliance played a central role in refugee assistance, exemplified through the employment of refugees in the High Commission for Refugees and Nansen Office, refugee funding of the Nansen Stamp Fund, ILO's employment-matching scheme and efforts to place refugees in urban or rural areas based on past livelihoods. After the Second World War, refugee self-reliance, and thus the role of refugees themselves, became ancillary, with the predominant focus shifting to host country development. Refugees were forced onto agricultural settlements that implemented block farming for cash crops, and were incarcerated if found engaging in alternative methods of self-reliance. In this way, the international refugee regime changed from being at least partially inclusive toward refugees to largely exclusive, further evidenced through the declining employment levels of refugees by assistance agencies as the League's High Commission was eventually replaced by UNHCR.

While interwar era assistance assuredly made use of refugees in ways that benefited both assistance agencies and states, it also necessitated the role of refugees as active participants in the fostering of their own self-reliance in both entrepreneurial and organizational capacities. However, the periods thereafter involved refugees more passively as beneficiaries. Refugees in Tanzanian settlements in the 1970s, for example, were part of 'hollow' leadership structures while Afghans in the 1990s were rarely in leadership positions within the very NGOs designed to promote their independence.[6]

Concomitant with changing discussions of refugees' agency has been the reconceptualization of refugees from capable workers in the interwar years to members of a vulnerable population after the Second World War. Since the new millennium the construction of refugees has arguably shifted back toward refugees as active agents with skills and value to contribute to host societies, with repeated calls for refugee 'participation'[7] and rising awareness

6 Weiner, M., Banuazizi, A., Barfield, T., Choucri, N., Gakenheimer, R., Moavenzadeh, F., and Rothenberg, J. (1991) 'A feasibility study prepared by the Reconstruction Group of the Center for International Studies of the Massachusetts Institute of Technology'. PN-ABS-658-90358, p 63.

7 See, for example, the language in: UNHCR (2017) 'A guide to market-based livelihoods interventions for refugees'. Geneva: UNHCR. The document opens with: 'Refugees are people with marketable skills and abilities, and a strong motivation to build their own livelihoods' (np).

of the work of refugees themselves as providers of protection and assistance through refugee-led organizations and initiatives. However, within formal humanitarian institutions, refugees are rarely embedded in assistance efforts in ways other than as beneficiaries and in this way the international refugee regime maintains largely exclusionary programming.[8] Growing efforts today to carve out spaces of 'meaningful' engagement by refugees in policymaking, as discussed in more depth, are promising and also slow to be taken up more widely.

Reflecting on older African settlements, a 1985 Refugee Policy Group report stated, 'Refugee participation may be the concept with the worst ratio of rhetoric to reality in the entire refugee assistance system'.[9] The relevance of this statement to refugee self-reliance assistance today makes it important to question how current practices within the sector address the abiding lack of affected community participation. Despite a contemporary emphasis on participatory approaches within refugee assistance, new partnerships have largely been forged outside of affected communities,[10] instead of evaluating and adjusting the structures through which assistance is provided. Findings from an Oxfam consultation of refugee-led and other civil society organizations in refugee-hosting countries found that local organizations continue to be neglected in policymaking and other decision-making processes surrounding refugees.[11] Similarly, UNHCR's 2019–2023 Global Strategy Concept Note for Refugee Livelihoods and Economic Inclusion aims to advocate for refugees' right to work, yet nowhere states refugees or other displaced people as potential partners in these endeavours.[12] In this way, despite a discourse of refugee capability in UNHCR's Livelihoods Unit and elsewhere, programme implementation is reminiscent of post-war administration in that it is still driven by actors other than refugees themselves.

The outcomes of refugee self-reliance assistance

Examining where solutions are needed in refugee assistance with knowledge of this history is important, for, in cases, the failed rural settlements of

---

8 Easton-Calabria, E. (2016) 'From participation to partnership: refugee-run organisations as important actors in development'. *FMR* 52: 72–74. Oxford: University of Oxford.

9 RPG (1985) 'Older refugee settlements in Africa: final report'. Washington, DC: Refugee Policy Group, p 104.

10 UNHCR, 'Global strategy for livelihoods'.

11 International Refugee Congress (2018) 'International Refugee Congress 2018 consultation report'. Istanbul: Oxfam Turkey. Available at: www.refugeecongress2018.org/resources-files/Consultation_Report_2018_March_03.05.2018.pdf (accessed 5 May 2018).

12 UNHCR (2019) '2019–2023 global strategy concept note for refugee livelihoods and economic inclusion'. Geneva: UNHCR.

the 1960s and 1970s have become the refugee camps of today, with many persisting practical challenges. Ongoing problems include inadequate planning for refugee camps, such as lack of soil testing, and a disregard for refugees' own methods of livelihoods creation. Kaiser's examination of long-term Sudanese refugees in Uganda, for example, discusses problems of soil quality and inadequate settlement plot size[13] – precisely the same issues as reported by Betts on the same population in Uganda in the 1960s.[14] In 2010, UNHCR cited 'lack of early planning' as a major issue in responding to displacement,[15] echoing discussions and disappointing results from previous decades. And 2020 monitoring by UNHCR found that over 60 per cent of refugees could not even meet *half* of their basic needs that year,[16] illustrating the dire effect of COVID-19 lockdowns on refugees' economic lives, in large part due to their informal nature.

Poverty and self-reliance

Despite widespread efforts to support refugees to engage economically, and regardless of whether they are in camps or cities, resettled in the Global North or living in the Global South, refugees are living in poverty. In the US today, for example, Indo-Chinese refugees, who constitute the largest resettled refugee population in the country beginning in the 1970s, still struggle with significant rates of poverty – 45 years after resettlement.[17] The situation globally of extreme poverty faced by many refugees is so dire that UNHCR helped form a Poverty Alleviation Coalition to address this.[18] Yet rather than tackle the structural factors and restrictions on rights that contribute to refugees' poverty today, the coalition promotes the Graduation Approach, which, while proven to be effective across countries and circumstances, constitutes an individualized approach that retains the onus on individual refugees to work their way out of poverty. However, in a world where an estimated 80 per cent of the global workforce is in the informal sector, lacking labour rights and at risk of exploitation, and many major refugee-hosting countries face some of the world's highest rates of

---

13 Kaiser, 'Between a camp and a hard place'. *The Journal of Modern African Studies* 44(4): 597–621.

14 Betts, T. F. (1969) 'Sudanese refugees in Uganda: the position in May 1969'. Report of Advice on Zonal Rural Development, Oxfam, 13 May.

15 UNHCR (2010) 'Concept note: Transitional Solutions Initiative—UNDP and UNHCR in collaboration with the World Bank'. Geneva: UNHCR, p 7.

16 UNHCR, '2020 global report'.

17 SEARAC (2020) www.searac.org/wp-content/uploads/2020/02/SEARAC_NationalSnapshot_PrinterFriendly.pdf.

18 www.unhcr.org/uk/poverty-alleviation-coalition.html.

unemployment, what type of work are refugees likely to engage in, and how far above the poverty line will many go? And – given all this – where do notions such as self-reliance, dignity, and protection fit in?

Viewing this history up to today, several take-aways are apparent. One – be it when learning about refugees in the 1920s or in 2022 – is that an over-reliance on livelihoods as a means to refugee integration (for example, a predominant focus on labour market integration) often comes at the expense of protection and, indeed, other rights. Implicitly and explicitly at different points in time, markets have been utilized both as a protection tool by humanitarians and as the endpoint of 'successful' refugee self-reliance, with the logic that refugees can achieve dignity through market-based activities and that once some form of income generation is found, humanitarian assistance can cease. We see this discursively but we do not find the evidence justifying this logic on a widespread scale in practice.

Previous chapters have explored both the benefits and harms of linking the process and outcome of refugee self-reliance to ulterior interests. For example, refugee self-reliance assistance during the interwar years sought to help refugees become commercial farmers able to grow cash crops such as tobacco to boost Greece's export economy. Refugees were encouraged to take out loans in order to do so, but faced challenges in both loan repayment and in feeding themselves and their families when cash crops such as tobacco rapidly dropped in price on the global market. The notion of instrumentalization, wherein an ulterior motive is achieved through efforts to foster refugee self-reliance, has come up repeatedly in different ways as the shape of refugee self-reliance assistance has changed over time.

In reality, many refugees over the past century have likely struggled to create or recreate livelihoods that generate enough income to live sustainably and well, or to find employment at all. Many countries have seen a restriction of refugee rights, including the right to work, over this time. Currently UNHCR estimates that 70 per cent of refugees live in countries with restricted or no right to work, 66 per cent live in countries with restricted or no right to freedom of movement, and 47 per cent live in countries with restricted or no right to bank accounts, effectively making almost half of the world's refugees an unbanked population.[19] Given that many refugees are not incorporated into host country national protection schemes (if these exist at all), the precarity of work becomes more evident and the expectation of refugee self-reliance as a panacea to global forced displacement seems even more far-fetched. And, given this disjuncture, livelihoods support risks becoming a policy of containment, wherein the idea rather than the

[19] UNHCR, 'Livelihoods and economic inclusion'. Available at: www.unhcr.org/livelihoods.html (accessed 1 April 2021).

outcome of refugee self-reliance is packaged and sold to eager donor states hoping to keep refugees from moving onward.

This thinking is faulty. The climate crisis is worsening, with the projected trend of more northern migration as temperatures rise. The economic fall-out from COVID-19 will continue. Aid budgets have already been significantly cut. Small-scale livelihoods trainings in sectors lacking markets in countries lacking employment opportunities, and individual introductions of refugees as gig workers and freelancers into the digital economy, are not enough to create refugee self-reliance on a widespread scale. They are certainly not enough to foster it with the dignity that current rhetoric states that it can bring.[20]

Next steps for refugee self-reliance

So what now?

Much of the work that has started must continue. There is a need to aim for practical and policy targets that are in reach, of which there are many. Continuing more recent efforts to conduct market assessments to inform livelihoods programming is one; ongoing efforts to define and measure self-reliance and track its outcomes, such as through the Self-Reliance Index led by the Refugee Self-Reliance Initiative,[21] is another.

As has been detailed in later chapters of this book in particular, there is a risk that the current individualized programmatic focus on refugee self-reliance blinds us to the way current realities are shaped by structural forces beyond any one refugee's control. Loosening the widespread restriction on refugees' rights, notably the rights to work, to freedom of movement, and to banking, are crucial building blocks for allowing refugees to engage economically. The initiative 'Let Them Work' led by the Center for Global Development and Refugees International is one promising example of research and advocacy pushing for expanded labour market access for refugees.[22]

---

20 See, for example, this excerpt from UNHCR's 2020 Global Report:

> Enabling refugees' resilience goes hand-in-hand with achieving durable solutions. Enhancing the self-reliance of refugees and other people of concern is a crucial component of the Global Compact on Refugees. Better self-reliance means refugees and host communities are better able to meet their essential needs, enjoy their human rights and live with dignity. Ensuring they have quality education, livelihoods opportunities and access to safe and sustainable energy benefits both host communities and people of concern to UNHCR. (p 110).

21 To learn more, see: www.refugeeselfreliance.org/.

22 To learn more, see: www.cgdev.org/sites/default/files/locked-down-and-left-behind-paper-71320.pdf.

At the same time there is an ongoing need to position refugees' economic independence within the broader contexts of host countries which arguably lack it themselves. Robert Cox wrote of the 'larger wholes' that critical examinations must encompass; ongoing trade and development asymmetry between the Global North and those countries in the Global South hosting most of the world's refugees is one 'whole' that refugee self-reliance is entwined within. High rates of unemployment in many of these countries, and global poverty levels, are two others.

There is also a need for a more radical reckoning of contemporary practices and discourses of self-reliance. The enduring existence of many refugees who are unable to work either due to disability, lack of assets, or other life circumstances illustrates that the right to work must be accompanied by the right *not* to work. This focus necessitates a decriminalizing of such situations, in part through a broader discursive shift that recognizes that vulnerability is not a problem to be fixed through self-reliance, and that resilience and vulnerability indeed often exist alongside each other.[23] Practically, taking the right not to work seriously means in practice ongoing commitments to incorporate refugees into national social protection schemes, and the expanded use of social transfers. Indeed, there is great value in offering assistance for refugees to not work at all if the only work available is dangerous and exploitative.

There is currently little academic scholarship or practical efforts linking refugee self-reliance to labour unions or labour collectives (perhaps reflecting the overall decline of unions in the last several decades). However, as both sociologists and activists remind us, rights are not won by individuals but by groups. To this end, there may be value in examining parallel situations involving migrants to better understand how advocacy platforms and alliances could be forged both nationally and transnationally to support the rights of refugee workers. National labour unions in the US have, for example, formally supported undocumented migrants since 2000, and in instances have offered legal support to represent union members at risk of deportation by immigration authorities. Understanding how this arose and the impact it has on migrant workers could offer insights for refugees facing similar restrictions elsewhere.

This brings us to another under-explored aspect of refugee self-reliance: its (non-)political construction. Despite examples of refugees being offered rights and livelihoods support in exchange for political allegiance, such as the case of Greek refugees and Prime Minister Venizelos in the 1920s, refugee self-reliance is rarely discussed as a political concept in current discourse. Notably, this element is missing in the UNHCR definition, which discusses ways self-reliance can help refugees be 'better able to enjoy their rights' but

[23] See for example: Krause, U. and Schmidt, H. (2020) 'Refugees as actors? Critical reflections on global refugee policies on self-reliance and resilience'. *Journal of Refugee Studies* 33(1): 22–41.

does not broach the often political ways these rights are obtained. Recent refugee-led advocacy initiatives such as the Global Refugee-Led Network (GRN) and Asia Pacific Refugee Rights Network (APRRN) bring this discussion into the sphere of humanitarianism and development through furthering awareness of the need for refugee self-governance in assistance and policymaking. The rising focus on refugee-led organizations as important actors in the assistance and protection of fellow refugees[24] illustrates the collective efforts of refugees around the world yet also reveals how political aspirations may be subsumed into more 'acceptable' forms of self-help such as livelihoods assistance. Yet engaging in politics is a requisite of civic life, and indeed a right unto itself; regardless of host country fears or humanitarians' discomfort, this should not be forgotten.

A crucial ongoing question is how refugees themselves define self-reliance and the assistance they see as necessary to attain it. Although this was explored to a certain extent in later chapters, extensive qualitative research on this would greatly add to contemporary discussions of refugee self-reliance and livelihoods. Likewise, an 'alternative history' of refugee self-reliance based on indigenous conceptualizations or documenting the assistance provided by grassroots refugee-led and national organizations would be a clear complement to the largely top-down focus here.[25] And, as mentioned in the introduction, the many other non-economic aspects of self-reliance deserve an equal seat at the table.

Final word

Ruth Palmeree provides a refugee in Greece with a loan to buy seeds in the 1920s. T. F. Betts advocates that another in 1970s' Tanzania sell his wood carvings, a craft he brought with him from Burundi. UNHCR employs an Afghan refugee in Pakistan in 1988 as a 'social animator'. The JRS trains a woman in Uganda in arts and crafts in 2015. Syrian refugees in Cairo develop a much-needed website offering advice and resources to fellow Syrians, and begin making money from it through Google ads.

[24] See: Pincock, K., Betts, A., and Easton-Calabria, E. (2020) *The Global Governed? Refugees as providers of protection and assistance*. Cambridge University Press.

[25] This would complement the small body of existing work focusing on refugee agency in relation to these topics. See Barbelet, V. and Wake, C. (2017) *Livelihood Strategies of Central African Refugees in Cameroon*. London: Overseas Development Institute (ODI); Field, J., Tiwari, A. D., and Mookherjee, Y. (2017) 'Refugee Self-Reliance in Delhi: The limits of a market-based approach', in J. Fiori and A. Rigon (eds) *Making Lives: Refugee self-reliance and humanitarian action in cities*. London: Humanitarian Affairs Team, Save the Children, pp 37–72; for non-academic explorations of refugee perspectives, see Ground Truth Solutions (2018) 'Should I stay or should I go?' 30 January. Available at: http://groundtruthsolutions.org/2018/01/30/should-i-stay-or-should-i-go/ (accessed 1 March 2018).

And then?

Based on the findings of this book, the purported intended endings of these stories – self-reliance – are not assured. Crops may go bad or the international market demand may suddenly drop. Settlement administrators may forbid particular livelihoods activities, or a host country may crack down on informal work. An international assistance agency may face funding cuts or withdraw completely. After three months, a new business may fail. Host country policies create restriction after restriction to refugees' entrepreneurship or, indeed, ability to work at all.

And so?

The stories in this book and its larger narrative demonstrate that refugee self-reliance is a dynamic concept and set of practices. Its institutional history in the 20th and 21st centuries reveal much – continuities and changes; suppression and resurgence; links to larger social, political, and economic processes. Different strategies have been preferred by host and donor governments and international assistance agencies over time, with varying motives and results. Archival research reveals that many contemporary practices have been employed, sometimes successfully, since the 1920s. Yet their structure and form of implementation have changed.

Self-reliance as a concept in itself has also changed meaning, at one point being defined as the 'natural' ability to live without institutionally provided aid, at another as food security in the face of cuts to assistance, and more recently as some form of income generation within host country labour markets, or perhaps the digital global economy. Its shift in wording, notably from the common term of 'self-sufficiency' to 'self-reliance' over time, as well as related terms such as 'rural animation' and 'self-help', demonstrates more of a repackaging than an authentic innovation of these practices. These terms may complicate its tracing but do not obscure its persistence as a valuable concept to a multitude of actors in the international refugee regime.

As we enter the next chapter of refugee self-reliance assistance, with self-reliance a 'pillar' of the Global Compact on Refugees, the COVID-19 pandemic ongoing, and remote work now a common term for us all, it would be wise to remember that definitions and practices of this assistance do little to explicate how refugees define and live out *their own* self-reliance. This book reveals the persistent neglect of refugee agency over a century of self-reliance assistance, and thereby the largest contradiction of this history. Indeed, following the interests and activities of refugees themselves, rather than those of instrumentalizing benefactors, may be the most successful means found yet to support refugees as agents rather than subjects of self-reliance.

Annex: A Note on Methods and Sources

Many of the documents I examined were project or settlement reports from UNHCR, the League of Nations, ILO, UNDP, World Bank, or national organizations such as the TCRS. These documents were often interim or final project reports which detailed the inception, funding, implementation, and outcomes of programmes. Thus, they likely targeted donors and senior organizational staff, and for this reason I treated them as valuable sources of information but not necessarily sources of 'truth'. I specifically took potential bias into account regarding records of project success, such as the UNHCR/World Bank project in Pakistan which employed both refugees and locals during the 1980s and was extended for multiple years. While project reports detailed the meeting of programme objectives (such as a certain percentage of refugees employed and local habitation restored), it was difficult to corroborate such statements without first-hand accounts from outside sources. However, I was able to find speeches from former UNHCR High Commissioner Hocké lauding the programme and depicting it as a model to be replicated. I also located contemporaneous secondary academic sources discussing the project as a success. What I garnered from this research of outside sources was not confirmation that the UNHCR/World Bank project was indeed a success, but instead that it was widely *presented* and *perceived* as one, including by arguably the most influential head of an institution representing refugee assistance (UNHCR). As this, after all, was the focus of my project – to examine programmes presented as models and successes, not necessarily *successful* programmes themselves – this project merited inclusion.

In contrast to many of the official reports I researched, sources such as journal entries and private letters appeared to hold more reliability due to the presumed intentions with which they were written. The copious journal entries and letters to family and friends by Ruth A. Palmeree in Greece in the 1920s and 1930s, for example, appeared to be written only for her intended audience as a form of regular communication and connection, as well as personal solace. The consistent style of letters across years, which often depicted the minutiae of daily life, such as how many babies were born in the hospital she ran or the furnishings of the new apartment she moved into, demonstrated the author as a reliable narrator whose depictions could largely be understood as true according to her. Similarly, private letters found in the T. F. Betts and Neldner Collections focusing on post-Second World War refugee assistance written between settlement commandants, staff, and other contacts often contained a directness that contributed to their air of reliability. One example (provided in depth in case study 2) is a letter by a programme supervisor of TCRS Agricultural Programme to Mr Neldner following a negative UNHCR appraisal of their programme: 'The people who have made the comments have talked much about the negative aspects in the settlements and not talked enough about the positive sides. This is a very important thing and the field staff should be told that they have to be careful about making negative remarks.'[1] Such frank statements about the need for control suggest a confidential correspondence where true feelings and perceptions about events were shared, thus making it a more reliable document.

A note on connecting historical and contemporary methods and cases

If appropriately undertaken, archival and contemporary research can be complementary approaches to learning of assistance to refugees. Both archival analysis and qualitative research, such as semi-structured interviews and (non-)participant observation, offer the means to gain information on specific topics as well as analyse discourse to learn of power dynamics and interests. Indeed, some have articulated the social process of archival research, describing an attempt to 're-create social worlds' through tracing 'histories … and the people who were represented in those histories'.[2] Contemporary research can be seen as having the opportunity to enter social worlds in 'real-time' – yet with a researcher still facing the significant task thereafter of 're-creating' them through analysis and writing up findings.

Ultimately, although my case studies are on historical time periods and actual events, this project follows a narrative that is my own. I sought to remain 'true' to my archival material and qualitative fieldwork through describing and sharing the information they contained while also using my own lens to examine material interests and power relations.

---

1 Jernaes, J. (1971) 'Letter to Mr. Neldner, regarding Mr. Feldman's report 25th September'. Neldner Archives, Bodleian Social Science Library, University of Oxford. RSP/NELD/ LT 59.44 FEL.

2 Lerner, N. (2010) 'Archival Research as a Social Process', in A. E. Ramsey, W. B. Sharer, B. L'Eplattenier, and L. Mastrangelo (eds) (2009) *Working in the Archives: Practical research methods for rhetoric and composition*. Southern Illinois: SIU Press, pp 195–205 (p 196).

References

Primary literature

Afghanistan Center Archives, Kabul University (Digital archive)

ARC (Austrian Relief Committee for Afghan Refugees) (1988) 'Annual report 1987'. FA/FP 61 ARC in Box FA/FP Afghans in Pakistan, 59.3–64.

Holtzman, S., Herbison, O., and Qayum, A. (1990) 'A discussion on Afghan involvement in reconstruction and relief activities'. Peshawar: GTZ (Deutsche Gesellschaft fuer Technische Zusammenarbeit)/ACBAR (Agency Coordinating Body for Afghan Relief).

Rädda Barnen (1992) 'Workshop on assistance to disabled refugees'. 4–8 October. Peshawar, Pakistan. Available at: www.tinyurl.com/yaeeaj75 (accessed 1 July 2016).

Brainerd P. Salmon Private Papers (Hoover Institution Archives, Stanford University)

Salmon, B. P. (1924) 'The Report', Folder 1, Writings, 1923–1924. Brainerd P. Salmon Papers, Hoover Institution Archives.

General Boxes, University of Oxford Refugee Studies Centre Grey Literature Collection (Oxford, UK)

ACBAR (1990) 'Overview of NGO assistance to the people of Afghanistan'. Agency Coordinating Body for Afghan Relief (ACBAR), Peshawar, Pakistan 1990. RSC Cardbox: FA/FP 59.3 ACB in FA/FP 59.3 A-Z.

Bennett, J. (nd) 'Afghanistan: cross-border NGO coordination'. ICVA. RSC Cardbox: FA/FP 59.4 BEN in Box FA/FP Afghans in Pakistan, 59.3–64.

Blomqvist, U. (1995) 'Follow-up study on the impact of the 1993 evaluations of the Rädda Barnen Training Unit [RBTU] in Peshawar, Pakistan'. The Emergency Standby Team (Swedish Save the Children), December. RSC Cardbox: FA/FP 625.25 BLO in FA/FP 62–62.25.

Boesen, I. (1983) 'From autonomy to dependency: aspects of the "dependency syndrome" among Afghan refugees'. Paper presented at the BIA (Bureau International d'Afghanistan) Conference on Afghan Refugees in Geneva, 4–6 November 1983. RSC Cardbox: FA/FP 65 BOE in FA/FP 65–65.25.

Christensen, H. and Scott, W. (1987) 'Survey of the social and economic conditions of Afghan refugees in Pakistan'. UNRISD. RSC Cardbox: FA/FP 65 CHR in FA/FP 65–65.25.

Clark, L. (1985) 'The refugee dependency syndrome: physician, heal thyself!' Refugee Policy Group. RSC Cardbox: RSP Documentation Centre, A 59.1 CLA.

IRC (International Rescue Committee) (1987) 'International Rescue Committee Pakistan program', August. RSC Cardbox: FA/FP 59.3 IRC in FA/FP 59.3 A-Z.

IRC (1988) 'Special report: integrating programs: education and self-reliance'. Quarterly Report April–June. International Rescue Committee Pakistan Programme. RSC Cardbox: A/FP 59.3 IRC in Box FA/FAP 59.3 A-Z.

Millwood, D. (1995) 'The Rädda Barnen Training Unit: community-based social work with Afghan refugees in Pakistan'. RSC Cardbox: FA/FP 64.14 MIL in Box FA/FP Afghans in Pakistan, 59.3–64.

Morton, J. (1992) 'The socio-economic status of Afghan refugees in Pakistan: an overview'. UNHCR Islamabad, May. RSC Cardbox: FA/FAP 65.1 MOR in FA/FP 65–65.25.

Rose, C. (1991) 'Biting the hand …'. ICWA Fellow, Institute of Current World Affairs. Peshawar, Pakistan, 15 September 1991. RSC Cardbox: FA/FP 60 ROSE in Box FA/FP Afghans in Pakistan, 59.3–64.

Ullrich, W. (1993) 'Long-term aid: GTZ projects for Afghan refugees'. Focus Section, gate 3/93 [Magazine]. RSC Cardbox: FA/FP 59.3 ULL D106904.

UNHCR (1986) 'The first income generating project for refugees areas: project overview'. RSC Cardbox: FA/FP 65.1 WOR in FA/FAP 65–65.25.

UNHCR (n.d.) 'UNHCR assistance programme for refugees in Pakistan'. Geneva: UNHCR. RSC Cardbox: FA/FP 59.3. UNHCR in FA/FP 59.3 A-Z.

US Committee for Refugees (1985) 'Afghan refugees: five years later'. January, RSC Cardbox: FA/FP Afghanis in Pakistan, 1–36.1/9; FA/FP 30 USCR.

World Bank (1983) 'Staff appraisal report, Pakistan: Income Generating Project for Refugee Areas'. World Bank, appraised on behalf of UNHCR. 6 December 1983. RSC Cardbox: FA/FP 65.1 WORLD BANK in FA/FP 65–65.25.

International Labour Organization Archive (UN, Geneva)

ILO (1926) Official Bulletin, Volume XI, January-December. Geneva: ILO.

ILO (1928) 'Refugee problems and their solution'. *International Labour Review*, 1768–1785.

ILO (1983) 'Tradition and dynamism among Afghan refugees: a report on income-generating activities for Afghan refugees in Pakistan'. Geneva: ILO.

League of Nations Archive (UN, Geneva)

Caphandaris, M. (1927) 'Annex. Letter from M. Caphandaris, Minister of Finance of Greece, to the Secretary-General of the League'. Geneva, 14 June 1927. League of Nations Archives, R397. C.322.1927.II.F.410.

Fanshawe, M. and Macartney, C. A. (1933) 'What the League has done: 1920–1932'. League of Nations Archives, O.LNU/1933(9).

Hansson, M. (1938) 'The Refugee Problem and the League of Nations'. Conference Given at the Nobel Institute Oslo on 7 January 1938. Geneva: Nansen International Office for Refugees.

LN (1923) 'Near East refugees, Western Thrace refugee settlement'. Report by Dr Nansen, High Commissioner for Refugees, to League of Nations, Communicated to the Council. Geneva, 22 April 1923.

LN (1925) 'Financial situation in Greece. Letter and note from the representative of the Greek Government'. Geneva, 3 September. League of Nations, Greek Delegation, No. 2935. League of Nations Archives, 10/46055/26389.

LN (1927) 'Settlement of Greek refugees. Report of the Financial Committee'. C.322.1927.II.F.410. Geneva, 14 June 1927. League of Nations Archives, R397, 10, 60557, 26389.

LN (1933) 'Human welfare and the League'. League of Nations Union, January 1933, No. 155. O.LNU/1933(8).

LN (1934) 'Human welfare and the League'. League of Nations Archives, O.LNU/1934(13).

LN (1945) 'Report on the work of the League: 1935–45'. League of Nations Archives, O.LNU/1945.

Macartney, C. A. (1930) *Refugees: The work of the League*. London: League of Nations Union.

Tsakalopoulos, I. (1926) [Letter from a Refugee] By Ignatios Tsakalopoulos (an exchanged person), Cavalla, 17 November 1926. To the President of the Council of the League of Nations, Geneva. League of Nations Archives, 10/55542X/263891.

Neldner Collection (University of Oxford Refugee Studies Centre Grey Literature Collection, Oxford, UK)

Feldman, D. (nd) 'Appraisal of the economic viability of four refugee settlements in Southern Tanzania confidential (final draft) report – for internal use only'. Neldner Archives, University of Oxford: RSP/NELD/LT 59.44 FEL.

Jernaes, J. (1971) 'Letter to Mr. Neldner, regarding Mr. Feldman's report 25th September'. Neldner Archives, University of Oxford. RSP/NELD/LT 59.44 FEL.

Ruth A. Palmeree Private Papers (Hoover Institution Archives, Stanford University)

AWH (American Women's Hospitals) (1923) 'AWH Bulletin 1923'. Ruth A. Palmeree Papers, Folder 3.13, Work Files, AWH 1923–1952. Hoover Institution Archives.

Palmeree, R. (1922) 'Letter to family and friends'. Ruth A. Palmeree Papers, Box 1, Folder 1.2, Notebook 1. Hoover Institution Archives.

Palmeree, R. (1922) 'Refugee work in Salonica, Greece. October 15–December 31, 1922'. Ruth A. Parmelee Papers, Box 3, Folder 3.12, Work Files, AWH 1922–1932. Hoover Institution Archives.

Palmeree, R. (1923) 'Untitled private letter'. Ruth A. Palmeree Papers, Folder 3.13, Work Files, AWH 1923–1952. Hoover Institution Archives.

Palmeree, R. (1923) 'Refugee work in Salonica, Greece'. AWH Report No. 2, May 1923. Ruth A. Parmelee Papers, Box 3, Folder 3.12, Work Files, AWH 1922–1932. Hoover Institution Archives.

Palmeree, R. (1925) 'American Women's Hospital for women and children'. Salonica, Greece. Report. Ruth A. Parmelee Papers, Box 3, Folder 3.12, Work Files, AWH 1922–1932. Hoover Institution Archives.

Palmeree, R. (1952) 'Dedication Piraeus Hospital, 1923'. Ruth A. Palmeree Papers, Folder 3.13, Work Files, AWH 1923–1952. Hoover Institution Archives.

T. F. Betts Collection, University of Oxford Refugee Studies Centre Grey Literature Collection (Oxford, UK)

Betts Collection (1967) 'Conference on the Legal, Economic and Social Aspects of African Refugee Problems Addis Ababa', 9–18 October 1967. Betts Collection, Bodleian Social Science Library, University of Oxford: Box No. 15, General Work.

Betts Collection (1971–1976) 'Compiled reports and reviews of East African Refugee Settlement Schemes (Burundi, Rwanda, Tanzania, 1971–1976)'. Betts Collection: General Box 1.

Betts, T. F. (1969) 'Sudanese refugees in Uganda: the position in May 1969'. Report of Advice on Zonal Rural Development, Oxfam, 13 May.

Betts, T. F. (1984) 'Evolution and promotion of the integrated rural development approach to refugee policy in Africa'. *Africa Today* 31(1): 7–24.

Betts, T. F. and Pitterman, S. (1984) 'Evolution and promotion of the Integrated Rural Development approach to refugee policy in Africa'. *Africa Today*, 31(1): 7–24.

Feldman, D. (1971) 'Report in Dependence/Initiative Section—1'. Betts Collection: Compiled Reports and Reviews of East African Refugee Settlement Schemes (Burundi, Rwanda, Tanzania, 1971–1976), Betts Collection: General Box 1.

ICVA (International Council of Voluntary Agencies) (1967) 'Assistance to African Refugees by Voluntary Organizations Conference on the Legal, Economic and Social Aspects of African Refugee Problems'. Addis Ababa, 9–18 October. Afr/Ref/Conf. 1967/No. 13, Betts Collection, Box No. 15, General Work.

ICVA (1969) 'Zonal Development Planning in Africa: Summary Record of an ICVA Ad Hoc Meeting, March 20', Betts Collection: J10.13(33r), Rural Development Background, Box No. 13.

ICVA (1970) 'ICVA Working Group on Integrated Rural Development: Summary Record of the Third Meeting International Council of Voluntary Agencies, January 6'. Betts Collection: A10.13.(33a), Rural Development Background, Box No. 13.

ILO (1969) 'Tanzania: Rural Prevocational and Vocational Training in Tanzania. A working paper resulting from the mission of Mr. P.F. Baldi and Mr. A.S. Nilsson, Experts of the International Labour Office, December 1968'. Geneva: ILO. Betts Collection, Box 53.

IORD (International Organization for Rural Development) (1971) 'International Organization for Rural Development: Annual Report 1970'. March, Brussels, Betts Collections: Background, Box 13: 37.

Morsink (1971) 'Report on training and employment (TRE)'. Betts Collection: Compiled Reports and Reviews of East African Refugee Settlement Schemes (Burundi, Rwanda, Tanzania, 1971–1976), Betts Collection: General Box 1.

Oxfam (1968) 'Tanzania: A Pilot Scheme of Agricultural Development for the Mwese Highlands in Tanzania'. Betts Collection, Refugee Research Project – Tanzania, Box 53A.

TCRS (Tanganyika Christian Refugee Service) (1967) 'Annual Report 1967'. Betts Collection, Bodleian Social Science Library, University of Oxford: Box 53. Tanzania: Rural Settlement Planning [394].

TCRS (1971) 'Annual Report 1971'. Betts Collection, Bodleian Social Science Library, University of Oxford: Box 53. Tanzania: Rural Settlement Planning [394].

TCRS (1972) 'Annual Report'. Betts Collection, Bodleian Social Science Library, University of Oxford: Box 53. Tanzania: Rural Settlement Planning [394].

Trappe, P. (1971) 'Social change and development institutions in a refugee population: development from below as an alternative: the case of the Nakapiripirit Settlement Scheme in Uganda'. Geneva: United Nations Research Institute for Social Development, Betts Collection: General Box 1.

UNHCR Archives (Geneva and online catalogue)

Getler, M. (1987) 'For Afghan refugees in Pakistan, welcome mat is wearing thin'. *Washington Post*, 11 September. UNHCR, 100.PAK.AFG.

Hartling, P. (assorted years) 'UNHCR High Commissioner speeches and statements'. Geneva: UNHCR. Available at: https://tinyurl.com/yd9fzyul.

Hocké, J. (1986) 'Statement by Mr. Jean-Pierre Hocké, United Nations High Commissioner for Refugees, at the Informal Meeting of Permanent Representatives in Geneva of States Members of the Executive Committee of the High Commissioner's Programme (ExCom), 13 June'. Geneva: UNHCR.

Hocké, J. (1988) 'Speech by Mr. Jean-Pierre Hocké, United Nations High Commissioner for Refugees, to the United Nations Administrative Committee on Coordination', New York, 24 October'. Geneva: UNHCR [np].

Hocké, J. P. (assorted years) 'UNHCR High Commissioner speeches and statements'. Geneva: UNHCR. Available at: https://tinyurl.com/ycpb3kbp.

Schnyder, F. (1964) 'Opening statement by Mr Felix Schnyder, United Nations High Commissioner for Refugees, to the Executive Committee of the High Commissioner's Programme, second special session, 28 January 1964'. Available at: www.UNHCR.org/uk/admin/hcspeeches/49f81111e/opening-statement-mr-felix-schnyder-united-nations-high-commissioner-refugees.html.

Schnyder, F. (1964) 'Statement by Mr Felix Schnyder, United Nations High Commissioner for Refugees, to the Thirty-seventh Session of the United Nations Economic and Social Council (ECOSOC), 1 May'. Available at: www.UNHCR.org/uk/admin/hcspeeches/3ae68fb81c/statement-mr-felix-schnyder-united-nations-high-commissioner-refugees-thirty.html.

Stein, B. (1994) *Returnee aid and development*. United Nations High Commissioner for Refugees (UNHCR). Central Evaluation Section. Geneva: UNHCR.

UNHCR (1962) 'Summary Report on the Refugee Problem in the Republic of Togo'. HCR/RS/23IRev.1, p 5.

UNHCR (1966) 'Saddrudin Aga Khan. Note for the File (Confidential)'. 4 August 1966. UNHCR Archives, [Sadruddin Aga Khan (Deputy High Commissioner)] Archives. 11/1-1/7/43. Fonds 11/Series 1/Box 69 ARC-2/A40.

UNHCR (1970) 'Report of the United Nations High Commissioner for Refugees, UNHCR Reports to General Assembly'. 1 January. United Nations General Assembly Official Records: Twenty-Fourth Session. Supplement No. 12 (A/7612). Geneva: UNHCR.

UNHCR (1997) 'The biggest caseload in the world. Afghanistan: the unending crisis'. *Refugees Magazine*, Issue 108. Available at: www.UNHCR.org/en-us/publications/refugeemag/3b680fbfc/refugees-magazine-issue-108-afghanistan-unending-crisis-biggest-caseload.html.

UNHCR (2003) 'Development Assistance for Refugees (DAR) for Uganda Self Reliance Strategy – way forward'. Report on Mission to Uganda 14–20 September 2003, RLSS/DOS Mission Report 03/11.

UNHCR Executive Committee of the High Commissioner's Programme (2001) 'Reintegration: a progress report'. Standing Committee 20th Meeting, 15 February. UN Doc. N. EC/51/SC/CRP.5.

UNHCR Policy Documents (contemporary, digitally accessed)

Lubbers, R. (2003) 'Op-ed by Ruud Lubbers, UN High Commissioner for Refugees'. 20 June. Geneva: UNHCR. Available at: www.UNHCR.org/uk/news/editorial/2003/6/3ef2e9094/op-ed-ruud-lubbers-un-high-commissioner-refugees.html (accessed 15 November 2017).

UNHCR (2000) 'The global report 1999'. Geneva: UNHCR.

UNHCR (2004) 'Framework for durable solutions for refugees and persons of concern'. Geneva: UNHCR, p 4.

UNHCR (2005) *Handbook for Self-Reliance*. Geneva: UNHCR.

UNHCR (2005) 'Progress report: Convention Plus'. High Commissioner's Forum, 8 November. FORUM/2005/6, p 2. Available at: www.UNHCR.org/uk/protection/convention/4371c24c2/progress-report-convention-plus-forum20056.html (accessed 15 November 2017).

UNHCR (2005) *Handbook for Implementing and Planning: Development Assistance for Refugees (DAR) Programmes*. Geneva: UNHCR. Available at: www.unhcr.org/44c484902.pdf.

UNHCR (2005) 'Putting refugees on the development agenda: how refugees and returnees can contribute to achieving the Millennium Development Goals'. High Commissioner's Forum. FORUM/2005/4. 18 May.

UNHCR (2009) 'UNHCR policy on protection and solutions in urban areas'. Geneva: UNHCR.

UNHCR (2011) 'Encouraging self-reliance'. Geneva: UNHCR.

UNHCR (2011) 'Livelihood programming in UNHCR: operational guidelines'. Geneva: UNHCR.

UNHCR (2011) 'Promoting livelihoods and self-reliance: operational guidance on refugee protection and solutions in urban areas'. Geneva: UNHCR.

UNHCR (2012) 'Livelihood programming in UNHCR: operational guidelines'. Geneva: UNHCR.

UNHCR (2014) '2014–2018 global strategy for livelihoods'. Geneva: UNHCR.

UNHCR (2014) 'Global strategy implementation report'. Geneva: UNHCR.

UNHCR (2015) Livelihoods. Webpage. Geneva: UNHCR.

UNHCR (2015) 'Operational guidelines on the minimum criteria for livelihoods programming'. Geneva: UNHCR.

UNHCR (2015) 'Uganda hosts record 500,000 refugees and asylum-seekers'. 18 December. Geneva: UNHCR.

UNHCR (2015) 'UNHCR planning figures for Uganda'. Geneva: UNHCR.

UNHCR (2015) UNHCR Country Operations Profile – Uganda. Webpage. Geneva: UNHCR.

UNHCR (2017) 'A guide to market-based livelihoods interventions for refugees'. Geneva: UNHCR.

UNHCR (2018) Livelihoods. Webpage. Available at: www.UNHCR.org/uk/livelihoods.html (accessed 14 September 2018).

Miscellaneously acquired archival documents (primary or secondary archival documents accessed online or through the Bodleian Library Collection, University of Oxford)

Armstrong, H. (1929) 'Venizelos again supreme in Greece'. *Foreign Affairs* 8(1): 120–129.

Denker, D. (1985) 'Along Afghanistan's war-torn frontier'. *National Geographic Magazine*, June.

Efimeris ton Syzitiseon (1930) 38th Session, Feb. 17, 1930, 650–665, 626, Library of the Greek Parliament in Athens. Cited in Kritikos (2005) 'The agricultural settlement of refugees', p 334.

IFAD (International Fund for Agricultural Development) (1987) 'International consultation on strengthening national agricultural research systems: wheat and rice research and training'. 26–28 January. Rome: International Fund for Agricultural Development. Available at: https://idl-bnc-idrc.dspacedirect.org/handle/10625/7872 (accessed 1 September 2016).

Martin, S. F. and Copeland, E. (1988) *Making Ends Meet*. Washington, DC: Refugee Policy Group.

Mears, E. G. (1929) *Greece Today: The aftermath of the refugee impact*. Stanford, CA: Stanford University Press.

Morgenthau, H. (1930) *I was sent to Athens*. Garden City, NY: Doubleday, Doran & Company.

Myers, M. G. (1945) 'The League Loans'. *Political Science Quarterly* 60(4): 492–526.

New York Times (1981) 'Reagan talk to World Bank and I.M.F.' 30 September. Available at: www.nytimes.com/1981/09/30/business/reagan-talk-to-world-bank-and-imf.html (accessed 24 February 2017).

Nyerere, J. (1967) 'The Arusha Declaration'. Dar es Salaam: Government of Tanzania.

Nyerere, J. (1967) 'The Arusha Declaration. Section: "Hard Work is the Root of Development"'. Available at: www.marxists.org/subject/africa/nyerere/1967/arusha-declaration.htm (accessed 1 November 2017).

Nyerere, J. (1968) *Ujamaa: Essays on Socialism*. Nairobi: Oxford University Press.

OAU (1978) Organization of African Unity: Final Report: Conference on the Legal, Economic and Social Aspects of African Refugee Problems, 9–18 October 1967, December 1978.

Pitterman, S. (1984) 'A comparative survey of two decades of international assistance to refugees in Africa'. *Africa Today* 31(1): 25–54.

Protonotarios, A. B. (1924) To Prosfygiko Provlima apo Istorikis, Nomikis kai Kratikis Apopseos, 88 [The Refugee Problem in Historical, Legal and State Perspective]; Efimeris ton Syzitiseon [Official Recording of the Debates], 65th Session, 24 June 1924, 458. Cited in Kritikos (2005).

Reagan, R. (1981) 'Inaugural Speech'. 20 January 1981. *Speaking My Mind: Selected Speeches*. London: Simon and Schuster.

Reagan, R. (1985) 'Address before a joint session of the Congress on the State of the Union', 6 February.

Regional Refugee Instruments and Related (1979) 'Recommendations from the Pan-African Conference on the Situation of Refugees in Africa'. Arusha (Tanzania). 17 May 1979. Available at: www.refworld.org/docid/3ae6b37214.html (accessed 26 September 2018).

Royal Institute of International Affairs (1937) *The Problem of International Investment: A report by a study group of members of the Royal Institute of International Affairs*. London, New York: Oxford University Press.

RPG (Refugee Policy Group) (1985) 'Older refugee settlements in Africa: final report'. Washington, DC: Refugee Policy Group.

Sinclair, M. (1993) 'NGO income generation programmes for Afghan refugees in Pakistan'. *Journal of International Development* 5(4): 391–399.

Stein, B. (1981) 'Refugees and economic activities in Africa'. Report prepared for the Office of Policy Development and Program Review, Bureau for Program and Policy Coordination. Agency for International Development.

Stein, B. (1990) 'Refugee integration and older refugee settlements in Africa'. Paper presented at the 1990 meeting of the American Anthropological Association. New Orleans: Michigan State University.
UNRRA (1946) *UNRRA: Structure and operations*. London.
UNRRA (1950) *UNRRA: The history of the United Nations Relief and Rehabilitation Administration*. New York: Columbia University Press.
US Government (1982) *United States Participation in Multilateral Development Banks*. Washington, DC: Department of the Treasury.
Weiner, M., Banuazizi, A., Barfield, T., Choucri, N., Gakenheimer, R., Moavenzadeh, F., and Rothenberg, J. (1991) 'A feasibility study prepared by the Reconstruction Group of the Center for International Studies of the Massachusetts Institute of Technology'. PN-ABS-658–90358.
Wilson, W. (1918) 'President Woodrow Wilson's Fourteen Points'. 8 January. Available at: http://avalon.law.yale.edu/20th_century/wilson14.asp

Qualitative interviews

Interviews, refugee informants 19–30, 1 May 2015–30 June 2015.
Interview, arts and crafts business member, 10 May 2015.
Interview, KCCA refugee informant, 10 May 2015.
Interview, Bondeko Centre leader, 15 May 2015.
Interview, HOCW leader, 16 May 2015.
Interview, InterAid protection officer, 20 May 2015.
Interview, training participant, 20 May 2015.
Interview, YARID leader, 20 May 2015.
Interview, FRC Project Officer, Kampala Urban Project, 10 June 2015.
Interview, Eugenie, JRS livelihoods trainer, 12 June 2015.
Interview, JRS livelihoods coordinator, 15 June 2015.
Interview, InterAid protection officer, 16 June 2015.
Interview, Bondeko Center, Kampala, 20 June 2015.
Interview, Jon Bennett, 24 November 2017.
Interviews, Alaa, 2019–2021.

Secondary literature

Ager, A. and Strang, A. (2008) 'Understanding integration: a conceptual framework', *Journal of Refugee Studies* 21(2): 166–191.
Aleinikoff, A. (2015) *From Dependence to Self-Reliance: Changing the paradigm in protracted refugee situations*. Washington, DC: Migration Policy Institute.
Altsitzoglou, F. (1929) *Oi giakades kai o kampos tis Xanthis* (Athens, 1941), 545; ESV, 9 December 1929, 177. Cited in Mazower 1991: 87.

Anwar, T. (2002) 'Impact of globalization and liberalization on growth, employment and poverty: a case study of Pakistan'. WIDER Discussion Papers-World Institute for Development Economics (UNU-WIDER), No. 17.

Arrighi, G. (1971) *The Relationship between the Colonial and the Class Structures: A Critique of AG Frank's Theory of the Development of Underdevelopment*. Dakar: United Nations African Institute for Economic Development and Planning. Available at: https://repository.uneca.org/handle/10855/42253 (accessed 20 November 2016).

Arrighi, G. (1978) 'Towards a theory of capitalist crisi's. *New Left Review 111*(3): 3–24.

Ashworth, J. (1987) 'The relationship between capitalism and humanitarianism'. *The American Historical Review* 92(4): 813–828.

Baitenmann, H. (1990) 'NGOs and the Afghan war: the politicisation of humanitarian aid'. *Third World Quarterly* 12(1): 62–85.

Barbelet, V. and Wake, C. (2017) *Livelihood Strategies of Central African Refugees in Cameroon*. London: Overseas Development Institute (ODI).

Barbelet, V. and Wake, C. (2017) *Livelihoods in Displacement: From refugee perspectives to aid agency response*. Humanitarian Policy Group Report, September. London: ODI.

Barnett, M. N. (2011) *Empire of Humanity: A history of humanitarianism*. Ithaca, NY: Cornell University Press.

Baron, N. and Gatrell, P. (2003) 'Population displacement, state-building, and social identity in the lands of the former Russian Empire, 1917–23'. *Kritika: Explorations in Russian and Eurasian History* 4(1): 51–100.

Barsky, R. B. and Kilian, L. (2004) 'Oil and the macroeconomy since the 1970s'. *Journal of Economic Perspectives* 18(4): 115–134.

Barton, J. (1930) *Story of Near East Relief (1915–1930): An interpretation*. New York: Macmillan.

Bartsch, D. (2004) 'Microfinance and refugees'. *Forced Migration Review* 20: 20.

Bates, T. (1997) *Race, Self-employment, and Upward Mobility*. Baltimore, MD: Johns Hopkins University Press.

Beck, U. (2000) *The Brave New World of Work*. Oxford: Blackwell.

Berger, M. T. and Beeson, M. (1998) 'Lineages of liberalism and miracles of modernisation: the World Bank, the East Asian trajectory and the international development debate'. *Third World Quarterly* 19(3): 487–504.

Betts, A. (2006) 'Comprehensive plans of action: Insights from CIREFCA and the Indochinese CPA'. UNHCR New Issues in Refugee Research Working Paper No. 120. Geneva: UNHCR, Evaluation and Policy Analysis Unit.

Betts, A. (2009) *Development Assistance and Refugees: Towards a North–South Grand Bargain?* Oxford: Refugee Studies Centre, Oxford Department of International Development.

Betts, A. (2009) *Protection by Persuasion: International cooperation in the refugee regime*. Ithaca, NY: Cornell University Press.

Betts, A. and Durieux, J. (2007) 'Convention Plus as a norm-setting exercise'. *Journal of Refugee Studies* 20(3): 509–535.

Betts, A., Bloom, L., Kaplan, J. D., and Omata, N. (2014) *Refugee Economies: Rethinking popular assumptions*. Oxford: Refugee Studies Centre, University of Oxford.

Bonaccorsi Di Patti, E. and Hardy, D. C. (2005) 'Financial sector liberalization, bank privatization, and efficiency: evidence from Pakistan'. *Journal of Banking & Finance* 29: 2381–2406.

Bousquet, F. (2018) 'Doing things differently to help refugees and their host communities.' *Voices: Perspectives on Development*. Washington, DC: World Bank Group.

Branson, R. (2018) How Business Can Make a Difference for Refugees. Webpage (18 July). Available at: www.virgin.com/richard-branson/how-business-can-make-difference-refugees (accessed 18 August 2018).

Cannadine, D. (ed) (2002) *Introduction: What is history now?* Basingstoke: Palgrave.

Caplan, P. (2007) 'Between Socialism and Neo-Liberalism: Mafia Island, Tanzania, 1965–2004'. *Review of African Political Economy* 34(114): 679–694.

Carpi, E., Field, J. A., Dicker, S. I., and Rigon, A. (2020) 'From livelihoods to leisure and back: refugee "self-reliance" as collective practices in Lebanon, India and Greece'. *Third World Quarterly* 42(2): 421–440.

Castles, S. (1998) 'Globalization and migration: some pressing contradictions'. *International Social Science Journal* 50(156): 179–186.

Castles, S. (2000) *Ethnicity and Globalization*. London: Sage.

Castles, S. (2005) 'Nation and empire: hierarchies of citizenship in the new global order'. *International Politics* 42(2): 203–224.

Castles, S. (2012) 'Cosmopolitanism and freedom? Lessons of the global economic crisis'. *Ethnic and Racial Studies* 35(11): 1843–1852.

Castles, S. (2013) 'The forces driving global migration'. *Journal of Intercultural Studies* 34(2): 122–140.

Chambers, R. (1976) *Rural Refugees after Arusha*. Mimeographed. Geneva: UNHCR.

Chaulia, S. S. (2003) 'The politics of refugee hosting in Tanzania: from open door to unsustainability, insecurity and receding receptivity'. *Journal of Refugee Studies* 16(2): 147–166.

Chimni, B. S. (1998) 'The geopolitics of refugee studies: a view from the South'. *Journal of Refugee Studies* 11(4): 350–374.

Chimni, B. S. (2000) 'Globalization, humanitarianism and the erosion of refugee protection'. *Journal of Refugee Studies* 13(3): 243–263.

Chimni, B. S. (2004) 'From resettlement to involuntary repatriation: towards a critical history of durable solutions to refugee problems'. *Refugee Survey Quarterly* 23(3): 55–73.

Chimni, B. S. (2009) 'The birth of a "discipline": from refugee to forced migration studies'. *Journal of Refugee Studies* 22(1): 11–29.

Coat, P. (1978) 'Material assistance: some policy problems reviewed in the light of Robert Chambers' evaluation reports'. Geneva: UNHCR.

Cooper, F. (1996) *Decolonization and African Society: The labor question in French and British Africa.* Cambridge: Cambridge University Press.

Corporaal, G. (2019) 'Intermediaries should be worried about the platform economy'. The iLabour Project, Oxford Internet Institute. Available at: https://ilabour.oii.ox.ac.uk/intermediaries-should-be-worried-about-the-platform-economy/.

Corporaal, G. F. and Lehdonvirta, V. (2017) 'Platform sourcing: how Fortune 500 firms are adopting online freelancing platforms'. Oxford Internet Institute, Oxford. Available at: www.oii.ox.ac.uk/blog/how-the-worlds-largest-companies-use-online-freelancing-platforms-new-report/ (18 December 2019).

Cowen, M. and Shenton, R. (1996) *Doctrines of Development.* London; New York: Routledge.

Cox, R. (1981) 'Social forces, states and world orders: beyond international relations theory'. *Millennium: Journal of International Studies* 10: 126–155.

Crisp, J. (2001) 'Mind the gap! UNHCR, humanitarian assistance and the development process'. *The International Migration Review* 35(1): 168–191.

Crisp, J. (2003) 'No solution in sight: the problem of protracted refugee situations in Africa'. Center for Comparative Immigration Studies (CCIS) Working Paper No. 68. CCIS: San Diego.

Crisp, J. (2010) 'Forced displacement in Africa: dimensions, difficulties, and policy directions', *Refugee Survey Quarterly* 29(3): 1–27. Available at: https://doi.org/10.1083/rsq/hdq031 (accessed 25 June 2018).

D'Souza, F. (1980) 'The Refugee Dilemma: International Recognition and Acceptance'. Report No. 43. London: Minority Rights Group.

Daley, P. (1989) 'Refugees and Underdevelopment in Africa: The case of Barundi refugees in Tanzania'. DPhil Thesis. Oxford: University of Oxford.

Daley, P. (2019) 'The Politics of the Refugee Crisis in Tanzania', in H. Campbell and H. Stein (eds) *Tanzania and the IMF.* London: Routledge, pp 125–146.

Detrez, R. (2015) 'Refugees as Tools of Irredentist Policies in Interwar Bulgaria', in H. Vermeulen, M. Baldwin-Edwards, and R. van Boeschoten (eds) *Migration in the Southern Balkans.* Cham: Springer International Publishing, pp 47–62.

Deutsch, J. G. (2002) 'Celebrating power in everyday life: the administration of law and the public sphere in colonial Tanzania, 1890–1914'. *Journal of African Cultural Studies* 15(1): 93–103.

Dritsa, M. (1990) *Βιομηχανία καί τράπεζες στήν 'Ελλάδα τοῦ μεσοπολέμου*. Athens: Educational Institution of the National Bank. Cited in Mazower (1992).

Duffield, M. (2002) 'Social reconstruction and the radicalization of development: aid as a relation of global liberal governance'. *Development and Change* 33(5): 1049–1071.

Duffield, M. (2006) 'Racism, migration and development: the foundations of planetary order'. *Progress in Development Studies* 6(1): 68–79.

Duffield, M. (2008) 'Global civil war: the non-insured, international containment and post-interventionary society'. *Journal of Refugee Studies* 21(2): 145–165.

Duffield, M. (2014) *Global Governance and the New Wars: The merging of development and security*. London: Zed Books.

Dunning, T. (2004) 'Conditioning the effects of aid: Cold War politics, donor credibility, and democracy in Africa'. *International Organization* 58(2): 409–423.

Dupree, N. H. (1988) 'Demographic reporting on Afghan refugees'. *Modern Asian Studies* 22(4): 845–865.

Easterly, W. (2005) 'What did structural adjustment adjust? The association of policies and growth with repeated IMF and World Bank adjustment loans'. *Journal of Development Economics* 76(1): 1–22.

Easton-Calabria, E. (2015) 'From bottom-up to top-down: the "pre-history" of refugee livelihoods assistance from 1919–1979'. *Journal of Refugee Studies* 28(3): 412–436.

Easton-Calabria, E. (2016) 'From participation to partnership: refugee-run organisations as important actors in development'. *FMR* 52: 72–74. Oxford: University of Oxford.

Easton-Calabria, E. (ed) (2017) 'Rethinking refugee self-reliance: moving beyond the marketplace'. RSC Research in Brief No. 7. Oxford: RSC.

Easton-Calabria, E. and Hakiza, R. (2021) 'In the interest of saving: Refugee-led microfinance in Kampala, Uganda'. *Development Policy Review 39*(1): 22–38.

Easton-Calabria, E. and Herson, M. (2020) 'In praise of dependencies: dispersed dependencies and displacement'. *Disasters* 44(1): 44–62.

Easton-Calabria, E. and Omata, N. (2016) 'Micro-finance in refugee contexts: current scholarship and research gaps'. Refugee Studies Centre (RSC) Working Paper Series No. 116. Oxford: University of Oxford.

Easton-Calabria, E. and Omata, N. (2018) 'Panacea for the refugee crisis? Rethinking the promotion of self-reliance for refugees'. *Third World Quarterly* 39(8): 1458–1474.

Edwards, M. and Gaventa, J. (2001) 'Global Citizen Action: Lessons and Challenges', in *Global Citizen Action*. London: Routledge, pp 275–287.

Ehtisham, A. and Mohammed, A. (2012) 'Pakistan, the United States and the IMF: great game or a curious case of Dutch Disease without the oil?' Asia Research Centre Working Paper No. 57. London: London School of Economics.

Eriksson, L. G., Melander, G., and Nobel, P. (eds) (1981) *An Analysing Account of the Conference on the African Refugee Problem, Arusha, May 1979.* Uppsala: Nordic Africa Institute.

Escobar, A. (1995) *Encountering Development: The making and unmaking of the Third World* (Princeton studies in culture/power/history). Princeton, NJ: Princeton University Press.

Esping-Anderson, G. (1990) *The Three Worlds of Welfare Capitalism.* London: Polity Press.

Fairlie, R. W. and Robb, A. (2008) *Race and Entrepreneurial Success: Black-, Asian-, and White-owned businesses in the United States.* Cambridge, MA: MIT Press.

Feldman, I. (2018) *Life Lived in Relief.* Oakland: University of California Press.

Ferguson, J. (2013) 'Declarations of dependence: labour, personhood, and welfare in southern Africa'. *Journal of the Royal Anthropological Institute* 19(2): 223–242.

FIC (Feinstein International Center) (2012) 'Refugee livelihoods in urban areas: identifying program opportunities: case study Egypt'. Boston, MA: Feinstein International Center, Tufts University.

Field, J., Tiwari, A., and Mookherjee, Y. (2017) 'Refugee Self-Reliance in Delhi: The Limits of a Market-Based Approach', in J. Fiori and A. Rigon (eds) *Making Lives: Refugee Self-Reliance and Humanitarian Action in Cities.* London: Humanitarian Affairs Team, Save the Children, pp 37–72.

Field, J., Tiwari, A., and Mookherjee, Y. (2017) 'Urban refugees in Delhi: identity, entitlements and well-being'. IIED Working Paper, October.

Flores, J. and Decorzant, Y. (2012) 'Public borrowing in harsh times: the League of Nations loans revisited'. Department of Economics Working Paper Series No. 2091. Geneva: University of Geneva.

Forced Migration Review (2018) 'Special Supplement on Refugee-led Social Protection'. Oxford: Refugee Studies Centre, University of Oxford.

Foucault, M. (1977) *Discipline and Punish: The birth of the prison.* New York: Pantheon.

Foy, D. (2006) 'The appropriateness and effectiveness of micro-finance as a livelihoods intervention for refugees'. London: Refugee Livelihoods Network.

Frank, A. G. (1966) *The Development of Underdevelopment.* Boston, MA: New England Free Press.

Fraser, N. (2003) 'From discipline to flexibilization? Rereading Foucault in the shadow of globalization'. *Constellations* 10(2): 160–171.

Garside, W. R. (2002) *British Unemployment 1919–1939: A study in public policy*. Cambridge: Cambridge University Press.

Giannuli, D. (1995) 'Greeks or "strangers at home": the experience of Ottoman Greek refugees during their exodus to Greece, 1922–1923'. *Journal of Modern Greek Studies* 13(2): 271–287.

Global Entrepreneurship Monitor (2015) '2014 global report'. GEM. Available at: www.babson.edu/Academics/centers/blank-center/global-research/gem/Documents/GEM%202014%20Global%20Report.pdf (15 June 2016).

Gorman, R. (1986) 'Beyond ICARA II: implementing refugee-related development assistance'. *International Migration Review* 20(2): 283–298.

Gorman, R. (1987) 'Taking stock of the Second International Conference on Assistance to Refugees in Africa (ICARA II)'. *Journal of African Studies* 14(1): 4–11.

Gorman, R. (1993) *Refugee Aid and Development: Theory and practice*. Westport, CT: Greenwood.

Gough, I. (1980) 'Thatcherism and the welfare state: Britain is experiencing the most far-reaching experiment in "new right" politics in the western world'. *Marxism Today*, pp 7–12.

Ground Truth Solutions (2018) 'Should I stay or should I go?' 30 January. Available at: http://groundtruthsolutions.org/2018/01/30/should-i-stay-or-should-i-go/ (accessed 1 March 2018).

Group of 77 (2017) 'About the Group of 77', *The Group of* 77. Webpage. Available at: www.g77.org/doc/ (accessed 3 November 2017).

Grover, D. C. (2003) ' "New Labour", welfare reform and the reserve army of labour'. *Capital & Class* 27(1): 17–23.

Haas, E. B. (1980) 'Why collaborate? Issue-linkage and international regimes'. *World Politics* 32(3): 357–405.

Hackl, A. and Gardiner, D. (2021) *Towards decent work for young refugees and host communities in the digital platform economy in Africa: Kenya, Uganda, Egypt*. Geneva: ILO.

Harrell-Bond, B. (1986) *Imposing Aid: Emergency assistance to refugees*. Oxford: Oxford University Press.

Harvey, D. (1985) *The Urbanization of Capital: Studies in the history and theory of capitalist urbanization*. Baltimore, MD: Johns Hopkins University Press.

Harvey, P. and Lind, J. (2005) *Dependency and Humanitarian Relief: A critical analysis*. London: Humanitarian Policy Group, Overseas Development Institute.

Haskell, T. L. (1985) 'Capitalism and the origins of the humanitarian sensibility, Part 1'. *The American Historical Review* 90(2): 339–361.

Haskell, T. L. (1985) 'Capitalism and the origins of the humanitarian sensibility, Part 2'. *The American Historical Review* 90(3): 547–566.

Hattem, J. (2017) 'Uganda may be best place in the world to be a refugee. But that could change without more money'. *The Washington Post*. June 20. Available at: https://tinyurl.com/ycfryldz (accessed 15 September 2018).

Hawley, E. (1984) 'Dedication to Tristram F. (Jimmy) Betts (1908–1983) scholar, humanitarian, gadfly'. *Africa Today, Refugees and Integrated Rural Development in Africa* 31(1): 3–5.

Hirschon, R. (1998) *Heirs of the Greek Catastrophe: The social life of Asia Minor refugees in Piraeus*. Oxford: Berghahn Books.

Horst, C. (2006) 'Introduction: refugee livelihoods: continuity and transformations'. *Refugee Survey Quarterly* 25(2): 6–22.

Housden, M. (2012) *The League of Nations and the Organization of Peace*. Harlow: Longman.

Howland, C. P. (1926) 'Greece and her refugees'. *Foreign Affairs* 4(4): 613–623.

Hunter, M. (2009) 'The failure of self-reliance in refugee settlements'. *Polis Journal* 2: 1–46.

Hyndman, J. (2000) *Managing Displacement: Refugees and the politics of humanitarianism*. London: University of Minnesota Press.

IFAD (2003) 'Five microfinance projects meet the rural pro-poor innovation challenge'. Available at: www.ifad.org/ ruralfinance/poverty/rppic.htm (accessed 11 August 2014).

ILO (2016) *Non-Standard Employment Around the World*. Geneva: ILO, p 18.

International Refugee Congress (2018) 'International Refugee Congress 2018 consultation report'. Istanbul: Oxfam Turkey. Available at: www.refugeecongress2018.org/resources-files/Consultation_Report_2018_March_03.05.2018.pdf (accessed 5 May 2018).

Irani, L. (2015) 'Difference and dependence among digital workers: the case of Amazon Mechanical Turk'. *South Atlantic Quarterly* 114(1): 225–234; Lehdonvirta, V. (2016) 'Algorithms that Divide and Unite: Delocalization, Identity, and Collective Action In "Microwork", in J. Flecker (ed) *Space, Place, and Global Digital Work*. London: Palgrave-Macmillan, pp 53–80.

IRC (International Rescue Committee) (2012) 'Urban refugees'. International Rescue Committee pamphlet. Available at:www.rescue-uk.org/sites/default/files/20.11.12%20Urban%20refs%20for%20ECHO%20advocacy%20event%20_0.pdf (accessed 11 August 2014).

Jacobsen, K. (2005) *The Economic Life of Refugees*. Bloomfield, CT: Kumarian Press, Inc.

Jacobsen, K., Ayoub, M., and Johnson, A. (2014) 'Sudanese refugees in Cairo: remittances and livelihoods'. *Journal of Refugee Studies* 27(1): 145–159.

Jamal, A. (2000) *Minimum Standards and Essential Needs in a Protracted Refugee Situation: A review of the UNHCR programme in Kakuma, Kenya*. Geneva: Evaluation and Policy Analysis Unit, UNHCR.

Jensen, J. (2013) 'US New Deal Social Policy Experts and the ILO, 1948–1954', in S. Kott and J. Droux (eds) *Globalizing Social Rights: The International Labour Organization and beyond.* Basingstoke: Palgrave Macmillan, pp 172–189.

JRS (2010) 'Uganda: JRS offers new training opportunities for refugees'. 16 April. Available at: http://en.jrs.net/news_detail?TN=news-20100421061545 (accessed 15 December 2017).

Kaiser, T. (2006) 'Between a camp and a hard place: rights, livelihood and experiences of the local settlement system for long-term refugees in Uganda'. *Journal of Modern African Studies* 44(4): 597–621.

Kaldor, M. (2005) 'Old Wars, Cold Wars, New Wars, and the War on Terror'. Lecture given to the Cold War Studies Centre, London School of Economics, 2 February.

Katz, Y. (1992) 'Transfer of population as a solution to international disputes'. *Political Geography* 11(1): 55–72.

Khan, A. H. and Hasan, L. (1998) 'Financial liberalization, savings and economic development in Pakistan'. *Economic Development and Cultural Change* 46: 581–598.

Khan, I. (1998) 'Afghanistan: A geopolitical study'. *Central Asian Survey* 17(3): 489–502.

Khan, S. R. and Aftab, S. (1994) 'Assessing the impact of financial reforms on Pakistan's economy'. *Pakistan Journal of Applied Economics* 10(1–2): 99–116.

Koser, K. (2007) 'Refugees, transnationalism and the state'. *Journal of Ethnic and Migration Studies* 33(3): 233–254.

Kritikos, G. (2005) 'The agricultural settlement of refugees: a source of productive work and stability in Greece, 1923–1930'. *Agricultural History* 79(3): 321–346.

Labman, S. (2010) 'Looking back, moving forward: the history and future of refugee protection'. *Chicago-Kent Journal of International and Comparative Law* 10(1): 2.

Lacroix, R. L. (1985) *Integrated Rural Development in Latin America* (Vol 716). Washington, DC: World Bank.

Lal, P. (2017) *African Socialism in Postcolonial Tanzania: Between the village and the world.* Cambridge: Cambridge University Press.

Lazaridis, G. (1994) 'The feminist movement in Greece: an overview'. *Journal of Gender Studies* 3(2): 205–209.

Lehdonvirta, V., Barnard, H., Graham, M., and Hjorth, I. (2014) 'Online labour markets – levelling the playing field for international service markets?' Paper presented at the IPP2014: Crowdsourcing for Politics and Policy conference, University of Oxford, 25–26, September 2014.

Lele, U. (1975) *The Design Of Rural Development: Lessons from Africa.* London: Johns Hopkins University Press.

Lerner, N. (2009) 'Archival Research as a Social Process', in A. E. Ramsey, W. B. Sharer, B. L'Eplattenier, and L. Mastrangelo (eds) (2009) *Working in the Archives: Practical research methods for rhetoric and composition*. Southern Illinois: SIU Press, pp 195–205.

Lillie, N. and Greer, I. (2007) 'Industrial relations, migration, and neoliberal politics: the case of the European construction sector'. *Politics and Society* 35(4): 551–581. doi:10.1177/ 0032329207308179.

Loescher, G. (2001) *The UNHCR and World Politics: A perilous path*. New York: Oxford University Press.

Loescher, G., Betts, A., and Milner, J. (2008) *The United Nations High Commissioner for Refugees (UNHCR): The politics and practice of refugee protection into the 21st century*. London: Routledge.

Lohrmann, U. (2007) *Voices from Tanganyika: Great Britain, The United Nations and the decolonization of a Trust Territory, 1946–1961*. Berlin: Lit Verlag.

Long, K. (2013) 'When refugees stopped being migrants: movement, labour and humanitarian protection'. *Migration Studies* 1(1): 4–26.

Malkki, L. H. (1995) *Purity and Exile: Violence, memory, and national consciousness among Hutu refugees in Tanzania*. Chicago: University of Chicago.

Mamdani, M. (1996) *Citizen and Subject: Contemporary Africa and the legacy of late colonialism*. Princeton, NJ: Princeton University Press.

Marrus, M. (1985) *The Unwanted: European refugees in the twentieth century*. Oxford: Oxford University Press.

Marshall, T. H. (1950) *Citizenship and Social Class* (Vol 11, p 69). Cambridge: Cambridge University Press.

Mazower, M. (1991) *Greece and the Inter-war Economic Crisis*. Oxford: OUP Catalogue.

Mazower, M. (1992) 'The refugees, the economic crisis and the collapse of Venizelist hegemony, 1929–1932'. *Deltion Kentrou Mikrasiatikon Spoudon [Bulletin of the Centre of Asia Minor Studies]* 9, 119–134.

Mazower, M. (1992) 'The Messiah and the bourgeoisie: Venizelos and politics in Greece, 1909–1912'. *The Historical Journal* 35(4): 885–904.

McDonald, J. G., Breitman, R., Stewart, B. M., and Hochberg, S. (eds) (2007) *Advocate for the Doomed: The diaries and papers of James G. McDonald, 1932–1935*. Vol 1. Bloomington: Indiana University Press.

Mendes, A. P. F., Bertella, M. A., and Teixeira, R. F. (2014) 'Industrialization in sub-Saharan Africa and import substitution policy'. *Revista de Economia Política* 34(1): 120–138.

Mentan, T. (2017). *Africa in the Colonial Ages of Empire: Slavery, capitalism, racism, colonialism, decolonization, independence as recolonization, and beyond*. Bamenda, Cameroon: Langaa RPCIG.

Merry, S. (2002) 'Ethnography in the Archives', in J. Starr and M. Goodale (eds) *Practicing Ethnography in Law: New dialogues, enduring methods*. New York: Palgrave Macmillan.

Meyer, S. (2006) 'The "refugee aid and development" approach in Uganda: Empowerment and self-reliance of refugees in practice'. UNHCR Working Paper Series No. 131. Geneva: UNHCR.

Migliorino, N. (2008) *(Re)Constructing Armenia in Lebanon and Syria: Ethno-cultural diversity and the state in the aftermath of a refugee crisis*. Oxford: Berghahn.

Mittelstadt, J. (2005) *From Welfare to Workfare: The unintended consequences of liberal reform, 1945–1965*. Chapel Hill: University of North Carolina Press.

Moore, B. (1990) 'Jewish refugee entrepreneurs and the Dutch economy in the 1930s'. *Immigrants & Minorities* 9(1): 46–63.

Moreno, L. and Bang Shin, H. (2018) 'Introduction: the urban process under planetary accumulation by dispossession'. *City* 22(1): 78–87.

Novak, P. (2011) 'The institutional incompleteness of empire'. *Central Asian Survey* 30(3–4): 389–406.

Novak, P. (2013) 'The success of Afghan NGOs'. *Development in Practice* 23(7): 872–888.

O'Connor, J. (1973) *The Fiscal Crisis of the State*. London: St James Press.

OED (Oxford English Dictionary) (2017) Definition: Gadfly. Oxford: Oxford University Press.

Omata, N. (2013) 'Repatriation and integration of Liberian refugees from Ghana: the importance of personal networks in the country of origin'. *Journal of Refugee Studies* 26(2): 265–282.

Omata, N. (2017) *The Myth of Self-Reliance: Economic lives inside a Liberian refugee camp*. Oxford: Berghahn.

Orde-Browne, J. (1946) *Labour Conditions in East Africa*. London: HMSO.

Parmelee, R. A. (2002) *A Pioneer in the Euphrates Valley*. Ann Arbor, MI: Gomidas Institute Books.

Payer, C. (1983) 'Tanzania and the World Bank'. *Third World Quarterly* 5(4): 791–813.

Pentzopoulos, D. (2002) *The Balkan Exchange of Minorities and Its Impact on Greece*. London: Hurst & Co.

Peters, M. (2001) 'Education, enterprise culture and the entrepreneurial self'. *Journal of Educational Enquiry* 2(2): 58–71.

Pettiss, S. (2004) *After the Shooting Stopped: The story of an UNRRA welfare worker in Germany 1945–1947*. Victoria, BC: Trafford.

Pierson, C. (1991) *Beyond the Welfare State? The new political economy of welfare*. Cambridge: Polity.

Pincock, K., Betts, A., and Easton-Calabria, E. (2020) *The Global Governed? Refugees as providers of protection and assistance*. Cambridge: Cambridge University Press.

Pironti, P. (2017) Post-war Welfare Policies. Encyclopedia Online, 1914–1918. Webpage. Available at: http://encyclopedia.1914-1918-online.net/article/post-war_welfare_policies (accessed 18 June 2017).

ProQuest (2014) 'Graph of search results: refugee livelihoods'. Available at: http://tinyurl. com/RefugeeLivelihoodsGraph (accessed 12 June 2014).

Psomas, A. (1974) 'The Nation, the State and the International System: The case of Modern Greece'. Thesis. Proquest Dissertation Publishing.

Putnam, R. D. (2002) *Democracies in Flux: The evolution of social capital in contemporary society*. Oxford: Oxford University Press.

Qureshi, S. (1980) 'Islam and development: the Zia regime in Pakistan'. *World Developmen*, 8(7–8): 563–575.

Rolfe, C. and Harper, M. (1987) *Refugee Enterprise: It can be done*. London: Intermediate Technology Publications.

Sachs, W. (ed) (1997) *The Development Dictionary: A guide to knowledge as power*. Hyderabad: Orient Blackswan.

Sauthier, I. L. (2013) 'Modern Unemployment: From the creation of the concept to the International Labour Office's first standards', in S. Kott and J. Droux (eds) *Globalizing Social Rights: The International Labour Organization and beyond* (International Labour Organization century series). Basingstoke: Palgrave Macmillan, pp 67–84.

Scheppele, K. L. (2004) 'Constitutional ethnography: an introduction'. *Law and Society Review* 38(3): 389–406.

Schuurman, F. J. (2009) 'Critical Development Theory: moving out of the twilight zone'. *Third World Quarterly* 30(5): 831–848.

Schwartz-DuPre, R. L. (2010) 'Portraying the political: *National Geographic*'s 1985 Afghan Girl and a US alibi for aid'. *Critical Studies in Media Communication* 27(4): 336–356.

Sharpe, M. (2011) 'Engaging with refugee protection? The Organization of African Unity and African Union since 1963'. UNHCR New Issues in Refugee Research, Research Paper No. 226. Geneva: UNHCR.

Silver, B. and Arrighi, G. (2000) 'Workers North and South', in L. Panitch and C. Leys (eds) *The Socialist Register 2001* (Vol 37). London: Merlin Press, pp 53–76.

Skran, C. (1985) 'The Refugee Problem in Interwar Europe, 1919–1939', MPhil thesis. Oxford: University of Oxford.

Skran, C. (1989) 'The International Refugee Regime and the Refugee Problem in Interwar Europe', DPhil dissertation. Oxford: University of Oxford.

Skran, C. (1995) *Refugees in Inter-war Europe: The emergence of a regime*. Oxford: Clarendon Press.

Skran, C. (2020) 'Refugee Self-Reliance and Entrepreneurship in Post-Conflict Reintegration: The case of UNHCR and Female Returnees in Sierra Leone', in a Special Issue on 'Rethinking Refugee Self-Reliance', Journal of Refugee Studies, forthcoming 2019.

Somers, M. R. and Block, F. (2005) 'From poverty to perversity: ideas, markets, and institutions over 200 years of welfare debate'. *American Sociological Review'*, 70(2): 260–287.

Soros, G. (2016) 'Why I'm investing $500 million in migrants'. *Wall Street Journal*, 20 September. Available at: www.wsj.com/articles/why-im-investing-500-million-in-migrants-1474344001 (accessed 1 August 2018).

Sporton, D. (2013) '"They control my life": the role of local recruitment agencies in East European migration to the UK'. *Population, Space and Place* 19(5): 443–458.

Stanford, J. (2017) 'The resurgence of gig work: historical and theoretical perspectives'. *The Economic and Labour Relations Review* 28(3): 382–401.

Stein, B. N. (1986) 'Durable solutions for developing country refugees'. *International Migration Review* 20(2): 264–282.

Tague, J. (2012) 'A War to Build the Nation: Mozambican Refugees, Rural Development, and State Sovereignty in Tanzania, 1964–1975'. Dissertation. University of California Davis. ProQuest UMI.

Terry, F. (2013) *Condemned to Repeat? The paradox of humanitarian action.* Ithaca, NY: Cornell University Press.

Thanes, P. (1988) 'The British welfare state: its origin and character'. *Refresh* 6(Spring): 5–8.

The Express Tribune (2016) 'Pakistan-IMF ties: a chequered history'. 5 August. Available at: https://tribune.com.pk/story/1156145/pakistan-imf-ties-chequered-history (accessed 30 November 2016).

The Telegraph (2012) 'David Cameron's welfare speech in full'. 25 June. Available at: www.telegraph.co.uk/news/politics/david-cameron/9354163/David-Camerons-welfare-speech-in-full.html (accessed 15 September 2018).

Tirado, L. (2015) 'America's "welfare state" is shameful: the UK shouldn't follow our lead'. *The Guardian*, 18 November. Available at: www.theguardian.com/politics/2015/nov/18/us-welfare-shameful-uk-public-services-private-profit (accessed 1 September 2018).

UNHCR (2016) 'Livelihoods and self-reliance'. Geneva: UNHCR. Available at: www.refworld.org/pdfid/585163cf7.pdf

UNHCR (2018) 'Comprehensive refugee response framework'. Geneva: UNHCR. Available at: www.unhcr.org/comprehensive-refugee-response-framework-crrf.html

UNHCR (2018) IKEA Foundation. Webpage, available at: http://www.unhcr.org/uk/ikea-foundation.html (accessed August 18, 2018).

UNHCR (2020) '2020 global report'. Geneva: UNHCR.

US Government (1998) Workforce Investment Act of 1998. Public Law 105–220-Aug 7. Available at: www.congress.gov/105/plaws/publ220/PLAW-105publ220.pdf (accessed 1 August 2018).

Van Hear, N. (2012) 'Forcing the issue: migration crises and the uneasy dialogue between refugee research and policy'. *Journal of Refugee Studies* 25(1): 2–24.

Wallerstein, I. (1974) 'Dependence in an interdependent world: the limited possibilities of transformation within the capitalist world economy'. *African Studies Review* 17(1): 1–26.

Ward, P. (2014) 'Refugee cities: reflections on the development and impact of UNHCR urban refugee policy in the Middle East'. *Refugee Survey Quarterly* 33(1): 77–93. Available at https://academic.oup.com/rsq/article-abstract/33/1/77/1570430 (accessed on 29 June 2018).

World Economic Forum (2018) 'Future of jobs report'. Geneva: WEF. Available at: www3.weforum.org/docs/WEF_Future_of_Jobs_2018.pdf

WRC (Women's Refugee Commission) (2009) *Building Livelihoods: A field manual for practitioners in humanitarian settings*. New York: Women's Refugee Commission.

Zetter, R. (2012) *Lands of No Return, Population Exchange and Forced Displacement in the 20th Century*. Athens: Anemon Productions.

Zetter, R. and Ruaudel, H. (2016) 'Refugees' right to work and access to labor markets – an assessment. Part I: Synthesis (Preliminary)'. KNOMAD Working Paper and Study Series. Washington, DC: World Bank.

Zolberg, A. (1983) 'The formation of new states as a refugee-generating process'. *Annals of the American Academy of Political and Social Science* 467: 24.

Zolberg, A. R., Suhrke, A., and Aguayo, S. (1992) *Escape from Violence: Conflict and the refugee crisis in the developing world*. Oxford: Oxford University Press.

Zwick, A. (2018) 'Welcome to the gig economy: neoliberal industrial relations and the case of Uber'. *GeoJournal* 83(4): 679–691.

Index

References to figures appear in *italic* type;
those in **bold** type refer to tables. References to footnotes
show both the page number and the note number (179n36).

A

Addis Ababa Conference 1967 63n11, 65, 67–68
Afghan refugees in Pakistan 23, 94–126
  dependency syndrome 105–108, 123–124
  domestic to international policy shifts 121–123
  instrumentalization of 100
  men returning home to participate in *jihad* 108
  psychosocial protection 108–109
  repatriation 113–114, 123
  self-reliance as a protection tool 96, 109–113
    cuts to food aid 110–111, 114
    gendered nature of self-reliance 111–113
  self-reliance assistance 96, 100–105, 125–126
    emergency relief 101
    UNHCR/World Bank project 94–95, 102–105, 206
    waged employment 101–102
Afghanistan
  'Afghanization' of NGOs 114–115, 122
  refugee camps 95–96
  Soviet invasion 98, 118
  US support for *mujahideen* agenda 120
Africa 59–93
  advent of refugee assistance 61–63
  agricultural settlements 66, 71–77, 82, 84
  colonialism and refugee self-reliance 89–91
  contrasting refugee assistance in Greece and 85–86
  control of refugee projects 66–67
  decolonization 61
  'development project' 65–68
  instrumentalization of refugee self-reliance 85, 93, 160–161
  refugee self-reliance, politics and exploitation 83–91
  restricting of refugee agency 66–68, 77–79, 80–82, 91
  'self-settled' refugees 67
  unequal burden-sharing 91, 97
  zonal development 64–65, 71, 84, 88–89, 93
African socialism (*ujamaa*) 68–69, 71, 86, 93
agency, refugee 197–199, 204
  East African restricting of 66–68, 77–79, 80–82, 91
  'self-help' and fostering of 109, 122
agricultural production and development 199
  cash crop schemes
    in Africa 66, 72, 76, 79, 84, 87, 90
    in Greece 38–39, 49, 52, 53
  coercion of refugees to participate in 75, 77–79
  feeding colonial and international capitalist aims 86–87
  political strategies of 88–89
  poor soil quality 79
  refugees as labourers in 66, 72, 75, 76, 77, 90
  for self-reliance of Tanzania 69
agricultural settlements 84, 198
  in Africa 66, 71–77, 82, 84
  in Greece 34–40, 49, 50, 52, 53
aid reduction 2, 121, 124–125, 154, 160, 201
Alaa 167, 169–173, 185, 191
Aleinikoff, A. 3, 154
American Women's Hospital (AWH) 32, 33, 42, 44
  provision of loans 43
  vocational training of refugees 45–47, *46*, *47*
Angolan refugees 77
Armenian refugees 9, 25, 43, 45, *46*, 49
arts and crafts
  businesses 148, 150–151
  training 146, 147
Arusha Conference 82, 83, 195
Arusha Declaration 69

B
bank accounts 169, 175, 183, 184, 201
Barbelet, V. 7
Betts, T.F. 59–60, 65, 76, 79, 200, 204
bond loans 50
Bondeko Refugee Livelihoods Centre 127, 140, **141**, 143, 144, 179n36
Bosnia 99
Branson, R. 4
Brazil 54, 55
Brookings Process 131–132
Bulgaria 31, 33, 37n47, 40, 50
burden and responsibility sharing 83, 91, 97, 97–98, 132, 136, 160–161, 203
  Global Compact on Refugees for fair 164–165
Burundian refugees 80–82, 129, 140, 182

C
Cameron, D. 155–156
Caphandaris, M. 51
capital, refugees' access to 145, 146–148, 157
capitalism
  crisis of 91–92
  incorporating refugees into systems of 53, 57
  integrating states into capitalist economy
    Africa 65, 75, 86–87
    Greece 27, 50–52
    Pakistan 119–120
  migration and 17–19
carpet industry, Smyrna 42
cash crop schemes
  in Africa 66, 72, 76, 79, 84, 87, 90
  in Greece 38–39, 49, 52, 53
Castles, S. 17, 18
Chambers, R. 67
charcoal burning industry 44
Chaulia, S.S. 90
Chimni, B.S. 17, 18
colonial trade relations 87
colonialism 60, 61
  and refugee self-reliance 89–91
Communism, resistance to 87, 88–89, 98, 120
Community Technology Access (CTA) 166
Comprehensive Refugee Response Framework (CRRF) 165
Conference on the Legal, Economic and Social Aspects of African Refugee Problems, 1967 (Addis Ababa Conference) 63n11, 65, 67–68
Congolese refugees 129, 140, 142, 143, 150, 182, 197
construction workers 40
contractors, independent 172, 188
Convention Plus Initiative 132–134
Convention Relating to the Rights of Refugees, 1951 9, 167, 197
cooperatives 74, 76, 78, 90
COVID-19 pandemic 3, 163, 192, 197, 200
Cox, R. 5, 203
craft
  businesses 148, 150–151
  training 146, 147
Crisp 130–131
critical development theory 11, 17, 194
critical theory 5–7, 193–194

D
Dadaab Freelancing Collective 179, 180, 184, 189–190
Daley, P. 67, 80
debt, refugee 39
dependency 123, 154
  syndrome 96, 105–108, 123–124
Deutsch, J. 90–91
development 11
  bridging gap between humanitarian assistance and 131–132
  East African project 65–68
  influence of neoliberal thought on 117–118
  linking of self-reliance and 94–95, 97, 99, 195, 196–197
  Targeted Development Assistance (TDA) 132–134
  UNHCR Refugee Aid and Development Strategy 96–100
  UNHCR/World Bank project foray into 94–95, 102–105, 206
  zonal 64–65, 84, 195
    in Tanzania 71, 88–89, 93
Development Assistance for Refugees (DAR) 55, 135–136
Development Studies 16–17
digital gig economy 24, 162–192
  actors promoting 176–179, *177*
  challenges and barriers to 182–185, 189
  digital access for refugees 166
  'enhancing' refugee self-reliance 164–167
  informal digital trade 178–179, 181–182
  landscape for refugees 173–176
    geography of digital work initiatives 174–175
    types of digital work 163, 175–176
  links to future of work 163, 186–187, 191–192
  online work platforms to support access to 178, 179–181, 186
  precarious work 187–188
  role for humanitarian and development organizations 163, 181, 187–191
  Tomooh case study 167–173
digital identities 166–167
digital training 163, 178, 187, 191
dignity through work 138, 155–156
documentation
  digital 166–167

lack of 128, 166–167, 181, 182, 184
refugee ID 169, 182, 184
training certificates 152
translation of 127, 128
Duffield, M. 18, 159

E

economic discourse, 'internationalization' of 116–121
economic subjects, refugees as 8–9
economy, integration into international
Africa 75, 86–87
Greece 27, 50–52
Pakistan 119–120
Egypt
refugees in 167–169
Tomooh 169–173, 191
Empact programme 181
employment, refugee
Afghan refugees' waged 101–102
and employment-matching scheme 48–49
expatriate contract staff preferred to 67–68
and fear of taking jobs away from citizens 157
focus on assistance to enable 29–30
in Great Depression 53–54
host country restrictions 168, 175, 182, 183, 184, 201, 203
projects to overcome dependency syndrome 106–107
in public works 84, 102, 104, 121–122, 195
in US 172–173
employment contracts 187–188
employment regulations 168, 184, 201
'employment-matching scheme' 48, 49
entrepreneurship, refugee 118, 128, 156, 165, 175, 196
digital 169–173, 181–182, 191
lack of practical support for 156–157, 161
self-reliance assistance and shift to 11–14, 106, 121, 122, 124, 135
UNHCR focus on support for 165
Europe
digital work projects for refugees 174
refugee crisis 162
refugees from 54, 59, 84
refugees redirected to outside 54–55
restrictionism 53, 54, 162, 164, 195, 197
exchanges of populations 25–26, 31–32

F

Facebook 172, 178, 182
farmers, refugee
Afghans forbidden from farming in Pakistan 102
coerced into alternative livelihoods 102, 151
in East Africa 74–75, 77
in Greece 34–40, 52, 53, 201
Figure 8 179, 181
financial reform
in Greece 50–52, 53
in Pakistan 119–120
Finnish Refugee Council (FRC) 139, **141**, 143, 144, 145, 149, 150, 151, 152
fishing 78, 79
food aid, cuts to 62, 110–111, 114, 125
forced migration 25–26, 31–32
Fortune 500 companies 186
France 49, 53
freelancing, online training in 179–181
funds, revolving 43

G

Gaza Sky Geeks 183, 184
gender
and digital training 180, 181
equality 99–100
and livelihoods trainings in Uganda 143–144
and self-reliance 111–113
Geneva Accords, 1988 109
Geneva Convention 184
geography of refugee self-reliance 19
Ghana 7, 181
gig economy *see* digital gig economy
Global Compact on Refugees (GCR) 2, 3, 162, 164–165, 192, 202, 205
Global Strategy Concept Note for Refugee Livelihoods and Economic Inclusion 2019–2023 166, 199
Global Strategy for Livelihoods 2014–2018 1, 129, 138, 154, 166
Global System for Mobile Communications Association (GSMA) 176, 178
Great Depression 53–55
Greco–Turkish war 31
Greece 21–22, 25–58
contrasting refugee assistance in Africa and 85–86
financial reform 50–52, 53
instrumentalization of refugee self-reliance 27, 30, 38, 52, 57
land reform 34–36
naturalization of refugees 38
population transfers 25–26, 31–32
Refugee Loans 50–53
self-reliance assistance 30–32, 57
self-reliance assistance practices 32–49
agricultural settlement 34–40, 49, 50, 52, 53
loans to refugees 38, 39, 43–44
revolving funds 43
small-scale industries 44–45
urban refugee settlements 40–42, 50
vocational training 44–48, 49
Greek National Bank 38, 43–44, 52

Greek Refugee Settlement Commission (GRSC) 22, 33, 42, 43, 44, 52, 56
accused of exploitation 39
bond loan 50
facilitating agricultural settlement of refugees 34–35, 36, 38, 49
mandate 45
Grover, D.C. 155n76

H
hairdressing, training in 140–142
handicrafts
businesses 148, 150–151
project for Afghan women 112
training 146, 147
Hansson, M. 54
Harrell-Bond, B. 9
Hartling, P. 96
Hatch-Dupree, N. 107
health education 85
High Commission for Refugees (latterly Nansen International Office for Refugees) 28, 29, 30, 198
Hirschon, R. 42
historical overview of refugee self-reliance assistance 11–14, **12–13**
historicizing refugee self-reliance 14–15
Hocké, J.-P. 94–95, 98, 99, 103
Hope of Children and Women Victims of Violence (HOCW) 140, **141**, 142, 143, 144
housing, Greek urban refugee 42
Hutu refugees from Burundi 80–82

I
ICT training 163, 178, 179, 187
Impact Sourcing 166
Indo-Chinese refugees 200
informal work 200–201
digital trade 178–179, 181–182
in Egypt 168
in Kampala 130, 145, 148–150, 151, 155, 156, 182
Innovation Unit 166
instrumentalization of refugee self-reliance 11, 194, 201
in Africa 85, 93, 160–161
in Greece 27, 30, 38, 52, 57
in Pakistan 100
integrated rural development (zonal development) 64–65, 84, 195
in Tanzania 88–89, 93
InterAid 127–128, 139–140, **141**, 143, 144, 149–150, 158
International Conferences on Assistance to Refugees in Africa (ICARA I and II) 83, 97
International Council of Voluntary Agencies (ICVA) 63, 70
International Labour Organization (ILO) 48, 54, 173
Decent Work Agenda 176
'employment-matching scheme' 48, 49
model of social insurance 28
on precarious work 187
proposals for Tanzania 72
report on Afghan refugees in Pakistan 101–102
report on rural settlements, 1969 72n50
International Monetary Fund (IMF) 117, 119, 121
international non-governmental organizations (INGOs) 102, 109, 121, 135, 143, 171, 174
International Rescue Committee (IRC) 106, 112, 144
International Trade Center (ITC) 179, 180
Iran 98

J
Jesuit Refugee Service (JRS) 139, 140–142, **141**, 143–144, 145, 147
job-matching platforms 178

K
Kaiser, T. 6–7, 136–137, 200
Kampala, Uganda 23, 127–161
business registration 148, 150
challenge of creating livelihoods after training 144–150
access to markets and capital 144–145, 146–148
KCCA and restrictions on livelihoods 148–150
discourses on self-reliance 151–152
fostering livelihoods 150–152
gap between rhetoric and reality 152–161
instrumentalization of refugee self-reliance assistance 160–161
lack of practical support for individual self-reliance 156–157
refugees as urban market subjects 155–156
self-reliance and quality of life 159
structural factors of self-reliance 157–159
informal work 130, 145, 148–150, 151, 155, 156, 182
non-economic benefits of livelihoods trainings 152
refugee employment statistics 128
refugee self-reliance assistance 135–144
providers of livelihoods assistance 139–140
self-reliance assistance practices 140–142
structure of livelihoods trainings 142–144
refugee-led organizations 127, 129, 140, 142, 143, 144
self-reliance strategy (SRS) 135–137, 159

Kampala City Council Authority (KCCA) 148–150, 151, 158
Kenya 87, 179, 181
  Dadaab Freelancing Collective 179, 180, 184, 189–190
  Dadaab refugee camp 166, 179
  informal digital trade 182

L
labour unions 203
lace industry 45, 48
Lacroix, R.L. 88
Lal, P. 86
land reform in Greece 34–36
Latin America 54–55, 88
League of Nations 1, 9, 33, 44, 56
  Greek refugee's letter to 39–40, *41*
  Refugee Loans 50–53
  refugee self-reliance and 27–30
Lebanon 40, 43, 48, 181, 183
letter, Tsakalopoulos' 39–40, *41*
LevelApp 175–176, 178
Liberian refugees 7
livelihoods 4, 130–135
  challenge of creating 144–150
  -focused projects in Africa 66
  gap between rhetoric and reality 152–161
  ignoring of constraints on assistance for 157–159
  KCCA and restrictions on 148–150
  lack of practical support for 156–157
  refugees seeking to continue urban 40–42
  research on 134
  restricting refugee initiatives on 75, 77, 78–79, 102
  UNHCR increase in budget for 134–135
livelihoods trainings 128–129, 137–138, 140–142, 202
  certificates 152
  digital 179, 180, 181, 183
  gap between rhetoric and reality 152–153, 156, 160, 161
  lack of assessment of most effective and viable 145, 146, 148, 156
  non-economic benefits 152
  providers of assistance for 139–140, **141**
  and reduction in aid 154, 160
  refugees' aims for joining 151–152
  structure 142–144
  see also vocational training
loans, refugee
  in Egypt 168
  in Greece 43–44
    for farmers 38, 39
  Nansen Stamp Fund 43, 47–48, 198
  in Pakistan 122
  for vocational training and small-scale industries 47–48
  see also micro-finance programmes
loans, state
  bond loans 50
  Refugee Loans 50–53
  structural adjustment 119
Long, K. 55, 84
Lutheran World Federation (LWF) 70, 78

M
Macedonia 35, 36–37
Malkki, L. 80–81, 82
markets
  access to 144–145, 146–148
  engagement with 118, 154, 196–197, 201
  refugees as subjects of urban 155–156
Mazower, M. 36, 39
Mears, E.G. 37
medical training 45–47, *46*, *47*
methodology 20, 206–207
micro-finance programmes 66, 96, 135, 156–157
  see also loans, refugee
Millwood, D. 108–109
mobile technology 175–176, 178
Mozambican refugees 70, 71, 77
mushroom growing 144
Mwese refugee settlement, Tanzania 71–77

N
Na Takallam 183
Nansén International Office for Refugees (formerly High Commission for Refugees) 29, 30, 53–54
  passport 43
Nansen Stamp Fund 43, 47–48, 198
National Geographic Magazine 105
nationalism 30–31
nation-states, interwar formation of 29, 31
naturalization of refugees 38, 70
Ndikumana, J.-M. 180
Near East Relief 45
neoliberalism, shift to 116–118, 123, 125, 188, 196–197
New York Declaration for Refugees and Migrants, 2016 164
non-governmental organizations (NGOs)
  'Afghanization' of 114–115, 122
  employing Western staff in Africa 67–68
  helping refugees into digital work 163, 174, 175–176, *177*, 178, 187, 189
  humanitarian assistance channelled through 121
  in Kampala 143–144, 149
  professionalization of, in Pakistan 123
  refugees working for 67–68, 173
  Tomooh working with 171
  working with Afghan refugees 101, 102, 109, 110–111
Norwegian Refugee Council (NRC) 179, 180

nurses
skilled refugee 127–128
training 45–47, *46*, *47*
Nyerere, J. 68, 69, 90, 92

O
Omata, N. 7
online freelancing, training in 179–181
online work platforms 178, 179–181, 186
Organisation of African Unity (OAU) 61, 167
outsourcing of work, international 188, 190

P
Pakistan
domestic to international policy shifts 121–123
financial reform 119–120
socialism 119n98
States and Frontier Regions Ministry 101, 104
Structural Adjustment Programmes 119
Western economic policies and welfare doctrine 115–116, 118–121
Western instrumentalization of 121
see also Afghan refugees in Pakistan
Palestine 32, 45, 58
refugees from 184
Pan-African Conference on the Situation of Refugees in Africa (Arusha Conference) 82, 83, 195
Paraguay 54
Parmelee, R. 25–27, 32–33, 43, 45, 46, 48, 56, 58, 206–207
Payer, C. 93
Peters, M. 117, 123, 156
Pierson, C. 10
Pironti, P. 28
politics and refugee self-reliance 38, 56–57, 83–91, 120–121, 203–204
poverty
neoliberalism and combating 118
refugees living in 42, 76, 145, 155, 200–202
private sector engagement with refugee self-reliance 4, 174, 176, 178, 190
problem-solving theory 5–6
protection 196–197
infringement in Kampala 150–152
psychosocial 108–109
self-reliance as a protection tool 96, 109–113, 201
Protocol Relating to the Status of Refugees, 1967 61
psychosocial welfare 108–109
public works projects 28–29, 84, 102, 104, 121–122, 195
purdah 111

Q
quality of life, self-reliance and 159
Quick Impact Projects 131

R
Reagan, R. 118
Refugee Aid and Development (RAD) 83, 96–100
Refugee Councils 91
'refugee dependency syndrome' 96, 105–108, 123–124
Refugee Employment and Skills Initiative (RESI) 179–180, 181
Refugee Law Project (RLP) 149
Refugee Loans 50–53
Refugee Policy Group 107, 199
refugee self-reliance 1–2, 196–197
colonialism and 89–91
definition 3
digital work 'enhancing' 164–167
future 202–204
gap between rhetoric and reality 156–157, 157–159
gendered nature 111–113
geography 19
instrumentalization 11, 194, 201
in Africa 85, 93, 160–161
in Greece 27, 30, 38, 52, 57
in Pakistan 100
League of Nations and 27–30
linking of development and 94–95, 97, 99, 195, 196–197
politics, exploitation and 83–91
poverty and 200–202
as a protection tool 96, 109–113, 201
scholarship 5–8
theoretical approaches 5–7, 15–19, 193–194
today 3–5
refugee self-reliance assistance 1, 21
Afghan refugees in Pakistan 96, 100–105, 125–126
continuity and change 194–196
in Greece 30–32, 57
practices 32–49
historical overview 11–14, **12–13**
historicizing 14–15
outcomes 199–200
and shift to entrepreneurship 11–14, 106, 121, 122, 124, 135
in Tanzania 68–70, 71–83
practices 71–83
targeting vulnerable groups 99–100, 110, 111, 115–116, 124–125
treating refugees as economic subjects 8–9
in Uganda 135–144
Refugee Self-Reliance Initiative 202
Refugee Studies 15–19, 194

refugee-led organizations 199, 204
in Afghanistan 115
in Greece 47–48
in Kampala 127, 129, 140, 142, 143, 144
refugee-led revolving funds 43–44
RefUnite 175
repatriation
of Afghan refugees 113–114, 123
and reintegration of returnees to country of origin 130–131
voluntary 83, 114, 123, 130
revolving funds 43
rights of refugees 75, 136, 137, 191, 197, 201
in Greece 38
right to work 6, 9, 38, 129, 131, 157, 184, 201, 203
in Uganda 129
Russian refugees 49
Rutamba Settlement, Tanzania 77–78, 80
Rwanda 99, 130
refugees from 62, 71, 77

S

Sarantis, F. 38–39
Schnyder, F. 62, 64
Schuurman, F.J. 17, 194
'self-help' 108, 109, 117, 122, 205
self-reliance strategy (SRS) 6–7, 135–137, 159
'Settlement Community Development Programmes' 77
settlements, refugee 62–63
collective self-reliance 85
evaluating self-reliance outcomes 82–83, 92–93
Mwese refugee settlement 71–77
number of self-sufficient 82
refugees' views on 80–81
Rutamba refugee settlement 77–78, 80
structure of self-reliance assistance 77–82
UNHCR report on East African 75, 78–79
urban 40–42, 49, 50
see also agricultural settlements
'Sister Sarra' 46, *46*
small-scale industries 44–45
smartphones, working from 175–176, 178
purchasing SIM cards 182
Social Welfare Cell 108–109
Somalian refugees 129
Somaliland 178, 179
sources 20, 206–207
South America 54–55
South Sudanese refugees 129, 140, 141, 143, 182
States and Frontier Regions Ministry (SAFRON) 101, 104
Stein, B. 124
structural adjustment loans 119
Structural Adjustment Programmes (SAPs) 69, 92, 119
subsistence farming 39, 49, 53, 72, 73, 74
Sudanese refugees 146, 168, 200
Syria 33, 43, 48
Syrian refugees 164, 167, 168, 173, 174
Alaa 167, 169–173, 185, 191

T

tailoring training 142, 143, 145
Tanganyika Christian Refugee Service (TCRS) 70, 73, 78–79, 85
Tanzania 22, 68–93
colonialism and refugee self-reliance 89–91
export markets 87
'progress' and welfare for refugees 85
refugee influxes 70
refugee self-reliance 86–88
refugee self-reliance assistance 68–70
refugee self-reliance assistance practices 71–83
evaluating outcomes of settlement self-reliance 82–83, 92–93
Mwese refugee settlement 71–77
structure of self-reliance assistance 77–82
Rutamba Settlement 77–78, 80
Structural Adjustment Programmes 69, 92
ujamaa (African socialism) 68–69, 71, 86, 93
US support for 89
zonal development 71, 88–89, 93
Targeted Development Assistance (TDA) 132–134
terminology 20–21
Terry, F. 100
theoretical approaches 5–7, 15–19, 193–194
tobacco 35, 38, 52, 53, 79, 87
Togo 64
Tomooh 169–173, 191
trade unions 203
Treaty of Neuilly 31
Treaty of Versailles 31
Tsakalopoulos, I. 39–40, *41*
Turkey 25–26, 31–32

U

Uber 178, 186
Uganda
COVID-19 pandemic 197
Development Assistance for Refugees 135–136
influx of refugees 129, 130
LevelApp 176
a progressive host country 129
Refugee Act 2006 137
refugee self-reliance assistance 135–144
self-reliance strategy (SRS) 6–7, 135–137, 159

Sudanese refugees in 200
see also Kampala, Uganda
ujamaa (African socialism) 68–69, 71, 86, 93
unemployment 28–29, 53, 117
United Kingdom (UK) 87, 116, 117, 123, 174
Unemployment Insurance Act 1920 29
welfare reform 155–156
United Nations Development Programme (UNDP) 70, 115, 131
United Nations High Commissioner for Refugees (UNHCR) 59, 174
in Africa 61–62, 64–65, 66–67, 78, 83–84, 87
limited budget 91
partnerships in Tanzania 70, 73
report on East African settlements 75, 78–79
assistance to Afghan refugees in Pakistan 100, 101, 102–105, 206
phasing out 109–110
Brookings Process 131–132
closure of a community centre 170, 173
Convention Plus Initiative 132–134
definition of refugee self-reliance 3
digital access and digital identities 166–167
digital work, connecting refugees with 166
Global Report 2020 197, 202n20
Global Strategy Concept Note for Refugee Livelihoods and Economic Inclusion 2019–2023 166, 199
Global Strategy for Livelihoods 1, 129, 138, 154, 166
Innovation Unit 166
livelihoods, focus on 2, 130–135, 153–155
'Livelihoods and self-reliance' 164
Livelihoods Unit 134–135
'local integration' policy 67
Poverty Alleviation Coalition 200
'Refugee Aid and Development Strategy' 96–100
a refugee reflecting on relations with 173
on self-sufficient settlements 82
Social Welfare Cell 108–109
Urban Refugee Policy 128, 137
Western control of 66
and World Bank project 94–95, 102–105, 206
United Nations Relief and Rehabilitation Administration (UNRRA) 58, 59
United Nations Research Institute for Social Development (UNRISD) 107–108
United States of America (US)
Indo-Chinese refugees 200
instrumentalization of Afghan refugees 121
labour unions 203
public works 28–29
Refugee Act 1980 172
refugees in 171, 172–173
support for *mujahideen* agenda 120
support for Tanzania 89
welfare-to-work programmes 117
Workforce Investment Act 1998 155
Upwork 179, 180, 181, 189
urban refugee settlements 40–42, 50
'employment-matching scheme' 49
US Committee for Refugees 106
US Department of the Treasury 118

V

Venezuela 54
Venizelos, E. 36, 37, 38
vocational training 135
for Afghan refugees in Pakistan 96, 110, 122
in Africa 77, 82, 83
in Greece 44–48, 49
see also livelihoods trainings
volunteering, refugee 127, 143, 170, 171
vulnerable groups 57–58, 121, 180
gendered nature of 111–113
psychosocial protection 108–109
targeting self-reliance assistance to 99–100, 110, 111, 115–116, 124–125

W

wages, low 76, 77, 108, 169, 187
Wake, C. 7
Ward, P. 158
welfare
development of state 28–29, 47, 84–85
extension to refugees 197, 203
'internationalization' of 116–121
notions of dependency and 123–124
parallels between assistance for refugees and trends in 84–85, 125, 155–156
self-reliance discourse in Western 117–118
WhatsApp 172, 178, 182
women
cultural restrictions on self-reliance of Afghan 111–113
digital training 180, 181
focus on 'vulnerable' groups of 99–100
fostering livelihoods without protection 150–151
livelihoods trainings in Kampala 143–144, 146, 147
vocational training 45–47, *46*, *47*
Women's Refugee Commission 2
work, future of 163, 186–187, 191–192
workers, shifting construction of refugees as 27, 55–58
'workfare' programmes 117

World Bank 3–4, 64, 117, 119, 132
/UNHCR project 94–95, 102–105, 206
in Tanzania 71, 72, 73–74, 92, 93
World Food Programme 70, 181

Y

Young African Refugees for Integral Development (YARID) 140, **141**, 143

Z

Zaire 70, 77
Zambia 70, 77, 133
zonal development (integrated rural development) 64–65, 84, 195
in Tanzania 71, 88–89, 93
Zwick, A. 187, 188